The Turns of Translation Studies

Benjamins Translation Library

The Benjamins Translation Library aims to stimulate research and training in translation and interpreting studies. The Library provides a forum for a variety of approaches (which may sometimes be conflicting) in a socio-cultural, historical, theoretical, applied and pedagogical context. The Library includes scholarly works, reference works, post-graduate text books and readers in the English language.

EST Subseries

The European Society for Translation Studies (EST) Subseries is a publication channel within the Library to optimize EST's function as a forum for the translation and interpreting research community. It promotes new trends in research, gives more visibility to young scholars' work, publicizes new research methods, makes available documents from EST, and reissues classical works in translation studies which do not exist in English or which are now out of print.

Volume 66

The Turns of Translation Studies: New paradigms or shifting viewpoints?
by Mary Snell-Hornby

The Turns of Translation Studies

New paradigms or shifting viewpoints?

Mary Snell-Hornby

University of Vienna

John Benjamins Publishing Company

Amsterdam/Philadelphia

™ The paper used in this publication meets the minimum requirements
of American National Standard for Information Sciences – Permanence
of Paper for Printed Library Materials, ANSI z39.48-1984.

Library of Congress Cataloging-in-Publication Data

Mary Snell-Hornby
The Turns of Translation Studies : New paradigms or shifting viewpoints? /
Mary Snell-Hornby.
p.   cm. (Benjamins Translation Library, ISSN 0929–7316 ; v. 66)
Includes bibliographical references and indexes.
1. Translating and interpreting--Research--History.

P306.5.S64 2006
418/.02072--dc22   2006045870
ISBN 90 272 1673 8 (Hb; alk. paper)
ISBN 90 272 1674 6 (Pb; alk. paper)

John Benjamins Publishing Co. · P.O. Box 36224 · 1020 ME Amsterdam · The Netherlands
John Benjamins North America · P.O. Box 27519 · Philadelphia PA 19118-0519 · USA

Es gibt dreierlei Arten Leser: eine, die ohne Urteil genießt, eine dritte, die ohne zu genießen urteilt, die mittlere, die genießend urteilt und urteilend genießt; diese reproduziert eigentlich ein Kunstwerk aufs neue.

(There are three kinds of reader: the first are those who enjoy without judging, the third those who judge without enjoying; the middle group judge with enjoyment and enjoy with judgement, and they actually reproduce a work of art anew.)

Johann Wolfgang von Goethe, 13th June 1819

Table of Contents

Preface

When I was asked by John Benjamins a few years ago whether I would consider presenting the book *Translation Studies. An Integrated Approach* (1988, 1995²) in a third revised edition, I spontaneously answered that I would rather write a completely new book. So much had meanwhile changed in Translation Studies that a revision would even then have been completely inadequate. Up to the mid-1980s, when the volume was compiled, the study of translation was still widely seen as a concern of either linguistics or literary studies, and my "integrated approach" set out to overcome the divisions between them and to present Translation Studies as an independent discipline. The response to that volume indicates that it served its purpose.

Seen from today's viewpoint, it seems that most accounts of the study of translation in those years were one-sided or fragmentary, mainly because what have meanwhile proved to be seminal works were often barely accessible: the conference papers of James Holmes are an outstanding example. In the meantime the discipline now institutionalized as Translation Studies has branched out in several directions, and a new perspective is needed to do it justice. This present book sets out to offer a critical assessment of such developments, concentrating on the last twenty years and focussing on what have turned out to be ground-breaking contributions (new paradigms) as against what may be seen in retrospect to have been only a change in position on already established territory (shifting viewpoints). Obviously, the borders are hazy (as in the earlier book we shall be thinking in terms of prototypes and not in rigid categories), and much is controversial, depending on the viewpoint of the scholar or reader: my aim is to stimulate discussion and to provoke further debate on the current profile and future perspectives of Translation Studies.

While endeavouring to view the discipline in the broad international perspective of today, I am aware that my viewpoint is a European one, and that any conclusions must by necessity be relative. The same however goes for any study of such a complex subject, even those which claim general – or global – validity. And here the use of English as a world-wide language of publication presents problems: there has been a disquieting trend in recent years for English to be used, not only as a means of communication, but also as part of the object of discussion (see 4.2.3). English publications frequently have a clear Anglo-American bias, and what are presented as general principles of translation sometimes prove to be limited to the area under discussion and to be caused by the specific status of English (cf. 4.3). Conversely, contributions written in languages other than English and on topics outside Anglophile interests tend to be ignored or over-simplified. The same goes for schools of thought or even entire traditions. After living and working in German-speaking countries for over forty years, I have become very aware of the complexity and wealth of the German tradition in translation over the centuries, also of the part played by the German-speaking scientific community in Translation Studies over the last twenty years, and of how inadequately all this is treated in the English-speaking Translation Studies debate. The only work I have read in English which does justice to the historical German tradition is André Lefevere's 1977 volume *Translating Literature. The German Tradition from Luther to Rosenzweig*, which is taken here as our starting-point. No discipline (or school of thought or individual scholarly investigation) arises in a vacuum, and it is often overlooked that much of the new paradigm of Translation Studies was (re)oriented against the older tradition (two names, Friedrich Schleiermacher and Walter Benjamin, were to be rediscovered in the US debate via English translation). A similar fate has befallen much work written in German – and languages other than English – over the last twenty years: when included in the English-speaking discussion, it is often over-simplified or the selection is limited to isolated work which happens to be available in English translation. This present profile of Translation Studies aims at correcting that deficit and will highlight such contributions alongside those more familiar through English publications. Every effort is made to situate all contributions in their specific historical or cultural context, and as far as possible the scholars concerned are cited in direct quotation, where necessary alongside the English translations (these, unless otherwise indicated, are mine).

This book is envisaged as a continuation of *Translation Studies. An Integrated Approach* (1988, 1995[2]) in that various issues are taken up from there, expanded and traced in their later development. Some sections take up topics and use material I have published elsewhere, but set out to bring it up to date with present developments. The book addresses a broad international readership of students, teachers and anyone generally interested in this challenging discipline, and it is written in a style of English that, as far as possible, atttempts to be jargon-free and accessible for the non-specialist.

Many of the ideas presented here go back to long discussions made possible by inspiring and dedicated colleagues, mainly in institutions they themselves have created or events they organized: Susan Bassnett and colleagues at the Centre for Translation and Comparative Cultural Studies, University of Warwick (with many outstanding conferences and seminars); Justa Holz-Mänttäri and colleagues from the Institute of Translation Studies, University of Tampere; Heidemarie Salevsky and her research seminars at the Humboldt University of Berlin; Christina Schäffner and her CILS seminars at Aston University Birmingham – to name but a few. My thanks go to them all, also to all those scholars who, before the days of sponsored and funded exchange, came to Vienna for our "Translation Summits" (notably Hans Vermeer, Paul Kussmaul and Hans Hönig) – leading to the foundation of the European Society for Translation Studies in 1992. Thanks too to Michaela Wolf for many hours of animated and stimulating discussion, to Mira Kadrić, here for help with the index, but especially for her loyal support through difficult times, to my former students of the University of Vienna, whose research is documented here – and then of course to Tony Hornby and Astrid, for all these years of patience, help and understanding.

And finally, my sincere thanks go once again to John Benjamins Publishing Company for their efficient and friendly cooperation.

Mary Snell-Hornby
Vienna, December 2005

Introduction

In September 2003 I attended the 11th Congress of the Latin American Association for Germanic Studies in Brazil. It lasted seven days in all and was held in three different places: the first three days with the ceremonial opening, several plenary lectures, panel discussions and papers in ten different sections, were spent at the University of São Paolo, the next two days, with more plenaries and panel discussions, at the historic colonial town of Paraty, birthplace of Julia da Silva-Bruhns, the mother of Heinrich and Thomas Mann, and it was concluded – with a final panel discussion, reports on the sections and closing lectures – in the imperial city of Petrópolis, where the Austrian writer Stefan Zweig lived for several months before taking his life in February 1942. It was a so-called *Wanderkongress* or "travelling congress", the idea being taken from *Wilhelm Meisters Wanderjahre* (*Wilhelm Meister's Travels*), the masterpiece Goethe wrote towards the end of his life, a work committed to social and technological progress, education reform, and a world no longer centred round Europe. The conference languages were Portuguese, German and Spanish. The general assessments made during the section reports and the closing lectures in Petrópolis were impressive: it was agreed that the Congress had broken new ground, above all through the perspectives gained by its interdisciplinary, intercultural approach. This was shown partly in the topics of some of the sections, such as "Literature and media" or "The challenge of Sigmund Freud – his works in translation" or "Discourses on megacities in a global context", but also in the new insights emerging from the links between Germanic Studies and Latin America: the despair of Stefan Zweig, for example, led to discussions on the "Transnational Holocaust discourse" and from there to the Latin American experience of dictatorship, as shown in the Memorial Park for the *desaparecidos* in Buenos Aires or in sculptures by a Colombian artist expressing the tragedy of civil war. All in all, as was observed in the concluding lecture, Germanic Studies has moved from its dogmatic, monolithic standing where German was the great language of scholarship and science, to a more relative but fruitful position among the plurality of languages and cultures in the globalized world of today with its need for international and intercultural dialogue.

This assessment was definitely justified, and indeed both the positions represented and the material dealt with at the Congress were a far cry from what I once had to assimilate for a British degree in German Language and Literature in the early 1960s (half of which was devoted to historical linguistics), and also from what was offered at German and English departments in Vienna and Munich later in the 1960s (primarily mainstream dogmas on canonized texts). But many of the insights and viewpoints which were acclaimed at the Brazilian Congress as being so innovative were for me actually not unfamiliar, as they have for many years been perspectives we have adopted in Translation Studies: the concept of intercultural communication, for example, the unlimited possibilities arising from interdisciplinary cooperation, the interweaving of discourse and cultural factors, and the relativity of all discourse to its immediate situation in time and place and its reception by a target audience. The motto of the Congress was "Blickwechsel" in its double meaning of "exchange of glances" (as in intercultural dialogue) and "change in viewpoint" (as in the shifting perspectives of interdisciplinary research). It is an unusually apt image to apply to any kind of translation, which always involves a *Blickwechsel* in both its senses and is hence always relative to the author, reader or situation concerned. Beyond that, it also seems highly appropriate for the new discipline of Translation Studies, which, in the fifty years of its development and in the many countries throughout the world where it has been established, has experienced innumerable "exchanges of glances" (including their intensified mode of clashing opinions) and changes of viewpoint, these varying from minor adjustments in familiar concepts to the presentation of completely new paradigms.

The topos of paradigms and progress was taken up by Hans Vermeer in his keynote lecture at the Translation Studies Congress in Vienna in 1992 with reference to the history of translation theory which, he felt, showed little progress:

> But what is progress? It is not a well-defined term in science. I can think of 3 types of "progress": the straightforward leap to a new idea or point of view, the extreme case which Kuhn (1970) called a paradigmatic change; the "peripatetic" spiral, which after many repetitions gets more or less away from its starting point; and ultimately the perfect circle, which undoubtedly is a movement, a going-on, peripatetically, but only to lead back to the very same question. (And it is hardly consoling to note that there are several circles side by side which differ in their respective starting points and therefore in their points of arrival.)
>
> There also seems to be a fourth type of progress. I mean the one which looks like a zigzagging spiral, advancing so to speak by leaps and bounds but at the same time going round in a circle, wasting a lot of breath and energy in fruitless repetitions, but ultimately managing to come to a conclusion some distance away from its starting point. (1994: 3–4)

Inspired by the conclusions of the Brazilian Congress on Germanic Studies (as against my memories of the 1960s), I started to trace the path of the young discipline of Translation Studies, following spirals, both peripatetic and zigzagging, and trying to identify what can be seen today as the "leaps" to a new paradigm. It soon became clear however how much was embedded in a complex historical development, how much depended on the language, affiliation and country of the individual researcher, and how much merely embroidered on statements that had already been made many years before. And yet, because times change, ideas and viewpoints usually take on a new relevance in their new historical context. With all this in mind, the idea for this book took shape.

The following chapters set out to offer a critical assessment of the discipline of Translation Studies over the last twenty years, not in the form of a general introduction, but by sketching a profile, highlighting what can now be assessed as groundbreaking contributions leading to new paradigms. While trying to see the discipline in the broad international perspective of today, I am aware that any conclusions must by necessity be relative to the viewpoint of someone working in Europe.

Even from a non-European perspective however, there is a broad consensus that many basic insights and concepts in Translation Studies today go back to the German Romantic Age, which forms our historical starting point. In Chapter 1 the path is traced from great precursors such as Goethe, Schleiermacher and Humboldt, then Benjamin and Rosenzweig, situating their basic statements in their specific historical context (1.1) to the pioneers of today's discipline, such as Levý, Nida and Reiss (1.2), as seen against the background of the crucial "pragmatic turn" in the 1970s (1.3). The work of James Holmes, who laid the foundation stone of the discipline with what now seem visionary powers, is discussed from today's perspective in 1.4. Chapter 2 analyzes the major movements during what became known as the "cultural turn" of the 1980s, which enabled Translation Studies to emancipate itself from literary theory and linguistics, and led to the establishment of the independent discipline: Descriptive Translation Studies (2.1), the skopos theory (2.2) and the theory of translatorial action (2.3), which together produced the *Neuorientierung* in Germany, and the functional anthropophagic (or "cannibalistic") approach in Brazil (2.4). The chapter closes with an overview of the 1980s in retrospect (2.5).

Chapters 3 and 4, the central chapters of the book, analyze major developments of the 1990s. Chapter 3 discusses Translation Studies as an interdiscipline that goes "beyond language" (3.1), concentrating on significant terms introduced or areas developed during the decade: Toury's notion of norms and Chesterman's concept of memes in their relation to translation ethics (3.1.1); non-verbal communication (3.1.2) and multimodal/multimedial translation as for stage and screen (3.1.3), with examples of texts and studies carried out during the 1990s. The section 3.2 discusses, again with examples, how Translation Studies has been "striking back" after the age of the "imperial eyes", both in postcolonial translation (3.2.1) and in gender-based Translation Studies (3.2.2). The chapter closes with a review of the various positions of the reader and the translator as reader (3.3), with illustrations from a study using an extremely productive model of translation critique (3.3.1). Chapter 4 deals with two essential turns within the discipline that took place during the 1990s. The first is a methodical one, resulting from the call for more empirical studies in the field of translation and interpreting (4.1). These led to the exploration of new areas, particularly in interpreting studies, such as court interpreting, community interpreting, sign language (4.1.1), but also in cognitive domains concerning the translation process (think-aloud protocols) and areas such as legal translation (4.1.2), and here individual studies will be discussed as examples. The second great turn was caused from without: globalization (4.2) and breath-taking advances in technology (4.2.1) were to create radical changes in the work of the translator, as exemplified here by the field of advertising (4.2.2). The role of English in this globalized world will be discussed, particularly International English as a lingua franca with regard to other languages and in its significance for translation (4.2.3). As an example of the latter, Venuti's plea for "foreignization" (a term adapted from Schleiermacher) will be analyzed, with reference to its relevance to languages and cultures other than English (4.3).

Chapter 5 takes a critical look at the state of the discipline at the beginning of the 21st century. On the one hand some tendencies are arising which seem to be retrogressive, such as the reappearance of views and linguistic concepts from the 1970s (5.1). On the other hand much progress has been made, and in 5.2 the various tendencies will be critically examined for genuine innovations. It transpires that Justa Holz-Mänttäri's model of translatorial action, and indeed several important contributions to the skopos theory, have a potential as yet not recognized in English publications. The reasons seem to be that the theoretical work was published in German and in a style often difficult to penetrate even for native speakers. It is hoped that the study presented here will contribute towards giving this work the international attention it deserves, as has already been achieved with think-aloud protocols, another method which originated in Germany. The closing section (5.3) sketches some insights of Translation Studies which could profitably be adopted elsewhere. The final chapter 6 summarizes the conclusions and ventures a prognosis for the future.

The sheer quantity of publications in the field of Translation Studies, as Hans Vermeer has repeatedly pointed out, makes it impossible to cover everything. But I hope to have included those publications, coming from various countries and schools of thought, that have made a significant contribution to the turns of Translation Studies over the past two decades. It remains for the reader to pass judgement, and, thinking of Goethe's phrase cited at the beginning of the book, it is hoped s/he will judge with enjoyment.

CHAPTER 1

Translation Studies

The emergence of a discipline

In the introduction to *Translating Literature: The German Tradition from Luther to Rosenzweig* (1977), André Lefevere divides the representatives of great traditions, following the classification of Gerard Radnitzky (1970), into four groups: precursors, pioneers, masters and disciples. The precursors are those often "appointed *ex post* by members of the tradition" (Radnitzky 1970: 9): the main precursor of the German tradition of translation theory in this sense would be Martin Luther (1483–1546). The pioneers are those "polemically oriented on other intellectual traditions flourishing in the intellectual milieu. They formulate the raw program of the tradition and often they formulate its manifesto..." (Radnitzky 1970: 9): for Lefevere pioneers of the German tradition are the Leipzig literary theorist Johann Christoph Gottsched (1700–66), his two Swiss antagonists Johann Jakob Bodmer (1698–1783) and Johann Jakob Breitinger (1701–76), along with the dramatist and critic Gotthold Ephraim Lessing (1729–81) and the philosopher and critic Johann Gottfried Herder (1744–1803), "whose polemical orientation on the German past and the concept of history profoundly affected the tradition as a whole" (Lefevere 1977: 1). The masters are those who "carry out part of the program and their work sets the standard by means of which the disciples measure their success" (Radnitzky 1970: 9): for Lefevere masters of the German tradition of translation theory are the poet, dramatist and all-round genius Johann Wolfgang von Goethe (1749–1832), the theologian Friedrich Schleiermacher (1768–1834), the language scholar and educational reformer Wilhelm von Humboldt (1767–1835), the early Romantic poet Novalis (pen-name of Friedrich von Hardenberg, 1772–1801) and the Shakespeare translator August Wilhelm Schlegel (1767–1845), while the leading disciples include Walter Benjamin (1892–1940), Franz Rosenzweig (1886–1929) – and "many German theorists of literary translation writing today" (Lefevere 1977:1).

Lefevere's book, which mainly consists of his own English translations, with commentaries, of the outstanding statements made by these leading personalities of the German tradition, concentrates on the the work of his "pioneers" and "masters". He is however fully aware of how intertwined many ideas of all four groups prove to be in retrospect:

> It is important to be aware of the tradition *qua* tradition. Positions taken by certain theorists become fully intelligible only when read in comparison with (or contrasted with) statements made by their predecessors. Thus Schleiermacher's well-known maxim that the translator should either leave the reader in peace and move the author towards him, or *vice versa,* appears first in Bodmer, and then in Goethe, whereas Benjamin's essay "The Task of the Translator", much glorified in an Anglo-Saxon world ignorant of the ramifications of the German tradition in translating literature, turns out to be an elaboration on certain thoughts to be found in Herder, Goethe, Schleiermacher, and Schopenhauer. (Lefevere 1977: 2)

1.1   Great precursors

Continuing from there Lefevere categorizes the German translation scholars of his day simply as disciples, because the tradition as such, he maintains, has only been criticized internally, it has never been entirely refuted or overturned by a rival paradigm. From the viewpoint of German literary translation only, this may even still be true (cf. Kittel and Poltermann 1998, also Hohn 1998). Seen from today's international perspective of Translation Studies as a whole however, Lefevere can be said to have presented a survey of great precursors in a field of scholarship which in the 1970s was already opening up into a new discipline with a separate identity of its own. But the call for such a discipline actually goes back to the early years of the 19th century and can already be heard from the ranks of Lefevere's "masters": in 1814 Friedrich Schleiermacher, the first Dean of the Faculty of Theology at the newly founded Humboldt University in Berlin, published an essay with the following observations:[1]

> Ueberall sind Theorien bei uns an der Tagesordnung, aber noch ist keine von festen Ursätzen ausgehende, folgegleich und vollständig durchgeführte, Theorie der Uebersetzungen erschienen; nur Fragmente hat man aufgestellt: und doch, so gewiß es eine Alterthumswissenschaft gibt, so gewiß muß es auch eine Uebersetzungswissenschaft geben. (cit. Salevsky 1994: 159)

> (Everywhere theories are the order of the day with us, but up to now no one has provided a theory of translation that is based on solid foundations, that is logically developed and completely worked out – people have only presented fragments.

---

1.   Friedrich Schleiermacher: „Alte Literatur. Ueber die Farbengebung des Alterthümlichen in Verdeutschung alter klassischer Prosa (Veranlasst durch Lange's Uebersetzung des Herodot. Berlin 1812 bis 1813)", published under the pen-name "Pudor" in the journal *Die Musen*, edited by Friedrich Fouqué and Wilhelm Raumann (1814, p. 104).

And yet, just as there is a field of scholarship called Archaeology, there must also be a discipline of translation studies.)

Such "fragments" must have included the age-old dichotomy of word and sense, faithful and free translation that goes back to Cicero and Horace (see Snell-Hornby 1988: 9–11, Robinson 1998 and 1998a), also A.W. Schlegel's Romantic concept of translation based on his own translations of Shakespeare's plays, which sought to be both faithful and poetic, hence to combine fidelity to the source text on the one hand with creative transformation as required by the target-text readership on the other (Kittel and Poltermann 1998: 423). In Germany the early years of the 19th century witnessed an outstanding intellectual exchange in the field of translation, and drawing on these debates, Schleiermacher presented his own concept of translation in his celebrated lecture "Ueber die verschiedenen Methoden des Uebersezens" (On the different methods of translating), delivered on 24th June 1813 to the Royal Academy of Sciences in Berlin (cit. Störig 1963). For a reader of today, almost two hundred years later, the text, with its exalted imagery and long convoluted sentences, may seem in one sense distant and antiquated. Some of it however sounds strangely familiar, such as the distinction between "das eigentliche Uebersezen" ("genuine translation") and "das bloße Dolmetschen" ("mere interpreting"), whereby the latter here refers to both oral and written translation of everyday business texts. For Schleiermacher this was a "mechanical activity", maybe worthy of mention, but not of extensive scholarly attention. Within the field of "genuine translation" he made a further distinction between "Paraphrase", generally of scholarly and scientific texts, and "Nachbildung" ("imitation"), which usually applies to literary works of art. From today's perspective his explanation of the difference between these two types of translation is striking:

> Die **Paraphrase** will die Irrationalität der Sprachen bezwingen, aber nur auf mechanische Weise. (...) Der Paraphrast verfährt mit den Elementen beider Sprachen, als ob sie **mathematische Zeichen** wären, die sich durch Vermehrung und Verminderung auf gleichen Werth zurükkführen ließen (...) Die **Nachbildung** dagegen beugt sich unter der Irrationalität der Sprachen; sie gesteht, man könne von einem Kunstwerk der Rede kein Abbild in einer anderen Sprache hervorbringen, das in seinen einzelnen Theilen den einzelnen Theilen des Urbildes genau entspräche, sondern es bleibe (...) nichts anders übrig, als ein Nachbild auszuarbeiten, **ein Ganzes**, aus merklich von den Theilen des Urbildes verschiedenen Theilen zusammengesetzt, welches dennoch **in seiner Wirkung jenem Ganzen so nahe komme**, als die Verschiedenheit des Materials nur immer gestatte. (Störig 1963: 45–6, emphasis added)

> (**Paraphrase** strives to conquer the irrationality of languages, but only in a mechanical way. (…) The paraphrast treats the elements of the two languages as if they were **mathematical signs** which may be reduced to the same value by means

of addition and subtraction (...). **Imitation**, on the other hand, submits to the irrationality of languages; it grants that one cannot render a copy – which would correspond to the original precisely in all its parts – of a verbal artefact in another language, and that (...) there is no option but to produce an imitation, a **whole** which is composed of parts obviously different from the parts of the original, but which would yet **in its effects come as close to that whole** as the difference in material allows. Lefevere 1977: 73, emphasis added)

With these statements Schleiermacher is already focussing on the distinction between translating literature and translating scientific language. Even though he describes both the "mere interpreting" of everyday business texts and the "paraphrasing" of scientific texts as "mechanical",[2] he was probably the first scholar to distinguish clearly between *Übersetzen* and *Dolmetschen* (cf. Salevsky 1992: 85), and the latter at least has a place in his conceptual world. His reference to the elements of languages as "mathematical signs" – a barb at theories of Gottsched (the "paraphrast") and Leibniz – can from today's viewpoint even be seen to anticipate concepts of structural linguistics, terminology and machine translation. For works of literature on the other hand, his "imitation" represents a holistic approach, which a hundred years later was to be developed in Gestalt psychology (Wertheimer 1912) and towards the end of the 20th century played a significant role in European Translation Studies (cf. Paepcke 1986, Stolze 1982, see too Snell-Hornby 1988: 29).

However, Schleiermacher is currently known above all for the central maxim of his academy lecture on the "roads" open to the translator:

> Meines Erachtens giebt es deren nur zwei. Entweder der Uebersezer lässt den Schriftsteller möglichst in Ruhe, und bewegt den Leser ihm entgegen; oder er lässt den Leser möglichst in Ruhe, und bewegt den Schriftsteller ihm entgegen. Beide sind so gänzlich von einander verschieden, dass durchaus einer von beiden so streng als möglich muss verfolgt werden, aus jeder Vermischung aber ein höchst unzuverlässiges Resultat nothwendig hervorgeht, und zu besorgen ist, dass Schriftsteller und Leser sich gänzlich verfehlen. (Störig 1963: 47)

> (In my opinion there are only two. Either the translator leaves the author in peace, as much as possible, and moves the reader towards him; or he leaves the reader in peace, as much as possible, and moves the author towards him. The two roads are so completely separate from each other that one or the other must be followed as closely as possible, and that a highly unreliable result would proceed from any mixture, so that it is to be feared that author and reader would not meet at all. Lefevere 1977: 74)

---

2.   Vermeer (1994a:166) points out that Schleiermacher uses the word *mechanisch* in the sense of "practical, goal-directed" as opposed to the aesthetic quality of fine arts.

Schleiermacher himself offered no definite terms to designate these two methods, which are now known in German as *Verfremdung* and *Entfremdung*, and have recently gained recognition in the English-speaking scientific community as *foreignization* and *domestication* (see 4.3 below). While he appears to be offering an alternative (*either/or*), Schleiermacher makes it clear during the course of his lecture that he far prefers the first course, and he is categorical in ruling out anything like a compromise. To be able to "move" the reader towards the author (a few lines later specified as "Roman", so the "movement" is not only across languages but back in time), the translator can of course translate word for word "like a schoolboy", but Schleiermacher recommends creating a language which has been "bent towards a foreign likeness" (Lefevere 1977: 78–79) – "einer fremden Aehnlichkeit hinübergebogen" (Störig 1963: 55) – hence "bending" the target language to create a deliberately contrived foreignness in the translation, particularly through the use of archaisms. Such a language was used by Schleiermacher himself in his translations of Plato, and by the poet Friedrich Hölderlin (1770–1843) in his German versions of Sophocles and other Greek poets. While the topic of a special sub-language for use in translation, as attributed to Schleiermacher, was to be taken up again repeatedly over the following two hundred years, as in Victorian England (see Bassnett 1980/2003: 70–74), in Germany of the 1920s (see discussion of Benjamin and Rosenzweig below), and finally by Venuti in the 1990s, the maxim on the relationship between author, reader and translator was not Schleiermacher's invention. It was at face value an elaboration of the maxims presented by Goethe, himself a prolific and enthusiastic translator (e.g. of Benvenuto Cellini, Voltaire, Euripides, Racine and Corneille), during his commemorative address for Christoph Martin Wieland, who died in 1813:

> Es gibt zwei Übersetzungsmaximen: die eine verlangt, dass der Autor einer fremden Nation zu uns herüber gebracht werde, dergestalt, dass wir ihn als den Unsrigen ansehen können; die andere hingegen macht an uns die Forderung, dass wir uns zu dem Fremden hinüber begeben und uns in seine Zustände, seine Sprachweise, seine Eigenheiten finden sollen. Die Vorzüge von beiden sind durch musterhafte Beispiele allen gebildeten Menschen genügsam bekannt. Unser Freund, der auch hier den Mittelweg suchte, war beide zu verhindern bemüht, doch zog er als Mann von Gefühl und Geschmack in zweifelhaften Fällen die erste Maxime vor. (cit. Tgahrt 1982: 270)

> (There are two maxims in translation: one requires that the author of a foreign nation be brought across to us in such a way that we can look on him as ours; the other requires that we should go across to what is foreign and adapt ourselves to its conditions, its use of language, its peculiarities. The advantages of both are sufficiently known to educated people through perfect examples. Our friend, who

> looked for the middle way in this, too, tried to reconcile both, but as a man of feeling and taste he preferred the first maxim when in doubt. Lefevere 1977: 39)

The wording may be similar, but the message differs markedly from Schleiermacher's. "Our friend" Christoph Martin Wieland was the first major translator of Shakespeare's plays into German (between 1762 and 1766 he published 22 plays in prose translation), and so Goethe's author was not one of distant Classical antiquity. Moreover, whereas Schleiermacher categorically sets one method against the other but strongly favours foreignization, Goethe commends Wieland in choosing the "middle way" and, "when in doubt", the method of naturalization (now known as "domestication").

The concept of the triad, consisting of the polarized approach (as presented by Schleiermacher) along with a "middle way", reminds us of another great figure in translation theory, this time from England. In his Preface to *Ovid's Epistles, Translated by Several Hands* (1680) John Dryden had distinguished between *metaphrase* (word-for-word translation) and its opposite *imitation* (which is confined by neither word nor sense, but represents a loose approximation of an author's emotions or passion), and between these two extremes is *paraphrase*, which expresses the sense of the original without being enslaved by the words. Though two of these terms seem the same as those later used by Schleiermacher, they are of course used by Dryden in a different sense. Like Schleiermacher however, Dryden makes it quite clear where his preference lies. For him the least desirable type of translation is "metaphrase", which he compares to "dancing on ropes with fettered legs" (1962: 269), but as both word-for-word translation and "imitation" are "the two extremes which ought to be avoided" (1962: 271), he clearly comes out in favour of sense-for-sense translation (cf. Snell-Hornby 1988: 11–12).

Over a hundred years later the tripartite classification of translations was to become a favourite model for the German Romantics. In 1798 the poet Novalis published an essay entitled "Blüthenstaub" ("Pollen") in the literary journal *Athenaeum* edited by Friedrich and August Wilhelm Schlegel (cit. Störig 1963: 33), where he describes a translation as being "grammatical, transforming, or mythical" (Lefevere 1977: 64). Mythical translations, as "translations in the highest style, (…) do not give us the real work of art, but its ideal". Examples would be Greek mythology as the translation of a national religion, or the myth of the "modern Madonna".[3] Grammatical translations are "translations in the ordinary sense. They require enormous erudition, but discursive abilities only." Transforming transla-

---

3.   Cf. Berman 1984/1992:111 „The allusion to the Madonna (...) refers to a visit by the Jena group to the museums of Dresden, where they were able to admire, among other things, Raphael's Madonnas."

tions require "the highest poetic spirit", but can easily degenerate into "mere trav-esties", examples being "Pope's Homer, and all French translations". For this type the translator must himself be an artist, the "poet's poet" ("der Dichter des Dich-ters"), and Novalis adds:

> In einem ähnlichen Verhältnisse steht der Genius der Menschheit mit jedem ein-zelnen Menschen. (Störig 1963: 33)

> (A similar relationship exists between every individual human being and the genius of mankind. Lefevere 1977: 64)

This concept of translation, particularly "mythical translation", clearly goes beyond the translation of verbal texts (cf. Vermeer 1994a: 4–6 and 3.1 below).

In 1819, in the Notes on his *West-Östlicher Diwan*, Goethe, while extending the horizon of interest to literatures outside Europe, was also to present a tripartite model, the "epochs" of translation, introducing what Lefevere calls "an evolution-ary component" depending on the stage reached in the relationship between source literature and target literature (1977: 35):

> Es gibt dreierlei Arten Übersetzungen. Die erste macht uns in unserm eigenen Sinne mit dem Auslande bekannt; eine schlicht-prosaische ist hiezu die beste. (…)

> Eine zweite Epoche folgt hierauf, wo man sich in die Zustände des Auslandes zwar zu versetzen, aber eigentlich nur fremden Sinn sich anzueignen und mit eignem Sinne wieder darzustellen bemüht ist. Solche Zeit möchte ich im reinsten Wortverstand die parodistische nennen. (…)

> Weil man aber weder im Vollkommenen noch Unvollkommenen verharren kann, sondern eine Umwandlung nach der andern immerhin erfolgen muß, so erlebten wir den dritten Zeitraum, welcher der höchste und letzte zu nennen ist, derjenige nämlich, wo man die Übersetzung dem Original identisch machen möchte, so daß eins nicht anstatt des andern, sondern an der Stelle des andern gelten soll. (Störig 1963: 36)

> (There are three kinds of translation. The first acquaints us with foreign countries on our own terms; a simple prosaic translation is best in this respect. (…)

> A second epoch follows in which (the translator) really only tries to appropriate foreign content and to reproduce it in his own sense, even though he tries to trans-port himself into foreign situations. I would like to call this kind of epoch the par-odistic one, in the fullest sense of that word. (…)

> Since it is impossible to linger too long either in the perfect or in the imperfect and one change must of necessity follow another, we experienced the third epoch, which is to be called the highest and the final one, namely the one in which the aim is to make the original identical with the translation, so that one would not be valued instead of the other, but in the other's stead. Lefevere 1977: 35–36)

For the first epoch of "prosaic", domesticating translations, Goethe suggests Luther's Bible translation as an example. As for the second, "parodistic" epoch, he remarks that "Wieland's translations are of this kind", and "The French use this method in their translations of all poetic works" (Lefevere 1977: 36). For the third epoch – Schleiermacher's ideal, later to be taken up by Walter Benjamin – Goethe names Johann Heinrich Voss, the celebrated translator of Homer into German hexameters, who was highly regarded by Goethe as an authority on Classical metres. At all events, his clear dichotomy of 1813 has, in this new progression or cline, been distinctly blurred.

In this context, the references to French translation must be explained. The translator specifically mentioned by Goethe as representative of his second epoch was Abbé Jacques Delille (1738–1813), a prolific French translator known in his day as the "French Virgil". The broader reference is however to the French tradition in general, going back to the French rationalism championed by Gottsched and to the free translations dating from the 17th century, notoriously dubbed "les belles infidèles". Although literalism was revived with the Romantic movement in the early 19th century, the French were generally seen by the German translators to "paraphrase and disguise". This was wittily sketched by A.W. Schlegel in 1798 in a dialogue called "Der Wettstreit der Sprachen" ("The Contest of Languages"), during which the Frenchman declares: "We look on a foreign author as a stranger in our company, who has to dress and behave according to our customs, if he desires to please." (Lefevere 1977: 50) This fits in exactly with Goethe's words of 1819 describing the "parodistic" French of his second epoch: "Just as the French adapt foreign words to their pronunciation, just so do they treat feelings, thoughts, even objects; for every foreign fruit they demand a counterfeit grown in their own soil." (Lefevere 1977: 36)

Wilhelm von Humboldt is represented in Lefevere's collection by an extract from the Introduction to his translation of Aeschylus' *Agamemnon*, published in 1816. This contains not only statements on translation, but also some of his principles of language in general, a field where he was a scholar of outstanding importance. George Steiner wrote of him: "Humboldt is one of the very short list of writers and thinkers on language – it would include Plato, Vico,[4] Coleridge, Saussure, Roman Jakobson – who have said anything that is new and comprehensive" (1975: 79). Essential for such an achievement was however the intellectual climate of his time and country:

---

4.   Giovanni Battista Vico (1668–1744), philosopher of cultural history and law in Italy, now recognized as the forerunner of anthropology and ethnology.

The short years between Herder's writings and those of Wilhelm von Humboldt were among the most productive in the history of linguistic thought. (…)

Humboldt was fortunate. An extraordinary linguistic and psychological process was occurring all around him: a major literature was being created. It brought to bear on language and national sensibility a concentration of individual genius together with a common vision for which there are few parallels in history. Goethe, Schiller, Wieland, Voss, Hölderlin, and a score of others were doing more than composing, editing, translating masterpieces. With a high degree of policy and proclaimed intent, they were making of the German language an exemplar, a deliberate inventory of new possibilities of personal and social life. *Werther, Don Carlos, Faust* are supreme works of the individual imagination, but also intensely pragmatic forms. In them, through them, the hitherto divided provinces and principalities of the German-speaking lands could test a new common identity. (Steiner 1975: 78–80)

It is against this background that we must see the work in and on language and translation by Humboldt (and indeed of the other scholars we have been discussing). He was among the first to make the vital connection between language and culture, language and behaviour. For him language was something dynamic, an activity (*energeia*) based on the consensus of its speakers rather than a static inventory of items as the product of activity (*ergon*), and the word itself is not merely a sign, but a symbol:

Alle Sprachformen sind Symbole, nicht die Dinge selbst, nicht verabredete Zeichen, sondern Laute, welche mit den Dingen und Begriffen, die sie darstellen, durch den Geist, in dem sie entstanden sind, und immerfort entstehen, sich in wirklichem, wenn man es so nennen will, mystischem Zusammenhange befinden, welche die Gegenstände der Wirklichkeit gleichsam aufgelöst in Ideen enthalten, und nun auf eine Weise, der keine Gränze gedacht werden kann, verändern, bestimmen, trennen und verbinden können. (Störig 1963: 82)

(All signs of language are symbols, not the things themselves, not signs agreed on, but sounds which find themselves, together with the things and concepts they represent, through the mind in which they originated and keep originating, in a real and, so to speak, mystical connection which the objects of reality contain as it were dissolved in ideas. These symbols can be changed, defined, separated and united in a manner for which no limit can be imagined. Lefevere 1977: 41–42)

His observation is therefore only logical that "if one excepts those expressions which designate purely physical objects, no word in one language is completely equivalent to a word in another." (Lefevere 1977: 40) As a translator Humboldt aims at clarity and fidelity to the text as a whole and emphasizes the need for empathy between translator and author; he tries to avoid "obscurity and un-Germanness" (Lefevere 1977: 3, "Undeutschheit und Dunkelheit" in Störig 1963: 84), and makes a distinction between translation and commentary:

> Eine Uebersetzung kann und soll kein Commentar seyn. Sie darf keine Dunkelheit enthalten, die aus schwankendem Wortgebrauch, schielender Fügung entsteht; aber wo das Original nur andeutet, statt klar auszusprechen, wo es sich Metaphern erlaubt, deren Beziehung schwer zu fassen ist, wo es Mittelideen auslässt, da würde der Uebersetzer Unrecht thun aus sich selbst willkührlich eine den Charakter des Textes verstellende Klarheit hineinzubringen.(Störig 1963: 84)

> (A translation cannot and should not be a commentary. It should not contain obscurities originating in vacillating use of language and clumsy construction; but where the original only hints, without clearly expressing, where it allows itself metaphors whose meaning is hard to grasp, where it leaves out mediating ideas, there the translator would go wrong if he were to introduce, of his own accord, a clarity which disfigures the character of the text. Lefevere 1977: 43)

The methods developed by the theorists of the German Romantic age, as attempts to empathize and understand rather than objectify, are based essentially on hermeneutics. This applies especially to Schleiermacher, who, quite apart from his academy lecture, also made a substantial contribution to the field of hermeneutics in general, writings which are undeservedly less well known today (see Schleiermacher 1993). This work, which was developed between 1805 and 1829, has been analyzed by Vermeer (1994a) and described in English by Salevsky (Rübberdt and Salevsky 1997). His basic concept is the hermeneutic circle, which describes the process of understanding as a circular movement involving a repeated return from the whole to the parts and vice versa, thus creating an ever-increasing spiral which "incorporates ever new sense connexions" (Rübberdt and Salevsky 1997: 301). Salevsky sums up Schleiermacher's basic ideas on hermeneutics as follows:

A. Any utterance can only be understood from the perspective of the entire life context to which it belongs, as an aspect of the speaker's life that is dependent on all other aspects of his life, and the latter can only be determined by taking into account the sum total of the settings which determine his development and future existence.
B. Any speaker can only be understood through the prism of his nationality and the age in which he lives. (Rübberdt and Salevsky 1997: 302)

Similarly, Vermeer identifies four factors in Schleiermacher's hermeneutic process: understanding the utterance itself, how it came into being, its immediate situation and how it relates to its background circumstances (including those of the speaker or author) as a whole. For Schleiermacher, understanding requires knowledge of the facts or objects under discussion, knowledge of the language used, and knowledge of the speaker (or author) himself (Vermeer 1994a: 174, cf. 3.3.1 below).

All this sheds light on how Schleiermacher would want his own utterances, as in the above quotations from his academy lecture, to be understood: not as isolated dichotomies, but within the immediate and broader context in which they were made. That is, as the words of a German scholar at the beginning of the 19th century, at the time when Napoleon was being forced back out of Central Europe (the Battle of the Nations was fought at Leipzig in October 1813); it was the early period of the Romantic movement, when German was beginning to emerge as a national language and Germany was emerging as a nation out of the patchwork of petty states it had been. It is in this context too that some further utterances from his lecture, meanwhile the object of considerable debate in Translation Studies (cf. 4.3 below), must be understood, particularly those on topics such as nationalism and linguistic purity. One such well-worn quotation is contained in the context of the "bent" and contrived, foreignized language which he recommends for translation, but he envisages problems because of the disadvantage involved for the writer's native language:

> Wer möchte nicht seine Muttersprache überall in der volksgemäßesten Schönheit auftreten lassen, deren jede Gattung nur fähig ist? Wer möchte nicht lieber Kinder erzeugen, die das väterliche Geschlecht rein darstellen, als Blendlinge?
> (Störig 1963: 55)

> (Who would not like to permit his mother tongue to stand forth everywhere in the most universally appealing beauty each genre is capable of? Who would not rather sire children who are their parents' pure effigy, and not bastards?
> Lefevere 1977: 79)

In our postcolonial days of hybrid texts (see 3.2.1) and European integration (4.2.3) these lines cannot be generalized as eternal principles of translation, but should be understood in Schleiermacher's own terms and "through the prism of his own nationality and age". This applies particularly to the metaphor of "siring children", which in our day and age seems blatantly racist. The word *Blendling* is now archaic, and it is not entered in the *Duden Universalwörterbuch* (Drosdowski et al 1996). It does appear in Friedrich Kluge's etymological dictionary of German (Kluge 1975) as a derivative of OHG *blendan* in the sense of *blend*, with the meaning "half-breed". Lefevere's English rendering "bastards", a word still common in colloquial usage, especially in its unspecified derogatory sense, is more than unfortunate and does not reflect the intentions of the German text of 1813.

Another frequently cited passage from Schleiermacher's lecture discusses "world citizenship" ("Weltbürgerschaft") and proficiency in foreign languages as against love of one's country and its national language, and it culminates in the following statement:

> Wie Einem Lande, so auch Einer Sprache oder der andern, muß der Mensch sich entschließen anzugehören, oder er schwebt haltungslos in unerfreulicher Mitte. (Störig 1963: 63)

> (Just as a man must decide to belong to one country, just so must he adhere to one language, or he will float without any bearings above an unpleasant middle ground. Lefevere 1977: 84)

It is not only the "middle ground" which was again to provide food for debate in future Translation Studies: from the viewpoint of today with all our hindsight on the development of nationalism in 20th century Germany, the imagery used by Schleiermacher, when analyzed outside its immediate context of time and place, could give and indeed has given grounds for misinterpretation (cf. 4.3).

In general however there is a consensus that the early 19th century German theorists have proved to be important precursors of modern Translation Studies, even for the English-speaking community. Lawrence Venuti opens his Introduction to the first part (1900s–1930s) of *The Translation Studies Reader* (Venuti 2000), which presents texts by Walter Benjamin, Ezra Pound, Jorge Luis Borges and José Ortega y Gasset, with these observations:

> The main trends in translation theory during this period are rooted in German literary and philosophical traditions, in Romanticism, hermeneutics, and existential phenomenology. They assume that language is not so much communicative as constitutive in its representation of thought and reality, and so translation is seen as an interpretation which necessarily reconstitutes and transforms the foreign text. Nineteenth-century theorists and practitioners like Friedrich Schleiermacher and Wilhelm von Humboldt treated translation as a creative force in which specific translation strategies might serve a variety of cultural and social functions, building languages, literatures, and nations. At the start of the twentieth century, these ideas are rethought from the vantage point of modernist movements which prize experiments with literary form as as a way of revitalizing culture. Translation is a focus of theoretical speculation and formal innovation. (Venuti 2000: 11)

Venuti's *Reader* opens with Walter Benjamin's essay "Die Aufgabe des Übersetzers" of 1923,[5] leaving a long gap after Schleiermacher and Humboldt. After the Romantic Age and during the course of the 19th century, the German tradition stagnated and was subject to some intense internal criticism. This started in effect

---

5.   „The Task of the Translator", translated by Harry Zohn.

with another lecture read at the Academy of Sciences in Berlin, this time on 21st October 1847 by Jakob Grimm: "Über das Pedantische in der deutschen Sprache" ("On the pedantic element in the German language") with the criticism that not even the words of Schlegel or Voss were able to recreate the "marvellous beauty" of Shakespeare or Homer. In this speech Grimm uttered his celebrated lines:

> Übersétzen ist übersetzen, traducere navem. Wer nun zur seefahrt aufgelegt, ein schif bemannen und mit vollem segel an das gestade jenseits führen kann, musz dennoch landen, wo andrer boden ist und andre luft streicht. (Störig 1963: 111)

> (To trans*late* ist to *trans*late,[6] *traducere navem*. Whoever has a talent for navigation, whoever is able to man a ship and lead it with full sail to the opposite shore, still has to land where the air and the soil are different. Lefevere 1977: 95)

The stress has changed noticeably since the days of Schleiermacher: no longer must the target language be "bent" to do justice to the source text, now the translator must accept that in the world of the target language "another breeze is blowing" ("andre Luft streicht"). Using yet another image, Grimm criticizes strict translations because they "pedantically strain themselves to weave a copy of the dress, and fall short of the source text whose form and content naturally and spontaneously agree" (Lefevere 1977: 95). In German the text reads: "…mühen sich die strengen das gewand nachzuweben pedantisch ab und bleiben hinter dem urtext stehn, dessen form und inhalt ungesucht und natürlich zusammenstimmen" (Störig 1963: 111) – clearly subscribing to the unity of form and content, which is not observable in translations which are too faithful.

In later years the criticism became harsher as German nationalism lost the freshness and enthusiam of the Romantic Age and became more aggressive. Friedrich Nietzsche (1844–1900), one of the most influential thinkers of the century was, in *Die fröhliche Wissenschaft* ("The joyful science", 1882), to dwell on the stiffness and pomposity of German translations (Störig 1963: 137) and attack translation as conquest – hence anticipating the arguments of postcolonial translation critics over a hundred years afterwards (2.4). Years later in 1925, Karl Vossler (1872–1949) lashed out at the "masters of translation" because "with the wolf's hunger of esthetic imperialism they grasp whatever they lust after" (Lefevere 1977: 97), likewise a kind of terminology which was to become familiar in postcolonial years (see 3.2.1 and 4.3).

The most well-known name in early 20th century German translation theory must however be Walter Benjamin (1892–1940), whose essay „The task of the

---

6.   Grimm's metaphor is based on a double meaning in the German which does not come across in this English translation: übersetzen (with the stress on the first syllable) means "to ferry across".

translator" has been the source of unusual inspiration and debate. "Die Aufgabe des Übersetzers" was published in 1923 as the Preface to his translation of Baudelaire's *Tableaux parisiens*. This was a time of great turmoil (Hitler's abortive *Putsch* took place on 23rd November 1923), with the monumental crises of inflation, Depression and the ensuing rise of Nazi dictatorship, which eventually led to Benjamin's suicide in 1940. An absolute contrast to such an experience of history are his mystical thoughts on translation as part of the "afterlife" (*Überleben*) which through transformation ensures the survival of the foreign text, and on "die reine Sprache" (pure language) as derived from Goethe's "third epoch" of translation. This is made possible in the translation by a radical form of literalism which, here in accordance with Schleiermacher, creates deviations from standard usage:

> Die wahre Übersetzung ist durchscheinend, sie verdeckt nicht das Original, steht ihm nicht im Licht, sondern lässt die reine Sprache, wie verstärkt durch ihr eigenes Medium, nur um so voller aufs Original fallen. Das vermag vor allem Wörtlichkeit in der Übertragung der Syntax, und gerade sie erweist das Wort, nicht den Satz als das Urelement des Übersetzers. (Störig 1963: 192)

> (Real translation is transparent, it does not hide the original, it does not steal its light, but allows the pure language, as if reinforced through its own medium, to fall on the original work with greater fulness. This lies above all in the power of literalness in the translation of syntax, and even this points to the word, not the sentence, as the translator's original element. Lefevere 1977: 102)

The logical conclusion comes in the final sentence of the essay:

> Die Interlinearversion des heiligen Textes ist das Urbild oder Ideal aller Übersetzung. (Störig 1963: 195)

> (The interlinear version of the Scriptures is the archetype or ideal of all translation.)

Completely different conclusions are reached by a contemporary of Benjamin's, Franz Rosenzweig (1886–1929), a Jewish theologian and one of the most influential religious philosophers of his age. From 1925 he worked with Martin Buber (1878–1965) on a new German translation of the Hebrew Old Testament, though he was already afflicted with a severe form of progressive paralysis and was unable to speak or write; however, using a system of signals and a specially constructed typewriter, he continued working as an active scholar. In 1926 he wrote his essay "Die Schrift und Luther" ("The Scriptures and Luther"), where he describes all speech as translation, and stresses, as Lefevere put it, that "literary translation is absolutely essential as an antidote against the aggressive, imperialist nationalism referred to above" (1977: 94, cf. 5.3 below). Rosenzweig was a staunch advocate of compromise and referred to Schleiermacher's dichotomy as a "blendende Antithese" (Störig 1963: 221), as "dazzling" in a double sense, both in its wit and in its tendency to distort "a very complex and entangled and never antithetically separated reality" (Lefevere 1977: 111). He suggested interpreting Schleiermacher's maxim, not as "either/or", but as a means of disentangling that complex reality, leading to the really essential question: "at which points in the work is the reader moved and at which points the original" (Lefevere 1977: 111).

With that we have yet again moved from the concept of two extremes to a complex terrain inbetween, and indeed the impression may be justified that we have been continually going in circles – Vermeer's "peripatetic spirals". George Steiner comments:

> List Saint Jerome, Luther, Dryden, Hölderlin, Novalis, Schleiermacher, Nietzsche, Ezra Pound, Valéry,[7] MacKenna,[8] Franz Rosenzweig, Walter Benjamin, Quine[9] – and you have very nearly the sum total of those who have said anything fundamental or new about translation. The range of theoretic ideas, as distinct from the wealth of pragmatic notation, remains very small. (1975: 269)

Of Steiner's thirteen personalities, seven have had a place in our overview of the German tradition. Conspicuously absent from the picture so far however are two outstanding figures from other traditions who are usually prominent in surveys of traditional translation theory: the French translator Etienne Dolet (1509–1546) and the Scottish lawyer and scholar Alexander Fraser Tytler (1748–1813), who, along with the poet Dryden, formulated some basic rules and principles for a good translator (see Snell-Hornby 1988: 12–13). In his *Essay on the Principles of Translation* of 1791 (see Tytler 1978), Tytler acknowledges his debt to Dryden, so it is not altogether surprising that their principles coincide. What is however remarkable is that both of them echo Etienne Dolet's 4-page treatise *La manière de bien traduire d'une langue en aultre* ("How to translate well from one language into another") published in 1540 (see Bassnett 1980/2002: 58–9 and Snell-Hornby 1988: 12–13). The three theorists state basic conclusions reached by their own work as translators, principles that are still stressed in translator training today: the need for mastery of both source and target language, for understanding the author's sense and meaning, and for translating in an appropriate and idiomatic style with all the ease of the original composition (cf. 2.4).

---

7.   Paul Valéry (1871–1945), French poet, critic and translator (see Steiner 1975: 346–7 and 478).

8.   Stephen MacKenna, translator of Plotinus' *Enneades* (published between 1917 and 1930), see Steiner 1975: 267–269.

9.   Willard V.O. Quine (1908–2000), American philosopher, (see Venuti 2000: 94–112, also Steiner 1975: 277).

1.2   Paving the way: from Jakobson to Paepcke

Having "appointed" some pioneers and masters of traditional translation theory as great precursors of modern Translation Studies, we should, following Radnitzky's model, now be looking for pioneers. However, reality seems to be more complicated, and as in former approaches (Snell-Hornby 1988: 31), we shall here abandon clear-cut groupings or typologies in favour of the prototypology, which permits blurred edges, overlappings – and even gaps. For the erratic history of translation studies the latter has particular relevance, especially for the years when scholarly exchange in translation theory, along with many other fields of scholarship, was harshly interrrupted by the Second World War.[10]

In post-war years activities were revived, whereby literary translation (viewed as a branch of Comparative Literature) was complemented by a burst of interest in the translation of non-literary language, then considered a subdivision of linguistics (see 1.3). During this period a number of outstanding scholars from various traditions in linguistics and other neighbouring disciplines made specific contributions to the debate, each of which may be seen as a flagstone, as it were, paving the way to the new discipline. This is the time of the "immediate precursors", often with a multilingual background and with intellectual roots in an environment that was particularly fruitful for translation.

One such environment was the so-called Prague School, developed in the mid-1920s by a group of scholars with specialities ranging from phonology and syntax to literary theory and covering a whole spectrum of European languages, including English and German, Czech and Russian. The focus was especially on contemporary language, stressing the function of elements within language, particularly as in contrast to each other, and the complete system or pattern as formed by these contrasts. One of its founders and principal members was Roman Jakobson (1896–1982), who spent his early years in Moscow, where he was known for his work in the movement called Russian Formalism: in 1928 he and Juri Tynjanov developed the concept of literature as a "system of systems" (see Prunč 2001: 208 ff. and 2.1 below). Later in Prague Jakobson addressed the nature of poetic language and the problems of verse translation (see Kufnerova and Osers 1998: 380). The political situation in Europe finally compelled him to emigrate, first to Scandinavia, then to the USA; here he taught first at Columbia University, then at Harvard, where he was professor of Slavic languages and literature and general

---

10. In Störig's anthology it is striking that the German translation of Ortega y Gasset's "Miseria y esplendor de la traducción", published in Spanish in 1937, appeared in 1956. Similarly, the next contribution, an essay by Martin Buber (collaborator of Franz Rosenzweig) was only published in 1954.

linguistics from 1949 to 1967. It was during this last period that he wrote the essay for which he is best known in Translation Studies, "On Linguistic Aspects of Translation" (1959). This presents another triadic system of translation, of a type which may seem familiar from our last section:

> We distinguish three ways of interpreting a verbal sign: it may be translated into other signs of the same language, into another language, or into another, nonverbal system of symbols. These three kinds of translation are to be differently labelled:
>
> 1. Intralingual translation or *rewording* is an interpretation of verbal signs by means of other signs of the same language.
> 2. Interlingual translation or *translation proper* is an interpretation of verbal signs by means of some other language.
> 3. Intersemiotic translation or *transmutation* is an interpretation of verbal signs by means of signs of nonverbal sign systems. (Jakobson 1959: 2)

What is striking about this model is however that it goes further than the traditional systems and sees translation from a semiotic viewpoint as a transfer of signs, as an interpretation of signs by means of other signs (particularly in the sense going back to Charles S. Peirce). The verbal sign is understood here as the lexical item or grammatical structure, and Jakobson discusses translation, as was usual for linguists of the time and as his examples show, mainly as a matter of words. What is significant for Translation Studies, as assessed from today's perspective, is however that he goes beyond language in the verbal sense and does not look merely across languages. His distinction between interlingual "translation proper" and intralingual translation (already familiar in summary, paraphrase, explanation or definition) is now for example fundamental in TV subtitling for the deaf and hard of hearing, whereas intersemiotic translation is an integral element in multimedial and multimodal transfer, whether software localization or translation for stage and screen (see 3.1.3 below).

Back in Europe, the Prague School tradition was to resurface during the 1960s in the person of the literary historian and translator Jiří Levý (1926–1967), who, until his early death at the age of 40, taught literary theory at the University of Brünn. For translation studies, Levý's main work was his book on literary translation, published in Czech in 1963 as *Umění překladu* (The Art of Translation) and then posthumously in 1969 in the German translation by Walter Schamschula with the title *Die literarische Übersetzung. Theorie einer Kunstgattung.*[11] With this book, which already succeeded in bridging the gap between theory and practice,

---

11. See Prunč (2001: 213–217) for extremely critical notes on Schamschula's translation, which have been considered in our discussion.

which discussed both linguistic and literary methods and introduced the aim of the translation as a decisive factor (see Prunč 2001: 213), Levý went beyond the role of precursor and proved to be one of the pioneers of modern Translation Studies. His material included drama translation, so long considered a stepchild of the discipline, with all the problems of speakability and performability that were to be debated in the 1990s, and one third of the book is devoted to verse translation. For Levý literary translation is a form of art in its own right, and has a position somewhere between creative and "reproductive" art; he divides the translating process into three phases: understanding, interpreting, transfer. The translated work is an artistic reproduction, the translation process is one of artistic creativity, which, by giving a concrete form to an already existent text, can best be compared to the art of acting on the stage. In this context Levý applies his notion of the translation norm (cf. 3.1.1), distinguishing between the "reproductive" norm, which requires fidelity as based on proper understanding of the text, and the "artistic" norm, which requires the fulfilment of aesthetic criteria (Levý 1969:68). For him fidelity and artistic style are by no means mutually exclusive. Translation norms are not static and absolute but always depend on their historical context, and like all artistic norms form part of their individual national culture.

Levý divides translation methods into two groups, the "illusionist" and the "anti-illusionist", as understood in contemporary theatre: conventional theatre tries to evoke the illusion that what is happening on the stage is reality, whereas the "epic theatre" of Bert Brecht with its method of alienation (*Verfremdung*) makes it clear that the play is only a copy of reality, thus provoking critical detachment towards the events on stage. Similarly, the translator can "hide behind the original" (Levý 1969: 31) and create the illusion that his translation is an original text. Or else he can refrain from imitating the source text and make it quite clear that his text is a translation, as for example by including "topical and personal allusions to the (intended) reader" (Levý 1969: 32, Prunč 2001: 215), although Levý points out that in fact such anti-illusionist translation is rare and would rather fall into the category of parody or travesty. However, even with the illusionist method, both in the theatre and in translation, everyone involved is in fact fully aware that an illusion is being created and upheld: in other words, the reader knows that the text is a translation, and that it at best only produces the same effect as the original. What is important is the holistic principle, the subordination of the parts and the details to the text as a whole, as seen in its function within the (literary) system, and within a cultural and historical context. Similar ideas were later to be expressed and elaborated in the functional and descriptive approaches of the 1980s.

With the role of the reader Levý broached another subject that was to become a central theme in literary studies in the 1970s (the theory of aesthetic response, see Iser 1976) and in Translation Studies from the 1980s (see 3.3 and 3.3.1). A literary work only has social relevance as a work of art when it is read, and the reader always understands it from the viewpoint of his own period in time. The reception process "normally" ends with the reconstruction of a literary work in the mind of its reader. But the translator differs from the "normal reader" in that he must form an idea of the work and put this into words for another reader, and, like the original, the translation only has social relevance when it is itself read. In a translation therefore, the material undergoes a change in all three subjective transformations by the act of reading: the remodelling of reality by the author, the visualization of the source text and its verbal expression by the translator, and finally the image (we shall be later discussing this as the "scene", see 3.3.1) that arises in the mind of the target reader. And this means, as was also to be stressed in the functional approaches of the 1980s, that the translator must work with the readership in mind and anticipate how his text can be visualized by them (Prunč 2001: 216–7).

In the English-speaking scientific community Levý is known for the essay "Translation as a Decision Process", published in the volume *To Honor Roman Jakobson* in 1967. Here again there are several aspects which anticipate developments of the 1980s and 1990s. From the teleological point of view Levý sees translation as a process of communication – Prunč correctly points out (2001: 219) that with the term *teleological* (from Greek *télos*, end, purpose) he is already anticipating the skopos theory (2.2). From the concrete working situation of the translator, translating is seen as a decision process, with moves, based on a series of consecutive situations, as in a game (Levý 1967/2000: 148), for which he has an unusually pragmatic, common-sense solution:

> Translation theory tends to be normative, to instruct translators on the OPTIMAL solution; actual translation work, however, is pragmatic; the translator resolves for that one of the possible solutions which promises a maximum of effect with a minimum of effort. That is to say, he intuitively resolves for the so-called MINI-MAX STRATEGY. (Levý 1967/2000: 156)

And here Prunč aptly observes (2001: 220) that Levý already anticipates the principle of relevance defined in Gutt 1991 as achieving maximum benefit at minimum processing cost.

Jiří Levý lived and wrote in Czechoslovakia of the 1960s, hence in an environment under the grip of communist rule: the short-lived Prague Spring was to take place during the year following his death. His exuberant pioneer spirit is all the more remarkable, as is the fact that his innovative ideas have in essence neither been refuted nor become outdated over the last forty years, many have on the contrary been confirmed, in Radnitzky's phrase, as part of the "raw program" of the future discipline of Translation Studies.

Other "immediate precursors" from the 1950s can be found in a completely different part of the world and outside the Central European mainstream. Canada has a long tradition in translation going back to early colonial times and involving both the interchange between colonists and indigenous people and the transfer between the two colonial languages English and French. This obviously concerned interpreting and matters of administration, legislation and commerce rather than literary texts or philosophy. But non-literary translation flourished, particularly against the bilingual background following Conferation in 1867, and Canada was to take the lead in such matters as organizing the profession, establishing a Translation Bureau and in translator training (see Delisle 1998). Pioneers in this field were Jean-Paul Vinay (1910–1999) and Jean Darbelnet (1904–90) with their *Stylistique comparée du français et de l'anglais* (1958), which was to gain international recognition and become a cornerstone in translation pedagogy world-wide.

In their Introduction the authors vividly describe the genesis of this seminal work. While driving on the highway from New York to Montreal, they were impressed by what they call the "caractère presque paternel et doucement autoritaire' ("the almost paternal and gently authoritarian character") of the English roads signs ('No passing', 'Slow – men at work', 'Slippery when wet'), which they say lack the "official resonance" of public signs in France (1958: 18). After crossing the Canadian border, they were irritated by the French-Canadian translations of the English signs ("Slow/Lentement", "Slippery when wet/Glissant si humide"), which differ basically from authentic, untranslated road signs in France: "Défense de doubler", "Ralentir travaux" (in Britain this would be "Slow – Road works ahead") or "Chaussée glissante sur 3 kilomètres" ("Road slippery for 3 km"). Vinay and Darbelnet concentrate on what they call the "génies différents" of the two languages (1958: 20): today one would rather speak of text-type conventions which are determined by both language and culture (see 3.1.1), but what is remarkable about their approach to translation is that it is based, not only on isolated words or signs from the language system, but on genuine parallel texts in concrete situations – later to become an invaluable tool in translator training and translation practice.

Vinay and Darbelnet concentrate on transposing structures as shown contrastively in a language pair. They call their approach "stylistic", though much of the material they cover (aspect, modality, derivation) is today included under grammar and semantics, and from today's viewpoint their "translation procedures", as based on such categories as borrowing, calque, transposition, explicitation and modulation and as applied to isolated lexical and grammatical items (or at best very simple sentences), seem atomistic and prescriptive. However, many of their observations still have a direct bearing on translation practice (their book appeared in an English translation in 1995), above all their insistence – innovative at the time – that language structures should be translated with respect to the communicative situation in which they occur: it is this situation and not signs or items in the language system which determine their notion of *équivalences.*

The term *equivalence* was to dominate the next two decades, though opinions differed considerably as to its exact meaning and application, a debate that was carried on in many different areas of translation. One of these was Bible translation, where the leading figure was Eugene A. Nida, whose seminal monograph *Toward a Science of Translating* (1964) made a substantial contribution towards developing the new field of scholarship. Nida's work for the American Bible Society, which he joined in 1943, concerned translation into indigenous languages, leading to an approach closely involved with anthropology and questions of culture; this was represented, as we have already seen, by Humboldt (1.1), also by the American ethnolinguists Edward Sapir (1884–1939) and Benjamin Lee Whorf (1897–1941). These two scholars viewed language as the direct expression of culture, and their names are known above all for the Sapir-Whorf hypothesis, or principle of linguistic relativity, which maintains that thought does not "precede" language, but on the contrary, the structure of a language conditions the way its speakers think. This too has been a subject of long debate, but the links between culture and language are undeniable, and Nida described language – like the skopos theorists after him – as an integral part of culture, words being symbols of cultural phenomena. As these symbols differ between cultures, and hence languages, translation cannot consist in providing exact equivalents of words in the source language, but rather:

> Translating consists in reproducing in the receptor language the closest natural equivalent of the source-language message, first in terms of meaning and secondly in terms of style. (Nida and Taber 1969:12)

This may well involve radical departures from the formal structure, leading to Nida's differentiation between formal and dynamic equivalence. Formal equivalence seeks to reproduce SL surface structures as exactly as possible, whereas dynamic equivalence focusses on evoking a similar response as in the source language (Nida and Taber 1969: 24). The much-quoted example of dynamic equivalence, whereby "Lamb of God" (symbolizing innocence) was translated into "seal of God" for the Innuit (unfamiliar with lambs), was in later years to be described by Nida as "apocryphal" (*Language International* 1996: 9). As an alternative we might take an example cited by Prunč (2001: 118): "Give us this day our daily bread", whereby "bread" might be rendered by "fish" or "rice" in cultures where these are the staple food.

Like Levý, Nida developed a three-step model for translation – analysis, transfer and restructuring – but based on a completely different approach deriving from Transformational Generative Grammar as the dominant linguistic theory of the day. Like Vinay and Darbelnet, he thought in terms of the "genius" of a language (Nida and Taber 1969: 3) – also echoing the imagery of the time. Since then he has been a prolific writer on various aspects of anthropology, language and translation, moving with and responding to the changes in attitude and thought, and yet preserving his basic culture-oriented approach. In 1996 he was profiled by *Language International* as the "Patriarch of Translation Studies" and a founder of the discipline (1996: 8–9).

Meanwhile, other "founders of the discipline" were active in the Eastern half of Europe. The University of Leipzig, where once Goethe had been a student, had now been named the Karl Marx University, and here a translators' training school was founded in 1957. In the same year the journal *Fremdsprachen* ("Foreign Languages") was launched, which, along with its Supplements and the series *Übersetzungswissenschaftliche Beiträge* ("Essays on Translation Studies"), published from 1977, was to gain an international reputation, as did the names of the three editors, Otto Kade, Gert Jäger and Albrecht Neubert: these, along with other colleagues, became known collectively as the "Leipzig School". Leipzig also had the merit of hosting, in 1965, what was probably the first scholarly conference devoted to translation (then otherwise merely a section in conferences of Applied Linguistics, see Wotjak 2000: 280 and cf. 1.4). From today's viewpoint we can say that the Leipzig publications, if one overlooks their ideological ballast and technical jargon, contain a great deal of pioneer work. This applies particularly to the writings of Otto Kade (1927–1980), whose monograph *Zufall und Gesetzmäßigkeit in der Übersetzung* ("Chance and Regularity in Translation"), published in 1968 as the 1st Supplement of the journal *Fremdsprachen*, is one of the seminal achievements of modern Translation Studies in Germany. Ironically, it first became known for what has with hindsight turned out to be probably its most dated feature, the system of four clearly delimited equivalence types (see Snell-Hornby 1988: 20), that central issue in translation of the time that tended to push all others aside. From the viewpoint of later years however, Kade has been honoured for other insights. Firstly, he was one of the first scholars to transcend the narrow linguistic limits dominant in the 1960s by introducing concepts from communication theory to explain the act of translation, particularly as regards non-literary texts. This involves:

1. The communication partners (the author of the source text, the translator, the user of the translation);
2. The language as means of communication;
3. The objective reality as object of communication and as context of situation in the broadest sense. (1968: 32)

The view of translation, not merely as switching elements of language, but as a concrete act involving participants and an extralinguistic situation, was then a novelty, at least in non-literary translation. It was to resurface later in the theory of translatorial action (2.3) and has now become a basic insight in functional translation studies.

From that starting-point Kade then undertook something that is crucial for any discipline: defining his basic terms so that they could be used as precise scientific tools. In English the words *translate* and *interpret* both have several senses in everyday usage, and the former is used as a technical term (but with different meanings) in physics and theology – and to this day both give reason for confusion and scholarly debate in the discipline of Translation Studies (cf. 1.4 and 6.). In German the same problem exists, but again with another focus and other shades of meaning. The difference between *Dolmetschen* and *Übersetzen* has varied over the centuries. *Dolmetschen* was used by Luther in his famous "circular letter" of 1530 to refer to translation in general (in this specific case Bible translation), whereas in 1813, as we have already seen, Schleiermacher distinguished between everyday communication, both oral and written (*Dolmetschen*)[12] and the translation of scholarly and literary texts (*Übersetzen*). The rough distinction was then developed between *Dolmetschen* as the oral variety and *Übersetzen* for written work, though in some contexts *Dolmetschen* was used as a generic term,[13] particularly for non-literary translation, and not without certain pejorative connotations. Translator training institutions in German-speaking countries used to be called *Dolmetscherinstitute*, with the insinuation of something "not really scholarly" – Kade's own institute in Leipzig bore that name when he was writing his monograph. One of Otto Kade's enduring achievements is to have presented technical terms for the discipline and to have provided rigorous definitions which in the German-speaking scientific community are still used today.

As the generic term for both oral and written translation, Kade suggested the term *Translation* (Lat. *translatio*), which, along with the (now archaic) verb *translatieren*, dates back to the 15th century (cf. Vermeer 2003: 20). The performer of the act involved is the *Translator* and its product is the *Translat* (1968: 33). In accordance with the spirit of the times, Kade defined *Translation* as the process of recoding from L1 to L2 (cf. 1.3). The two subdivisions of *Translation*, *Übersetzen* and *Dolmetschen*, are defined as follows:

---

12.   Hence in this context it is not equivalent to Engl. *interpret*, and Lefevere's (1977) translation is misleading.

13.   Note that in English *translation* is widely used in this generic sense.

> *Übersetzen*: die Translation eines fixierten und demzufolge permanent darge-
> botenen bzw. beliebig oft wiederholbaren Textes der Ausgangssprache in einen
> jederzeit kontrollierbaren und wiederholt korrigierbaren Text der Zielsprache.
>
> *Dolmetschen*: die Translation eines einmalig (in der Regel mündlich) darge-
> botenen Textes der Ausgangssprache in einen nur bedingt kontrollierbaren und
> infolge Zeitmangels kaum korrigierbaren Text der Zielsprache. (1968: 35)
>
> (*Übersetzen* (translation): the rendering of a source-language text that has been
> preserved (in writing) and is hence permanently available or can be repeated at
> will in a target-language text which can be checked any time and can be repeatedly
> corrected.
>
> *Dolmetschen* (interpretation): the rendering of a source-language text which is
> presented only once (usually orally) in a target-language text which can only be
> checked to a limited extent and which due to lack of time can hardly be corrected.)

This careful description of the two activities is to my knowledge still unsurpassed
and certainly merits scholarly attention in the international debate.[14] If we replace
the concept of *text* by *discourse* in the above translation describing *Dolmetschen*,
we have a contrastive definition which might well be a candidate for use in the
English-speaking Translation Studies community today.[15] It is significant however
that Kade specifically ruled out the term "Translationswissenschaft" for a "linguo-
semiotic discipline" which could not cover all the aspects of translation (1973:
184). It was not until the 1980s that functional approaches were developed
embracing these other aspects of translation and the term *Translationswissenschaft*
was adopted (cf. 2.2). For the "linguo-semiotic" approach of the 1960s the term
"Übersetzungswissenschaft" was meanwhile retained, alongside the strictly formalistic Leipzig term "Translationslinguistik", which was associated with the
abstract approach of Gert Jäger (1975) and rather disrespectfully dubbed by students as "TraLaLi".

As was the case with Jiří Levý, Kade's monograph contains various concepts
which were ahead of their time and anticipate future developments. One of these

---

14. In the *Routledge Encyclopedia of Translation Studies* the only reference in the index to a
comparison between translation and interpreting is the first part of Gile's article on Conference
and simultaneous interpreting (1998: 41–42), where he distinguishes between interpreting as the
"oral translation of oral discourse" and sight translation as "the oral translation of written texts".
He describes the differences between translation and interpreting practice which "arise from the
fact that translators deal with written language and have time to polish their work, while interpreters deal with oral language and have no time to refine their output." Otto Kade is mentioned
in the *Encyclopedia* only for his lexical equivalence types mentioned above (Kenny 1998a: 77–78).

15. Note however that Kade's definition of *Dolmetschen* (referring specifically to conference interpreting), does not cover dialogue interpreting (see 4.1.1).

was what he called the "character of the text" according to three different components (1968: 44–47). Like any act of communication, translation consists both of content – with an intellectual component (K1) and an emotional component (KII) – and expression, with a component of form (KIII). In the case of non-literary or – to use Kade's own term – pragmatic translation, K1 is usually more dominant than KII, which in some cases (as in a scientific report) can be reduced to nil. In the case of propaganda or advertising however, KII can be decisive. In literary translation KIII is more dominant than in pragmatic translation, where the form has solely communicative value; in literary translation the form can also be a means of artistic expression. Apart from discussing pragmatic translation (which since Schleiermacher had been virtually lying dormant in European translation theory) as a fully-fledged scientific category, Kade was here anticipating the basic text-types in translation that were to be further developed by Katharina Reiss. Another important connection he made was between human translation and machine translation, the latter then being very much en vogue in the scientific debate. Kade's contribution in this field has been analyzed by his Leipzig colleague Albrecht Neubert (1992), another early pioneer in Translation Studies (much of whose work, especially that published since the demise of communism, is also available in English). Neubert soon integrated sociolinguistic components, for example (1977), and he was one of the first scholars to use the concept of prototypology (personal communication, Brussels 1984), which he applied to lexicography (Neubert 1986). The Leipzig School continued its activities after Kade's death in 1980, and during the 1980s German scholars from "East" and "West" began a process of rapprochement and even cooperation: the 12th and last issue of *Übersetzungswissenschaftliche Beiträge*, with the theme "Interference in Translation", edited by Heide Schmidt, was published in 1989, and contained contributions, not only by Švejcer (Moscow), Neubert (Leipzig) and Klaudy (Budapest), but also by Wilss (Saarbrücken), Kussmaul (Mainz-Germersheim), Holz-Mänttäri (Turku) and Snell-Hornby (Zürich).

Many ideas from the Leipzig School had already been taken up elsewhere in the Western stream of translation theory, as in the work of Peter Newmark (cf. Newmark 1981). What is not so well known is Kade's contribution to the then still embryonic field of interpreting studies. As a practising conference interpreter Kade made a substantial contribution to interpreter training (e.g. Kade 1965) and also to interpreting theory (e.g. Kade 1970), and took up contact with Danica Seleskovitch in Paris, whose institute, the École Supérieure d'Interprètes et de Traducteurs (ESIT), was founded in 1957, the same year as the one in Leipzig. Years later Seleskovitch was to describe similarities and differences between herself and Kade (Seleskovitch 1992), and it is noteworthy that she too worked with a group of scholars, particularly Marianne Lederer and Florence Herbulot (collectively known as the Paris School), who developed the *théorie du sens* or "interpretive approach" that was to become a cornerstone of interpreting studies (Seleskovitch and Lederer 1984 and cf. 4.1 below). Seleskovitch's work also goes back to the 1960s, and it is remarkable that with her emphasis on non-verbal sense and her three-phase definition of the translating process (interpretation of discourse, deverbalization, reformulation) she was to emancipate herself even more than Kade from the linguistic approach of the time.

Seleskovitch explicitly describes Kade as "un précurseur" (1992: 38), but if we take up Radnitzky's definition of the pioneers as those "polemically oriented on other intellectual traditions flourishing in the intellectual milieu" and who "formulate the raw material of the tradition", it would seem that both Kade and herself already bridge the gap to the pioneers. The other intellectual tradition was in this case linguistics – then flourishing as Transformational Generative Grammar (1.3) – and the "raw material" was with Kade above all the communicative approach, with Seleskovitch the concept of interpreting based on non-verbal sense. Another early pioneer of this kind is the German scholar Katharina Reiss, whose book on translation critique (1971), now available in English as *Translation Criticism – The Potentials and Limitations. Categories and Criteria for Translation Quality Assessment* (2000), is still celebrated as the first substantial contribution to modern (West) German translation studies. The "raw material" provided by Reiss was above all her "text typology for translators" (2000: 24–47) based on Karl Bühler's organon model distinguishing the three basic language functions of representation, expression and persuasion (cf. Snell-Hornby 1988: 30). From these Reiss derived three corresponding text-types: informative texts focussed on content (such as scientific reports), expressive texts focussed on form (such as lyric poetry and literary texts in general) and operative texts focussed on appeal (such as advertising and propaganda). Based on these text-types Reiss then developed a model of translation critique with specific criteria for evaluating translations. This is divided into two main sections: the linguistic components within the text and the extra-linguistic determinants behind the text. Linguistic components are defined as semantic equivalence, lexical adequacy, grammatical correctness and stylistic correspondence, while the extra-linguistic determinants are the immediate situation, the subject matter, the factors of time, place, audience and speaker, and finally affective implications (Reiss 2000). For decades this approach was used in innumerable German diploma theses as the classic model of translation critique. Reiss also mentioned a fourth group of texts which she called the "audiomedial" type: this – along with many other of her new ideas – provoked lively debates in scholarly journals right into the 1990s (cf. 3.1.3). She was then to join Hans Vermeer in "formulating the manifesto" of the skopos theory (Reiss and Vermeer 1984) – and she is now generally celebrated as the doyenne of German Translation Studies.

A monumental work of the 1970s was George Steiner's *After Babel. Aspects of Language and Translation* (1975), already mentioned above for his appraisal of Humboldt and the outstanding figures of traditional translation theory, particularly in the Romantic Age – it is significant that his Select Bibliography, "a checklist of material which the student of translation will find of particular use, ... set out chronologically" (1975: 475), begins with Schleiermacher's academy lecture of 1813. In all however, Steiner divides the literature on the theory, practice and history of translation into four periods. The first, with what he calls an "immediate empirical focus" (1975: 236), begins with Cicero and ends with Tytler's *Essay* of 1791; the second, one of "theory and hermeneutic inquiry", lasts up to Valéry Larbaud's "inspired but unsystematic" *Sous l'invocation de Saint Jérôme* in 1946 (1975: 237). The third period, beginning with the work on machine translation in the late 1940s, introduces structural semantics and information theory into the discussion and partially overlaps in time with the fourth period: this goes back to the early 1960s with the influence of the philosophers Martin Heidegger (1889–1976) and Hans-Georg Gadamer (1900–2002), causing "a reversion to hermeneutic, almost metaphysical inquiries into translation and interpretation" (1975: 238). While these four divisions may in themselves be debatable (cf. Bassnett 1980/2002: 46–47), it was Steiner who, when writing his book in the early 1970s, recognized the interdisciplinary potential in translation as a "point of contact between established and newly evolving disciplines", and consequently situates it within a framework of subjects including ethnography, sociology and formal rhetoric which clarify the process of "life between languages" (1975: 238).

In the spirit of hermeneutic inquiry characteristic of his fourth period, Steiner develops his concept of hermeneutic motion, which is strongly reminiscent of Goethe's three epochs of translation. Steiner's concept sees translation as a movement through four stages. The first is initiative trust (*élancement*) "in the 'other', as yet untried, unmapped alternity of statement" (1975: 296), after which comes aggression (or penetration), an "incursive and extractive" move in the sense of Heidegger (1975: 297), whereby "the translator invades, extracts, and brings home" (1975: 298). The third move is incorporation (or embodiment) and involves "bringing back" what has been appropriated, and the last one is restitution, whereby the translator "endeavours to restore the balance of forces, of integral presence, which his appropriative comprehension has disrupted" (1975: 302). With this view of translation Steiner sought "to overcome the sterile triadic model which has dominated the history and theory of the subject" (1975: 303). While his own model is in essence debatable (see Robinson 1998 and Stolze 2003), it not only echoes the ominous words of Nietzsche and Vossler quoted above, but also anticipates much of the debate on postcolonial translation (3.2.1). From today's viewpoint one can say that Steiner's work on translation has a double edge. On the one hand he is "polemically oriented" both on traditional translation theory, as already quoted, and on the static views of linguistics and translation dominant at the time, which he counters with his incomparable rhetoric. In the chapter of his book entitled "Word against Object" – contradicting Quine's *Word and Object* (1960) – he discounts the Chomskyan dogma of language universals then en vogue (see 1.3):

> But it is its great untidiness that makes human speech innovative and expressive of personal intent. It is the anomaly, as it feeds back into the general history of usage, the ambiguity, as it enriches and complicates the general standard of definition, which give coherence to the system. A coherence, if such a description is allowed, 'in constant motion'. The vital constancy of that motion accounts for both the epistemological and psychological failure of the project of a 'universal character'. (1975: 203)

On the other hand he showed prophetic insight by being "polemically oriented" to future developments: *After Babel*, written in the early 1970s, closes with an uncannily accurate vision of the internationalization of English as a "'pre-packaged' semantic field", and a warning against the global diffusion of English as a "principal agent in the destruction of natural linguistic diversity" (1975: 470). This topic will occupy us in 4.2.3 and 6.

If "polemic orientation" to the flourishing tradition is the mark of a pioneer spirit, the German translation scholar Fritz Paepcke (1916–1990) can be described as a typical pioneer. Paepcke was both a scholar of Romance languages with a background in the Classics and a translator, and the scope of his work ranged from philosophy and lyric poetry to legal texts and advertising. He too was an ardent advocate of the hermeneutic approach, particularly as based on the concepts and methods of Hans-Georg Gadamer, with whom he was personally acquainted. Paepcke's polemics were directed both against the Chomskyan linguistics of the 1960s and 1970s and against the linguistically oriented schools of translation theory then developing in Germany (see 1.3). "Die Sprachwissenschaft", he used to say, "ist eine Wissenschaft ohne Sprache" (The science of language is a science without language). Hence it was only logical that he was one of the few people of the time who seriously questioned the concept of equivalence: the "illusion of equivalence" was a phrase coined by the author (see Snell-Hornby 1988: 13–22) in conversation with Fritz Paepcke.

Most of Paepcke's work appeared in German or French in the form of essays, the most important of which were collected by Klaus Berger and Hans-Michael Speier in a volume entitled *Im Übersetzen leben* (Living in Translation) and published in 1986. The perspective of these essays, written or given as lectures for var-

UNIVERSITY OF CHESTER 18⁷

Supplier   Dawson Books (UK)
Order Date   04/06/2013
Quantity   1
Unit Price   28.00
Instructions E*418.02 SNE*

Author   Snell-Hornby, Mary.
Title   THE TURNS OF TRANSLATIO

Volume
Format
Shelf Mark   418.02 SNE
Site   UMA4N
Fund   F
Sequence
Loan Type
Quantity   1

ious occasions and in many different places, is interdisciplinary, multilingual and distinctly European. Paepcke played an active part in cultural exchange programmes in many different directions: he soon recognized the immense potential for translation studies in Finland, for example, and – during years characterized by the Cold War and the division of Europe – was a staunch supporter of colleagues in Poland and Hungary. He was fascinated by language as an instrument of expression, and his own style of writing – not unlike George Steiner's English – was complex, intense and often paradoxical. The motto of his laudatio to the Polish-German translator Karl Dedecius in 1981 is characteristic: "Hinter allen Sprachen steht das Unsägliche" (Behind all languages is the unutterable).

He was one of the first people of his generation however to emphasize that translation is not just a matter of language or languages:

> Wir übersetzen weder Wörter noch Sprachen, sondern Texte. Textübersetzen verweist auf eine Begrenzung, weil jeder Text in eine Situation eingebettet ist, die selbst nicht Sprache ist. Diese Situation ist der kulturelle, geschichtliche oder wirtschaftlich-soziale Raum, in dem ein Text zu uns redet. (1986: 159)

> (We translate neither words nor languages but texts. Text-translation indicates a demarcation, because every text is embedded in a situation which itself is not language. This situation is the cultural, historical, economic or social space in which a text speaks to us.)

In content if not in style this was the message of the skopos theory which was later developed in Germany. For Paepcke the preliminary for text-translation is "text-understanding" (*Textverstehen*) in the sense of Hans-Georg Gadamer:

> Textverstehen ist die Fähigkeit, das Gemeinte einer Textaussage zu klären, sowie die Wirkungsabsichten des Autors in einen neuen Kontext zu integrieren. (Paepcke 1986:XV)

> (Text-understanding is the ability to clarify the message of a statement and to integrate the author's intended effect into a new context.)

The key element in Paepcke's hermeneutic approach is therefore not the linguistic structures of the text, as was generally the case in the 1960s and 1970s, but its message (*das Gemeinte*):

> Entgegen allen Verkehrungen hat das Übersetzen seinen Grund im Verstehen und vorzugsweise nicht im Theoretischen. Es bewegt sich nicht allein in sprachlichen Verhaltensmustern, es reagiert auch nicht zuverlässig in spracheigenen Reflexen, ihm steht das unabgegrenzte offen. (1986:158)

> (Despite all contrary assertions translation is based on understanding and not pri-
> marily on theoretical reasoning. It does not move only in linguistic behaviour pat-
> terns or react in set linguistic reflexes, it is open for what has not been delimited.)

Hence Paepcke was a declared opponent of all the "analyzing, factorizing and operationalizing" (1986: 158) which characterized the methods of linguistically oriented translation studies (cf. Wilss 1977), and he had a deep aversion to rigid systematizing and to the additive checklist stance of the day (see 1.3) He was a leader of his time in emphasizing the notion of *Übersummativität*, the holistic con-cept which views a text as more than the mere sum of its parts (cf. Snell-Hornby 1988: 43). Another cornerstone of Paepcke's approach was Gadamer's notion of *Horizontverschmelzung* (1960), the "merging of horizons" between the familiar and the new that occurs during the process of reading (cf. 3.3 below). Gadamer also provided his metaphor of the game, leading to the comparison of translation with sport, particularly with the act of throwing a javelin (1986: 87) as an activity "zwischen Regel und Spiel" (between rules and play) – see Cronin 1998 for later elaborations of the game theory – while his concept of *Leibhaftigkeit* ("body feel-ing") anticipates exactly what Robinson was to describe at length as "body or somatic response" (1991: 10).

Paepcke's hermeneutics is inseparable from his understanding of culture, par-ticularly against the background of western and European history. This embraces both unity of tradition and the diversity of languages and customs, perspectives later to be enshrined in the development of the European Union. Paepcke was one of the few translation scholars of his generation who could bridge the gaps between scholarship and practice, training and profession (the POSI project of the 1990s[16] goes back to his initiative), and he was already fascinated by questions which were to be the subject of intense debate in the 1990s, questions of identity and otherness for example, and the phenomenon of European multilingualism, as seen in his own endeavours to learn Hungarian in his later years:

> Für mich war ein neuer Perspektivenwandel eingetreten, als mir das Ungarische
> zunächst eine unüberwindlich erscheinende Widerstandskraft entgegensetzte.
> Dadurch dass ich mit dem radikal Anderen des Ungarischen konfrontiert wurde,
> vermochte ich in die Beschreibung dessen, was Übersetzen ist, die Kategorie der
> Nichtidentität oder der Andersheit einzuführen. Während eine lange Geschichte
> interkultureller Gemeinsamkeiten das Französische und das Deutsche anein-

---

16.   "PraxisOrientierte StudienInhalte für die Ausbildung von Übersetzern und Dolmetschern" (practice-oriented study content for the training of translators and interpreters), see "POSI takes shape. A project to 'Europeanise' translator training" in *Language International* (1996) 8(4): 7–9.

ander gebunden hat, kehren die Meridiane, die durch die Pole der Sprachen gehen, offenbar in sich zurück und wandern. (Paepcke 1986: XVII)

(For me it was a new shift in perspectives when Hungarian first showed me a power of resistance which seemed insurmountable. By being confronted with the radical otherness of Hungarian, I was able to introduce the category of non-identity or Otherness in my description of the nature of translation. Whereas French and German are connected by a long history of intercultural common ground, the meridians passing through the poles of languages apparently turn back on themselves and move away.)

1.3   The pragmatic turn in linguistics

As we have seen, our pioneer figures in translation studies were more or less united in their polemical stance against the linguistics of the day. To clarify this further, we need to examine the state of the discipline of linguistics during this time – and the crucial "pragmatic turn" which encouraged the emancipation of translation studies both from linguistics and from comparative literature.

The discussion goes back to the years immediately after the Second World War, when translation emerged as a topic of scientific interest through the issue of machine translation, a subject debated with what strikes us today as incredible naiveté and euphoria. For modern Translation Studies the conclusions reached may serve as a kind of negative starting-point. In his essay 'Translation, a memorandum' of 15th July 1949, published in Locke and Booth's volume *Machine Translation of Languages* (1955), Warren Weaver stated categorically that while mere word-for-word translation would be inadequate, only a few items on the left or right of the word concerned need be considered to ensure a correct translation (Weaver 1955). The researchers of the time seriously believed that detailed syntactic rules, an extensive lexicon and high-speed processing of ambiguities would be an adequate basis for a perfect type of machine translation known as "fully automatic high quality translation" (FAHQT). But by 1960 the linguist Bar-Hillel had realized that such an MT-system would have to include a model of human knowledge, and he came to the conclusion that translation was not after all a purely mechanical activity (Bar-Hillel 1960) – an assertion that no serious translator of today would ever dispute (cf. Moser-Mercer 1986: 311). Among linguists however the debate continued until 1966, when the Automatic Language Processing Advisory Committee published its results in the influential ALPAC report, which tended to support those who considered the pursuit of fully automatic translation systems a waste of time and concluded "...that it is wise to press forward undaunted, in the name of science, but that the motive for doing so cannot sensibly be any foreseeable improvement in practical translation" (ALPAC 1966: 24).

Nearly four decades later, our view of machine translation is very different (see 4.2.1). For the present section it is important to emphasize that when the ALPAC report was published in 1966, non-literary translation was seen quite indisputably as part of linguistics, and this was at the time dominated by Noam Chomsky's Transformational Generative Grammar, particularly through his publications *Syntactic Structures* (1957) and *Aspects of the Theory of Syntax* (1965). In this view, language is the result of a universal innate facility (*competence*), and Chomsky offered a system of language analysis in terms of (a finite number of) specific rules that ideally generate (a potentially infinite number of) grammatical sentences (the production of these being *performance*). The approach was extremely abstract, and the rules were formalized in mathematical terms by means of symbols, equations and diagrams. The upper limit of analysis was the sentence, which was viewed as a string of items, and where examples were offered these were of extreme simplicity, a prototype being "John hit the ball". As a system of language analysis, generative grammar (after many years of a predominantly historical approach to language) was then thought revolutionary, and it was even considered "a serious candidate for an adequate theory of human language"[17] as a whole. Given the approach of the time, this would also mean that generative grammar would provide a theory of translation, and some attempts were made in this direction, as for example in Catford 1965. However, translation scholars – and even some linguists – protested that in fact language in its concrete realization was far more complicated (Steiner's "great untidiness of language") than in Chomsky's linguistics (which Paepcke called the "science without language"), particularly as anything which did not conform strictly to the orthodox view of "well-formed sentences" (based on rigid selection restrictions) was considered deviant and hence negligible. This included all forms of metaphor, for example, a view which even then provoked protest and led the linguist Uriel Weinreich to declare that "a semantic theory is of marginal interest if it is incapable of dealing with poetic uses of language, and more generally, with interpretable deviance" (1966: 471).

However, in 1955, while Chomsky was developing his theory of transformational grammar, the British philosopher John L. Austin gave a series of lectures at Harvard University which in 1962 were to appear in book form under the title *How to do Things with Words* – in every sense a far cry from the Chomsky school with its intensely abstract approach and its verbose and convoluted jargon. But like Chomsky, Austin was also to open new perspectives and bring about radical changes in our view of language, albeit of a totally different nature. His pragmatic

---

17.   The quote is taken from the opening lines of the Statement of Purpose in the first issue of the journal *Linguistic Inquiry* in 1971.

speech act theory, further developed by John Searle (1969), sees utterances in terms of both making statements and performing specific acts (cf. Hatim 1998), and it can be said to be one of the major forces in the "pragmatic turn". This was continued in the following years with the inclusion of social and communicative aspects of language and the emergence of text-linguistics, which all favoured a holistic, interdisciplinary approach to translation, more critical and appreciative investigations of the process and product of translation and hence the development of the discipline of Translation Studies as such.

The many contributions to the pragmatic turn within the mainstream of linguistics are well documented and it is not our aim to debate them here. There are however some outstanding linguists whose work had a pragmatic orientation from the outset, who had an intense interest in translation and who indirectly influenced the development of Translation Studies in Europe without being translation scholars themselves.

One of these was the Romanian-born linguist Eugenio Coseriu (1921–2002), best known for his work in Romance languages at the University of Tübingen. From today's viewpoint we might say that Coseriu's basic contribution towards the turn that led to Translation Studies was twofold. Firstly, in a study that first appeared in 1951 in Spanish under the title "Sistema, norma y habla" but had its major impact in a later German form "System, Norm und Rede" (Coseriu 1970), he challenged the then unquestioned Saussurean dichotomy of *langue* and *parole*, adding the concept of *norm* between that of *system* on the one hand and that of *text* or *discourse* on the other. As a linguist, Coseriu was referring strictly to a concept of language norm, but in a much broader context, and with varying forms of usage, the notion of norm later became central for Translation Studies: as had already been anticipated by Levý (1.2), afterwards as social and cultural norms in the functional approach of Vermeer and Nord (2.2), and finally as was to become famous in the form of translation norms in Descriptive Translation Studies (3.1.1). However, Coseriu's language norm is relevant in itself as a basic component of the translator's material. Whereas the language system provides a fund of rule-governed abstract possibilities, the norm is the concrete, socially accepted realization of the system: the one is a code, the other is behaviour, part of a culture with all its social constraints. The norm is hence far more dynamic than the system, changing with time and varying regionally. (The pronunciation norms of British English might serve as an example: whereas once only the "Queen's English" passed muster in public life, now all kinds of local variants are socially acceptable and in fact more usual than the old "received pronunciation".) Coseriu's second contribution concerns literary language and again revolves round the notion of norm. In a short essay "Thesen zum Thema Sprache und Dichtung" (Theses on the topic of language and poetry) (1971), he states categorically that poetry is not to be considered as "deviant language" but "Sprache schlechthin, als Verwirklichung aller sprachlichen Möglichkeiten" (1971:85), in other words it is the epitome of language, the realization of the entire potential of a language, against which ordinary language represents a reduction of the total language potential. So in this view, literary language does not simply deviate from a static and prescriptive linguistic norm, but is the creative extension of the language norm, in its flexible sense of rule-governed potential. For Translation Studies this insight is of fundamental importance: one of the literary translator's most difficult choices is deciding how such creative extensions of the source-language norm can be rendered in the target text without actually infringing the rules of linguistic acceptability (cf. Snell-Hornby 1989a).

The Swiss linguist Ernst Leisi, known for his pioneer empirical studies at the English Department of the University of Zurich, paved the way for future approaches to Translation Studies above all with his work in contrastive lexical semantics. Basic to his approach was the operational definition of meaning which he published in 1953 (as it happened, concomitant with the philosopher Ludwig Wittgenstein), whereby the meaning of a word is equated with its use (Leisi 1953: 15 ff., Wittgenstein 1953: 20 ff.). This resolved the difference between denotation, then thought to be the only form of meaning adequate for semantic analysis, and connotation, then thought to belong to "extralinguistic reality" and hence to lie outside the scope of serious objective description. For Leisi the definition of a word is only adequate:

> ...wenn sie alle für den Gebrauch des betreffenden Wortes relevanten Bedingungen nennt und andererseits nichts als diese Bedingungen. Die Definition ist also zugleich ein Minimum und ein Maximum. (1973: 134)
>
> (...if it names all the conditions relevant for the use of the word concerned, but on the other hand nothing beyond these conditions. A definition is therefore both a minimum and a maximum at the same time.)

Leisi's "Gebrauchsbedingungen" (or "conditions of use") were to become the concept immediately associated with his work and that of his "Zurich School", and they were a corner-stone of some of the first empirical semantic studies which investigated real-life language by means of corpus analysis and interviews (see Leisi 1973). It soon became clear on the one hand that connotative, emotive and evaluative elements are sometimes basic to the meaning of a word, but above all that the semantic content of words, and in particular the structure of semantic fields, vary considerably from one language to another (see Snell-Hornby 1983 and cf. 3.1.2). In other words, the concept of equivalence, during the 1960s and 1970s the basic criterion of work on translation, was soon called into question even within linguistics, and it was only a logical step from Leisi's functional approach to language to the functional theories of translation developed in the 1980s.

Common to all those involved in the "pragmatic turn" of the 1970s – and in particular those who made constructive contributions towards the development of Translation Studies – is, as with the early translation scholars discussed in 1.2, their "polemical orientation" or resistance to the school of generative grammar. This applies particularly to the concept of "scenes-and-frames semantics" developed by Charles Fillmore, once a zealous disciple, then an equally ardent critic of Chomsky's linguistics. During the 1970s Fillmore developed his own holistic theory of meaning – "an integrated view of language structure, language behaviour, language acquisition" (1977:55) – based on the notion of prototype semantics proposed by the psychologist Eleanor Rosch (1973), as against the then prevalent reductionist "checklist theory" of generative grammar. The "frame" is a "system of linguistic choice", such as words or grammatical structures, and as such it triggers off a "scene" in the mind, "a coherent segment of beliefs or experiences or imaginings" (Fillmore 1977:63) and vice versa. In other words, the "scene" is the experienced or otherwise meaningful situation or scenario that finds expression in linguistic form. Scenes and frames constantly activate each other (frame-scene, scene-frame, scene-scene, frame-frame); this means that a particular linguistic form, such as a phrase found in a text, evokes associations which themselves activate other linguistic forms and evoke further associations, whereby every linguistic expression in a text is conditioned by another one, these combining during the course of the reading process to form a "scene behind the text" (see 3.3.1).

Crucial both for the "pragmatic turn" in linguistics and the ensuing development of Translation Studies was the role of text-linguistics. One might even say that the realization that the sentence was not after all the upper limit for language research amounted to a quantum leap in the field. As in most areas of linguistics, some approaches were more applicable to translation than others. From today's perspective it seems that in the English-speaking community M.A.K. Halliday was the main driving force – his systemic functional grammar, for example (1976, cf. Munday 2001: 90–91), and his study on cohesion (Halliday and Hasan 1976) – while in the German-speaking world the outstanding text-linguists were Robert de Beaugrande and Wolfgang Dressler. Their introduction to text-linguistics (1981) provides what is for translation one of the most apt definitions of the term "text" yet offered: it is – in contrast to earlier structuralist or linguistic descriptions involving strings of words and sentences – a "communicative occurrence", and their seven criteria of textuality (coherence, cohesion, intentionality, acceptability, informativity, situativity and intertextuality) have meanwhile found their way into translator training courses as basic tools. Similarly their definition of the literary text as one whose world bears a systematic alternative relation to the accepted version of the "real world" (1981:191) has provided an essential point of comparison and differentiation between "literary" and "other" translation.

The pragmatic turn in linguistics as reflected in the speech-act theory, the rise of text-linguistics, the functional approach to language with the inclusion of its social and communicative aspects, clearly indicated the general trends of the 1970s. There was firstly the broadening of perspectives within linguistics (and other disciplines) and secondly the breakdown of barriers between the individual fields. The first led to the reorientation from the isolated concept of the linguistic sign and the abstract concept of the language system as described above (with the polarized dichotomies involved) to a holistic notion of the text as part of the world around, and the second trend led to an invaluable process of cross-fertilization, whereby the study of language was enriched by insights from anthropology, philosophy, sociology and psychology. This was the spirit of the 1970s, and how ripe it proved to be for the development of Translation Studies in the 1980s will occupy us in Chapter 2.

1.4   The legacy of James Holmes

Meanwhile however the ground was being prepared elsewhere by a central pioneer of modern Translation Studies, one who was not merely "polemically oriented" towards the existing intellectual tradition, but above all one who was deeply committed to securing an independent academic status for his field. Towards this end, he was the scholar who both formulated the "raw program" and presented the "manifesto" of today's discipline.

James Holmes (1924–1986) was for his time a most unusual personality, and from today's perspective he incorporated the frequently described but rarely attained ideal of the bilingual and bicultural translator and translation scholar. As a US citizen, he lived in the Netherlands from the late 1940s, and was hence "a participant in two cultures, at home both with their languages and with the literatures written in those languages, he was thus the ideal mediator between the Low Countries and the Anglo-American world" (Van den Broeck 1988: 1). Holmes was himself a poet and an acclaimed and impassioned translator of poetry, and he was also a literary scholar specializing in translation theory and the history of translation: he was in fact the founder and general editor of the series *Approaches to Translation Studies,* of which André Lefevere's study of the German tradition so often quoted here was the fourth volume.

James Holmes was a regular participant at the world conferences of the Applied Linguistics Association and the International Comparative Literature Association, these then representing two clearly separate disciplines, non-literary translation being defined as a subdivision of the first, and literary translation a branch of the second. As we have already seen, the world of scholarship was up to the late 1960s characterized by rigid frontiers, and during the years of the Cold War and the Iron Curtain these themselves precisely reflected the spirit of the times: alongside a typically buoyant self-confidence (at least in the Western half of Europe), there was a dogged consolidation of the status quo. James Holmes was an independent and innovative spirit moving in two such separate worlds, both in the academic and the geographical sense, and he succeeded in bringing them closer together through translation.

A seminal paper given by Holmes in 1972 in the Translation Section of the Third International Congress of Applied Linguistics, held in Copenhagen in August 1972, was entitled "The Name and Nature of Translation Studies". The author designed this as the "map" of an empirical "disciplinary utopia" (or rather a description of the impediments in the way of its development), but from today's viewpoint the paper is a visionary blueprint of the future discipline. It has been available in two expanded versions, both published posthumously in the late 1980s: one in the collection of papers called *Translated!* (Holmes 1988), the other in a special issue of the *Indian Journal of Applied Linguistics* (1987) edited by Gideon Toury, who also uses it as a starting-point in Toury 1995.[18] It is this latter version (Holmes 1987) we are using here.

The first impediment in the way of the development of the "disciplinary uto-pia" was "the seemingly trivial matter of the name for this field of research" (Holmes 1987: 11), whereby Holmes was referring mainly to translation (rather than interpreting), in particular literary translation. He rejects the vague terms of traditional theory, which referred to the "art", the "craft" or the "principles" of translation, and at the same time he questions the more "learned" terms of (then) recent years. These originated outside English and resulted in neologisms of two kinds. There are firstly those formed by the addition of a suffix, as in the now established French term *traductologie*. The German form *Translatologie* was later to be used by Justa Holz-Mänttäri (2.3), and it still exists as the translation of Slavonic terms for the discipline (as in the names of translator training institutes), but to my knowledge it has not been related to literary translation. The compara-ble English term *translatology*, rejected by Holmes on purely philological grounds, has hardly caught on at all, being too abstract in connotation to include descriptive

---

18. Here Toury states: "... the sad fact is that Holmes' pioneering paper was hardly ever men-tioned by other authors, especially in books and articles which became standard works in the field" (1995: 8). His list includes Snell-Hornby (1988) and other work written before Holmes' pa-per was made generally available. Since then however the situation has changed noticeably (cf. Munday 2001). For Katharina Reiss' German version of Holmes' "map" of the discipline see Snell-Hornby and Kadrić (1995: 14).

studies of texts. Secondly there are those terms that have arisen by formation of a compound, such as *Übersetzungswissenschaft* on analogy with other disciplines in German like *Literaturwissenschaft*, whereby the semantic range of the word *Wissenschaft* is broader than that of the English word *science*, which Holmes rightly rejects for translation, as this is usually limited to the exact or natural sciences and implicitly excludes literary studies and the arts subjects in general (1987: 12). The term "Translation Studies" suggested by Holmes in 1972 for adoption as the standard term for the discipline, is the one now unquestioningly used in English today, albeit implying translation only, as against the discipline of Interpreting Studies which has meanwhile developed beside it (4.1.1).

In his search for precise terminology Holmes was treading a similar path to that already marked out by Otto Kade on the other side of the Iron Curtain in 1968 (1.2). However, while presenting the German term *Translation* as the generic term for the activity (and clearly defining its two subdivisions), Kade continued to use the term *Übersetzungswissenschaft* for the scholarly study of both translation and interpreting. As explained above, he explicitly avoided using the term *Translationswissenschaft*, and it only emerged as the generic German term for the discipline in the course of the 1980s (2.2).

As the second, and greater, impediment to the development of his disciplinary utopia, Holmes named "the lack of any general consensus as to the scope and structure of the discipline" (1987:13). He then put forward his own plan for such a structure which, in its diagram form (1987:21) is today basic material for introductory university courses. In a paper given at the "James S. Holmes Symposium on Translation Studies" held in Amsterdam in 1990 (Snell-Hornby 1991), I discussed his proposals, naming scholars who had meanwhile worked in the "utopian" fields concerned, particularly in non-literary areas. I would here like to take up this material again, where relevant bringing the references up to date for the first years of the new century.

For the basic macrostructure of his empirical discipline of "Translation Studies", Holmes used the classical distinctions of "Pure" and Applied. The latter was further divided into Translator Training (teaching methods, testing techniques and curriculum planning), Translation Aids (lexicological and terminological aids, also grammars) and Translation Policy and Criticism, all of which were to become objects of intense interest and a vast amount of activity in the 1980s and 1990s (see 4.1.2, 4.2.1 and 3.3.1). But it was the "Pure" branch that was to prove especially fruitful: this was subdivided into Theoretical and Descriptive, the latter, as Descriptive Translation Studies (DTS) nowadays frequently used synonymously with literary translation studies as such – at least in the English-speaking community (see 2.1). In Holmes' model, Descriptive Translation Studies fell into three groups: product-oriented, process-oriented and function-oriented DTS. The first was described as involving corpus analyses, comparative surveys, "and one of the eventual goals of product-oriented DTS might possibly be a general history of translations – however ambitious such a goal may sound at this time" (1987: 14). In 1972 such a goal was indeed utopian, but meanwhile a respectable amount of the then virgin territory has been covered (e.g. Vermeer 1992, Delisle and Wood-sworth 1995, Baker 1998, Singerman 2002). There has also been a prolific output in other fields of product-oriented DTS, especially in the English-speaking community and in the Low Countries (2.1). The other two branches met with particular interest in Germany and Finland: process-oriented studies, based on think-aloud protocols investigating what takes place in the "black box" of the translator's mind, were carried out by Krings (1986), Jääskeläinen (1989) and Tirkkonen-Condit (1990), Hönig (1991) and Lörscher (1991), to name only a few, while function-oriented description is typically represented in Germany, as by Hönig and Kuss-maul (1982), Nord (1988) and Hönig (1995). The Theoretical branch is divided into "General Theory" on the one hand, where Hans Vermeer's skopos theory (see Reiss and Vermeer 1984) deserves a central position (2.2), and into six types of "Partial Theories", which today are of varying interest. "Medium-restricted theories" are now mostly relevant in the field of Machine Translation or Machine-Aided Translation (4.2.1), but were intended by Holmes to include "oral translation" or interpreting (which later blossomed into a field of study in its own right, see 4.1.1). "Area-restricted theories" concern work carried out with specific language pairs, or in specific multi-lingual areas such as Switzerland or Belgium. "Rank-restricted" problems focussing on sentences or words are today of less interest than in the early linguistic approach – Holmes himself encouraged the development of "rank-free theories" (1987: 17) – whereas "text-type restricted theories" concern areas such as Bible translation (of constant interest in translation theory) or then neglected areas such as translation for stage and screen (3.1.3), which over the last twenty years have experienced a genuine boom. "Time-restricted theories" involve the translation of texts bound to a particular, usually older period, whereas "problem-restricted theories" range from questions of equivalence, now of less interest in the discipline than in 1972 (but cf. 5.1), to the translation of metaphor, which developed into another flourishing area of research (cf. Newmark 1985, Kurth 1995, Schäffner 1998).

While Holmes presented his categories Theoretical, Descriptive and Applied as "three fairly distinct branches of the entire discipline" (1987: 20), he saw their relationship as dialectical, each branch providing material for the other two:

> Translation theory, for instance, cannot do without the solid, specific data yielded by research in descriptive and applied translation studies, while on the other hand one cannot even begin to work in one of the other two fields without having at least an intuitive theoretical hypothesis as one's starting point. (1987: 22)

Holmes concluded his epoch-making paper with the remark: "Translation studies have reached a stage where it is time to examine the subject itself. Let the meta-discussion begin." (1987: 22) And, as we can see from this brief overview, it began indeed.

James Holmes did not only move between the separate worlds of linguistics and literature, he also managed to bring together scholars from various countries lying ideologically or geographically far apart. In particular he established many international contacts through the conferences, congresses and colloquia he attended – and in those days these were by no means as frequent or self-evident as they are today. It was in fact through conference papers that he sketched his "manifesto" of Translation Studies, as we see in those reprinted in Holmes 1988. These are, in addition to the Copenhagen paper, his contribution to the Leuven Conference of 1976 (see 2.1), a short plenary address with the title "Translation Theory, Translation Theories, Translation Studies, and the Translator" presented at the 8th FIT World Congress in Montreal in May 1978 (1988: 93–98, see 4.1.2), an even shorter paper with the title "The Future of Translation Theory: A Handful of Theses" presented at an "International Symposium on Achievements in the Theory of Translation" held in October 1978 in Moscow and Yerewan (1988: 99–102), and finally a paper with the title "The State of Two Arts: Literary Translation and Translation Studies in the West Today" presented at the 10th FIT World Congress in Vienna in August 1984 (1988: 103–111). These papers put forward proposals that now might seem self-evident, but in the 1970s they ranged from the progressive to the revolutionary, as for example: replacing the term *equivalence* by a "network of *correspondences*, or *matchings*" (1988: 101) which might be seen to anticipate Vermeer's concept of "intertextual coherence" (2.2, 3.3.1); encouraging linguists to stop thinking at last in terms of "the sentence and linguistic phenomena below the sentence level" (1988: 94) and to start thinking in terms of texts; launching a "translation sociology" which shows "how a translated text functions in the society into which it comes" (1988: 95), or how texts "function communicatively in a given sociocultural setting" (1988: 100), anticipating the future trends of both Descriptive Translation Studies and of the skopos theory. Most importantly, Holmes made a plea for cooperation, not only between translation theorists and practising translators, but also between different scholars and schools, especially in the form of interdisciplinary teamwork – "text studies, linguistics (particularly psycho- and socio-linguistics – literary studies, psychology, sociology" (1988: 101). It may have been one of Holmes' most significant achievements to have brought together scholars with similar interests but from various parts of the world: Itamar Even-Zohar from Tel Aviv, Israel, Anton Popovič from Nitra, Slovakia, Susan Bassnett from Warwick, England and of course various colleagues in the Low Countries (see 2.1). Van den Broeck draws the conclusion:

These contacts made possible a fruitful collaboration, whose results are to be seen. A succession of three international colloquia, at Leuven (1976), Tel Aviv (1978), and Antwerp (1980) respectively, were the direct result of these contacts. If not the driving force behind these high-level academic encounters, Holmes certainly provided the inspiration behind them, and much experienced advice. The group of scholars at present becoming internationally known, from the circuit Amsterdam-Anwerp(*sic!*)-Leuven-Nitra-Tel Aviv, can with a certain pride call itself Holmes' progeny. (1988: 4)

A matter of special concern for Holmes was communication between scholars in the West and behind the Iron Curtain. He was, as he stated explicitly in his Moscow paper, aware of a "major lacuna" in his readings on translation theory:

> Since I do not know Russian, I have read only that small tip of the vast Soviet translation-theory iceberg that juts above the surface of Western thinking by having been translated. Far too little *has* been translated, far too much has *not*, and hence the work of a great many theorists, from Cukovskij via Revzin and Rozencveig to Koptilov and Kommisarov (to mention but a few), remains for me little more than hearsay. (1988:99)

What applied to the extraordinarily well-read James Holmes, was of course true for most scholars in the West, and what applied to Russian, went for other Slavonic languages too. Thus it came about that the prolific and innovative Slovak scholar Anton Popovič (1933–1984), mentioned above as one of Holmes' "inner circle", did not achieve the international fame of his Czech colleague Jiří Levý because much of his work appeared in Slovak and was not translated into a Western language. At the beginning of the 21st century such problems may be less acute (see 4.2.3), but it is a great merit of James Holmes to have stressed during the Cold War how much scholarship was lost to the West by not being made available through translation.

Holmes' lecture at the FIT World Congress in 1984, "The State of Two Arts: Literary Translation and Translation Studies in the West Today", dedicated to the memory of Popovič, is – as seen from the perspective of twenty years later – a brilliant resumé of the position of (largely literary) translation studies at the time. It first sums up the sad position of the literary translator and the then prevalent policy of publishing houses (and over the last twenty years neither has really improved). The state of the art of translation studies in 1984 seems rather more promising. Praise is first given to the new generation of linguists for freeing themselves from the limitations of structuralism (with its premise that the upper limit for research was the sentence) and venturing a change of paradigm into the world of communication, text and discourse. Literary scholars however come in for a good deal of criticism, because:

> ...there is not really a disciplinary paradigm at all, but rather a far-too-rapid suc-
> cession of fashions and frills of the moment, from New Criticism to literary struc-
> turalism to literary sociology to post-structuralism to reception studies to
> deconstruction. The one thing that most (though by no means all) of these mod-
> ish approaches have shared has been that the "literature" of a cultural area is a
> question of a corpus of texts that have been canonized, that is to say, accepted by
> the community as of high literary worth, and that the task of the literary scholar is
> to develop methods for the better understanding of texts in the canon. (1988: 106)

This is a clear example of "polemical orientation" to the then flourishing tradition
of literary studies, and Holmes openly challenges the dogma of only concentrating
on the canon. To answer the crucial questions of translation studies, he sees the
most promise in the approach of deconstructionism (cf. 2.4). He continues by
describing the (then) new conceptual framework of the polysystemic approach
championed in Tel Aviv by Itamar Even-Zohar and his colleagues, praising it as an
alternative to the traditional dogma and as a better model for the study of literary
translations (2.1).

Finally, he turns to translation scholars, in the 1960s "a somewhat wild-eyed
band of scholars" from various fields, but meanwhile (1984) "the band has grown,
split into camps, held colloquia and conferences, and almost become accepted"
(1988: 109). Above all however it is split down the middle, on the one hand there is
the normative approach of the translator training institutes, on the other the
empirical/historical/descriptive approach as supported by Holmes (an issue that
was to rage for many years and which is still not resolved). For the latter group
Holmes indicates research achievements "that could change the face of literary history, with the role of translating and translations within that history for the first
time really coming into its own" (1988: 10).

There is a final negative note on the need to improve translator training, to do
research into "what really goes on inside the black box of the translator's brain" and
to compile better translation aids, because "our bilingual dictionaries and grammars are still a disgrace and a despair" (1988: 10, cf. 4.1.2 and 4.2.1). The final verdict: "The state of the art of translation studies is better than ever before. It is not
good. There is still so much to be done" (1988: 110).

CHAPTER 2

The cultural turn of the 1980s

If it was the pragmatic turn of the 1970s that made the made the emergence of Translation Studies as an independent discipline possible, it was what later became known
as the "cultural turn" of the 1980s that largely established its basic profile. The "cultural turn" is a name later given to a development that several of the various camps of
the now generally (if grudgingly) accepted band of translation scholars like to claim
as their own. This chapter traces the course of the cultural turn in Translation Studies during the 1980s, in the Low Countries, Israel and England, also in Germany,
Finland and Brazil, following the four different streams of the decade. In Radnitzky's
typology we are now crossing the threshold where Translation Studies leaves the territory of the pioneers and enters the domain of the masters, those who carry out
their portion of the programme, those whose work sets the standard by which the
disciples later measure their own success. It has turned out to be a wide, if rocky
domain, and to say that the material is in itself well-documented would be an understatement: the literature, particularly on Descriptive Translation Studies and the skopos theory, has meanwhile reached immense proportions, and it is not my aim to
repeat its content. What follows is again an assessment of the ground-breaking contributions, as seen from today's perspective, which led to a fundamental change of
paradigm, enabling Bassnett and Lefevere to conclude in 1990: "The growth of
Translation Studies as a separate discipline is a success story of the 1980s." (1990: ix)

2.1   Descriptive Translation Studies: The "Manipulation School" revisited

To put the development of Descriptive Translation Studies in perspective, let us
again take up the threads of James Holmes' 1984 paper, and his presentation of
what was then the new conceptual framework in literary translation studies:

> Building on the groundwork of the Russian structuralists, and availing themselves
> of work on metatexts and the literary communication process done in Slovakia
> and the Low Countries, Itamar Even-Zohar and scholars grouped around him at
> Tel Aviv have in recent years provided us with a conceptual framework in their
> ongoing definition of the fortunes of literary texts as a "polysystem". This polysys-
> temic approach, which has been heralded with a great deal less fanfare than has
> deconstructionism, is today gaining more and more adherence in the West as a
> framework for explaining what takes place in the literary culture. Making use of

insights from the field of general systemics, the study of how systems work, Even-Zohar and his colleagues have posited that "literature" in a given society is a collection of various systems, a system-of-systems or polysystem, in which diverse genres, schools, tendencies, and what have you are constantly jockeying for position, competing with each other for readership, but also for prestige and power. Seen in this light, "literature" is no longer the stately and fairly static thing it tends to be for the canonists, but a highly kinetic situation in which things are constantly changing. (1988:107)

This introduction to the concept of the polysystem for those translators and translation scholars then assembled in Vienna was to remain one of its most cogent and coherent descriptions ever offered. The work Holmes was referring to had been going on from the mid-1970s, and was presented at the colloquia in Leuven (1976), Tel Aviv (1978) and Antwerp (1980), but for outsiders much of it remained virtually inaccessible. Some of it was only available in Dutch and Hebrew, and the rest existed mainly in the form of mimeographed manuscripts, unpublished doctoral theses or local publications with only a limited circulation. The proceedings of the legendary Leuven conference (Holmes et al. 1978) were out of print after only a few years (cf. Snell-Hornby 1988: 37).

The breakthrough came in 1985 with the publication of that volume of essays edited by Theo Hermans, with the now famous title *The Manipulation of Literature* (Hermans 1985). The aim, as the editor stated in his introduction was, "quite simply, to establish a new paradigm for the study of literary translation, on the basis of a comprehensive theory and ongoing practical research" (1985: 10), and from today's perspective one can say right away that this aim was achieved (cf. Snell-Hornby 1995[2]: 22ff.). The authors included Gideon Toury with an exposition of Descriptive Translation Studies, José Lambert and Hendrik van Gorp with a model for describing translations (cf. 3.3.1), Susan Bassnett(-McGuire) on drama translation (cf. 3.1.3) and André Lefevere on rewrites (cf. 3.3). While Hermans emphasized that the group of authors consisted of scholars sharing "some basic assumptions", but "is not a school" (1985: 10), that is precisely how they became known. The title of the volume, along with the editor's statement "From the point of view of the target literature, all translation implies a certain degree of manipulation of the source text for a certain purpose" (1985: 11), soon led to them to be dubbed the "Manipulation School".[19]

---

19. I can even recall how this came about. The Göttingen Research Project 309 on Literary Translation, where in 1986–1987 I had the uneasy role of "Guest Linguist" (cf. Snell-Hornby 1988: viii), organized a conference early in 1987 and invited several of the Low Countries group to give papers. The name "Manipulation School" was created during an especially lively discussion after one of these papers.

It is their basic assumptions that were then innovative:

> What they have in common is, briefly, a view of literature as a complex and
> dynamic system; a conviction that there should be a continual interplay between
> theoretical models and practical case studies; an approach to literary translation
> which is descriptive, target-oriented, functional and systemic; and an interest in
> the norms and constraints that govern the production and reception of transla-
> tions, in the relation between translation and other types of text processing, and in
> the place and role of translations both within a given literature and in the interac-
> tion between literatures. (Hermans 1985: 10–11)

The key words from our point of view are *descriptive, target-oriented, functional*
and *systemic*, particularly as they were diametrically opposed to the dogmas on
translation of the time, which, as the domain of the translator training institutes,
were essentially *prescriptive, source-text oriented, linguistic* and *atomistic*. This was
the great rift mentioned by Holmes in 1984, which, with the growing success of the
new functional approaches, only deepened over the next decade (and not only in
the Low Countries), and it has still not been completely resolved.

Not the linguistic features of the source text are then the central issue, but the
function of the *translation in the "target culture"*: that was the essential premise of
the new paradigm, as Gideon Toury expounded in his essay "A Rationale for
Descriptive Translation Studies" (Toury 1985):

> Semiotically speaking, it will be clear that it is the *target* or *recipient culture*, or a
> certain section of it, which serves as the *initiator* of the decision to translate and of
> the translating process. Translating as a teleological activity *par excellence* is to a
> large extent conditioned by the goals it is designed to serve, and these goals are set
> in, and by, the prospective receptor system(s). Consequently, translators operate
> first and foremost in the interest of the culture *into* which they are translating, and
> not in the interest of the source text, let alone the source culture. (1985: 18–19,
> emphasis Toury)

With "culture" Toury is implying the entire social context involved in the translation, along with the norms, conventions, ideology and values of that society or
"receptor system", and the concept tends to be used in Toury's work in the abstract
sense of a systemic background or network (as implied above by Holmes and in
the sense of the polysystem theory). However, it was the starting-point for the
sociological approach already represented in the 1985 volume by André Lefevere's
contribution "Why Waste our Time on Rewrites?", where the categories *patronage,
poetics* and *ideology* (Lefevere 1992) are presented (cf. 3.2.1). Toury himself was to
concentrate on the theory and method of Descriptive Translation Studies, with
which his name is inextricably linked, and he presented some ideas which at the
time seemed outrageous and gave rise to lengthy debate. One was the hypothesis

that "translations are facts of one system only: the target system" (1985: 19), thus negating a relationship to the source text; another was his view that any text can be counted as a translation if it is accepted as such in the target culture (cf. Snell-Hornby 1988: 25, and 2.2 below). Meanwhile Toury has become associated above all with his concept of translation norms (3.1.1), and his approach is not concerned directly with the phenomenon of culture as such. It is significant that of the contributors to the "Manipulation" volume, those most closely associated with the concept of the "cultural turn" during the 1980s were to be André Lefevere and Susan Bassnett (cf. 5.3).

In the volume "Translation, History and Culture" jointly edited by Bassnett and Lefevere (1990), which consists of papers presented at a conference held in Warwick in 1988, the "cultural turn" is a central concept. It is included in the title of their introduction (Lefevere and Bassnett 1990: 1), and is described as the abandoning of the 'scientistic' linguistic approach as based on the concept of the *tertium comparationis* or "equivalence" and moving from "text" to "culture", a "cultural turn" which they say all the contributions to the volume have taken (1990: 3–4):

> The 'cultural turn' also explains why this volume, as opposed to so many others in the field, displays a remarkable unity of purpose. All contributions deal with the 'cultural turn' in one way or another, they are so many case studies illustrating the central concept of the collection. (1990: 4)

In this volume "culture" takes on a broader and more concrete sense than with Toury: it includes innovative contributions in the postcolonial field (Sengupta, see 3.2.1), in feminist discourse (Godard, see 3.2.2) and on ideological misreading in translation (Kuhiwczak, see 3.3).

In 1998 there appeared a collection of essays written by Bassnett and Lefevere – published after Lefevere's death in 1996 – with the title *Constructing Cultures* (cf. 5.3). In his Foreword Edwin Gentzler refers to the 1990 volume, saying that "it was then that translation studies officially took the 'cultural turn'" and "while many scholars were inching toward the cultural turn in the early 1990s, Bassnett and Lefevere were the first to articulate the position" (1998: xi). The achievements of both these scholars in the discipline and the value of their joint publications are beyond dispute, but in the next section we shall assess Gentzler's above remarks, also the cultural turn as reflected in the 1990 volume, in the light of what was going on elsewhere.

2.2   The skopos theory and its functional approach

In 1976, the same year as the historic conference in Leuven, other scholars were engaged in heated debate in a lecture-hall in Germersheim, Germany. In what was to be one of his last publications, Hans Hönig (1941–2004) and Paul Kussmaul recall these developments, each from their individual viewpoint (Hönig 2004, Kussmaul 2004).

Once again, the point of resistance was the paradigm of (applied) linguistics, which was then producing its own "science of translation", drawing on a background of contrastive linguistics, curricular management and machine translation (cf. Wilss 2004). In 1977 Wolfram Wilss published his book *Übersetzungswissenschaft. Probleme und Methoden* (which appeared in English in 1982 with the title *The Science of Translation*), where he compiled an inventory of the factors involved in translation as based on linguistics and communication theory, and with reference to concepts from the Leipzig School. This book has often been described as the beginnings of the discipline in (West) Germany, and it did indeed do much to make the study of translation acceptable to an academic environment which had till then dismissed it as a "merely practical" activity – in the climate of the time an undoubted achievement. But it did not bring about a radical change of paradigm. This, according to Hönig and Kussmaul (both 2004), was initiated by Hans J. Vermeer during the academic year 1976–77 in a lecture course describing a "General Theory of Translation". The ideas were so new and so exciting that the younger colleagues Hönig and Kussmaul were motivated to attend and join in the discussion. The result was Vermeer's seminal essay "Ein Rahmen für eine allgemeine Translationstheorie" (A framework for a general theory of translation, Vermeer 1978), which laid the foundations for the skopos theory.

Kussmaul, who recalls that the idea of attaching more importance to the target culture had already been "in the air" among the colleagues at Germersheim, describes the approach as follows:

> Eine Kernthese des Aufsatzes bestand darin, dass Ziel und Zweck einer Übersetzung von den Bedürfnissen und Erwartungen des Lesers in seiner Kultur bestimmt wird. Vermeer nannte dies "Skopos", und die sogenannte "Treue gegenüber dem Original", also die Äquivalenz, war diesem Skopos untergeordnet. Wir empfanden dies als Befreiungsschlag, so als sei die Übersetzungstheorie endlich vom Kopf auf die Füße gestellt worden. (2004: 223)

> (A central idea of the essay was that the aim and purpose of a translation is determined by the needs and expectations of the reader in his culture. Vermeer called this the "skopos", and the so-called "faithfulness to the original", equivalence in fact, was subordinated to this skopos. This gave us a real sense of release, as if translation theory had at last been put on its feet.)

On the basis of Vermeer's ideas, Hönig and Kussmaul then compiled their book *Strategie der Übersetzung. Ein Lehr- und Arbeitsbuch (Strategy of Translation. A coursebook)*, which appeared in 1982 and, as the title indicates, was written for students, in a lively and lucid style and illustrated by many examples. The Greek word *skopos* was avoided, as at the time it was largely unknown in the translation context, and instead the authors used the word *function* – which earned them, and others of similar convictions, the title of the "Germersheim Functionalists". In their book, which soon became a bestseller, the concept of culture has a central role; their definition of the text, which for translation purposes rivals that of Beaugrande and Dressler (1981), is "the verbalized part of a socioculture" (1982:58): the text is embedded in a given situation, which is itself conditioned by by its sociocultural background (for the diagram of these relations see Kussmaul 1986: 209). The translation is then dependent on its function as a text "implanted" in the target culture, whereby there is the alternative of either preserving the original function of the source text ("functional constancy"), or of changing the function to adapt to the specified needs of the target culture.

Vermeer was to restate and elaborate his theoretical principles in a collection of lectures he published in 1983, then at a colloquium held in Saarbrücken in 1983 (Vermeer 1984), and above all in the book he wrote with Katharina Reiss which became the "manifesto" of the skopos theorists: *Grundlegung einer allgemeinen Translationstheorie (Foundations of a General Theory of Translation*, Reiss and Vermeer 1984), where, like James Holmes before him, he discussed the name of the discipline involved. Taking over Kade's generic terms *Translation, Translator* and *Translat*, he suggests (among other possibilities) the derivative *Translationswissenschaft*, which has meanwhile gained acceptance in the German-speaking scientific community.[20] In his model, language is not an autonomous "system", but part of a culture, hence the translator should not be only bilingual, but also bicultural. Similarly, the text is not a static and isolated linguistic fragment, but is dependent on its reception by the reader, and it invariably bears a relation to the extra-linguistic situation in which it is embedded, it is therefore "part of a world-continuum" (1983: 48).

This approach relativizes both text and translation: the one and only perfect translation does not exist, any translation is dependent on its skopos and its situation. Whereas Toury's concept of a translation is "a text that is accepted as such" (2.1), the skopos approach has identified five broad translation types. The *interlinear version* (or word for word translation), as once used by Bible translators in the form of glosses, merely reproduces the linear sequence of words, irrespective of

---

20. Even here, however, with exceptions (cf. Preface to Pöckl 2004).

any rules of the TL language system. The *grammar translation*, as used in foreign language classes to test knowledge of vocabulary and grammar, observes the rules of TL syntax, and the linguistic meaning itself is clear, but it functions at sentence level, and there is no context. The *documentary* or "scholarly" translation reflects Schleiermacher's maxim of "moving the reader towards the author" (1.1): the text is here seen in its entirety, but the translation is oriented towards the source text and aims at informing the reader of its content, even by "alienating" or "foreignizing" the target language. The *communicative* or "instrumental" translation is oriented towards the target culture, using its conventions and idioms; the text function typically remains unchanged (as with instructions for use – cf. 2.3) and the text is not immediately recognizable as a translation. With the *adapting* or "modifying" translation, the source text functions as raw material to serve a particular purpose, as with multimedial or multimodal translation (3.1.3) or when news reports are used by press agencies. (Cf. Reiss and Vermeer 1984: 134–136, also Reiss 1995: 21–23, see too Gawlas 2004). With this approach a translation is seen in terms of how it serves its intended purpose, and the concept of translation, when set against the former criterion of SL equivalence, is more differentiated and indeed closer to the realities of translation practice.

Vermeer expanded his ideas in a lecture given in Zurich on 21st May 1984, which was published in a later version as "Übersetzen als kultureller Transfer" ("Translation as a cultural transfer", Vermeer 1986). Here he states his own definition of translation:

> …ein Informationsangebot in einer Sprache z der Kultur Z, das ein Informationsangebot in einer Sprache a der Kultur A funktionsgerecht (!) imitiert. Das heißt ungefähr: Eine Translation ist nicht die Transkodierung von Wörtern oder Sätzen aus einer Sprache in eine andere, sondern eine komplexe Handlung, in der jemand unter neuen funktionalen und kulturellen und sprachlichen Bedingungen in einer neuen Situation über einen Text (Ausgangssachverhalt) berichtet, indem er ihn auch formal möglichst nachahmt. (1986: 33)

> (…an offer of information in a language t of the culture T,[21] which imitates an offer of information in a language s of the culture S according to its specified function. In other words, a translation is not the transcoding of words or sentences from one language into another, but a complex form of action in which someone gives information about a text (source language material) under new functional, cultural and linguistic conditions and in a new situation, while preserving formal aspects as far as possible.)

---

21.   T/t = target (German Z/z = Ziel), S/s = source (German A/a = Ausgangs-…).

This is an explicit rejection of the then still influential linguistic definition of translation as an "equivalent" version of the source text.[22] The most important factor is the *skopos* (Greek for *aim, purpose, goal*), hence the purpose or function of the translation in the target culture, as specified by the client (in a translation brief) or the envisaged user-expectations; translation is hence prospective rather than, as had hitherto been the case, retrospective. The skopos can apply to both the process and the product of translation, and a distinction is made between the *Translationsskopos* (the translator's intended purpose) and the *Translatskopos* (the function of the translation as seen in the receiving culture): in everyday practice these differ, and only in ideal cases is there complete agreement between them. The second important factor is *intratextual coherence*: a message has been understood when the reader (or user) can make sense of it both in itself and in relation to his/her given situation. That is more important than *intertextual coherence* (or fidelity to the source text), which pertains if the function of source and target texts remain the same. If a change of function is required, the translation should fulfil the criteria specified in the *skopos*. In the heated discussion following the Zurich lecture, Vermeer spoke of "de-throning the source text", which he merely considered a "means to a new text", ideas which were anathema to the assembled linguists and which even among translation scholars provoked stormy debate.

Vermeer's approach was essentially dynamic and holistic, actually in keeping with the trends of the times, and today it might seem strange that it met with such opposition. His ideas harmonize with those of James Holmes (for whose disciplinary utopia he provided a General Theory), as for example his concept of "intertextual coherence" (cf. 3.3.1) which replaces the orthodox "equivalence" and refines Holmes' notion of the "network of matchings" (1.4). Similarly the concepts of "documentary" and "instrumental" translation – compatible with Newmark's "semantic" and "communicative" translation (1981) – are placed in context with leading, linguistically oriented, works of the time (House 1977 and Diller and Kornelius 1978, cf. Reiss and Vermeer 1984: 92).

Basically however, as we see from the title of his 1986 essay, Vermeer views translation as a cultural transfer rather than a linguistic one, language being part of culture. The definition of culture, taken over from his Germersheim colleague Heinz Göhring, itself based on that of the American ethnologist Ward Goode-

---

22. Cf. Koller (1972: 69–70): „*Linguistisch* kann die Übersetzung als Umkodierung oder Substitution beschrieben werden: Elemente a1, a2, a3... des Sprachzeicheninventars L1 werden durch Elemente b1, b2, b3....des Sprachzeicheninventars L2 ersetzt." (In linguistic terms translation can be described as transcoding or substitution; elements a1, a2, a3… of the language system L1 are replaced by elements b1, b2, b3… of the language system L2."

nough (1964: 36, see Snell-Hornby 1988: 39–40), has meanwhile become standard among German-speaking translation scholars supporting the functional approach:

> Kultur ist all das, was man wissen, beherrschen und empfinden können muss, um beurteilen zu können, wo sich Einheimische in ihren verschiedenen Rollen erwartungskonform oder abweichend verhalten, und um sich selbst in der betreffenden Gesellschaft erwartungskonform oder abweichend verhalten zu können, sofern man dies will und nicht etwa bereit ist, die jeweils aus erwartungswidrigem Verhalten entstehenden Konsequenzen zu tragen. (Göhring 1977: 10)

> (Culture consists of everything one needs to know, master and feel, in order to assess where members of a society are behaving acceptably or deviantly in their various roles, and in order to behave in a way that is acceptable or deviant for that society, as far as one wishes to do so and is not prepared to take the consequences arising from deviant conduct.)

Later Vermeer was to modify this definition as:

> ...die Gesamtheit der Normen, Konventionen und Meinungen, nach denen sich das Verhalten der Mitglieder einer Gesellschaft richtet, und die Gesamtheit der Resultate aus diesem Verhalten (also z.B. der architektonischen Bauten, der universitären Einrichtungen usw. usw). (Vermeer 1989a: 9)

> (...the totality of norms, conventions and opinions which determine the behaviour of the members of a society, and all results of this behaviour (such as architecture, university institutions etc. etc)

This concept of culture as a totality of knowledge, proficiency and perception (in particular the notions of *norm* and *convention*) is basic to the functional approach to translation as a special form of communication and social action[23] in contrast to abstract code-switching, and it was later extended by Heidrun Witte (1987) in a discussion of the translator's "cultural competence" as "competence between cultures". The concept of culture is central to the skopos theory (described more fully in Schäffner 1998b), and as such already gave rise to the "cultural turn" in Germany during the mid-1980s. The "new orientation" was so clear that in 1984 (the same year in which the volume by Reiss and Vermeer was published) I started asking colleagues for contributions to an anthology reflecting this change (Snell-Hornby 1986): they include essays by Vermeer, Kussmaul and Hönig. The exciting new developments in the German scientific community then formed the topic of the paper I gave at the Warwick Conference in 1988, "Linguistic Transcoding or

---

23. For a more recent and detailed discussion of the concept of culture and its relevance for translation see Schmid 2000.

Cultural Transfer? A Critique of Translation Theory in Germany" (Snell-Hornby 1990), which begins with these remarks:

> In recent years there has been a ferment of new ideas on translation in the German-speaking countries, many of them hotly debated in countless publications, but in the English-speaking world the household names of German translation theory remain virtually unknown. As an attempt to counteract the deficit, this paper presents an overview of the two main streams in translation theory that have developed in Germany since the war: the linguistically oriented *Übersetzungswissenschaft* as represented in particular by the theorists of the Leipzig School, along with Wolfram Wilss and Werner Koller, and the culturally oriented approach of scholars such as Hans J. Vermeer. (1990: 79)

In the introduction to their 1990 volume Lefevere and Bassnett use the notion of the "cultural turn" (1990: 4, quoted in 2.1) with explicit reference to that paper – which describes developments in Germany of the 1980s. All the more perplexing is Gentzler's assertion, likewise quoted in 2.1, that it was with the 1990 anthology "that translation studies officially took the 'cultural turn'" (1998: xi). When the turn was "officially" taken is difficult to say: "unofficially" I would suggest that it was taken by Hönig and Kussmaul in 1982, and then followed up by Vermeer and his colleagues through the following years, definitely contributing towards what Bassnett and Lefevere themselves were so famously to describe as the "success story of the 1980s" (1990: ix).

2.3   The model of translatorial action

The year 1984 was to mark a major turning point in Translation Studies. Apart from Holmes' Vienna paper and the volume by Reiss and Vermeer, there appeared, in a small academic publishing house in Helsinki, a book by Justa Holz-Mänttäri called *Translatorisches Handeln. Theorie und Methode (Translatorial Action. Theory and Method.)* This too was the result of thought processes going back for years, and it was also an act of rebellion against ruling dogmas on translation, but whereas the Manipulation School grew out of academic conference activities and the skopos theory was born in the lecture-room, Justa Holz-Mänttäri's theory reflects the everyday routine of the practising translator.

Holz-Mänttäri, a native of Hamburg who has lived for many years in Finland, worked both as a professional translator and a teacher of translation at the universities in Turku and Tampere. She presented her own theory of translation both at the Congress of the International Association of Applied Linguistics (AILA) in Lund, Sweden in 1981 and at the AILA Colloquium in Saarbrücken in 1983, in itself an irony of fate, because she believed that translation was fundamentally not a matter of language at all. In that respect her approach was even more radical than that of Hans Vermeer. For Holz-Mänttäri translation is basically action, a form of intercultural communication (whereby language is not content or goal but the necessary instrument). Her form of "polemical orientation" was against the Finns' practice of qualifying and evaluating their professional "language translators" (Finnish *kielenkääntäjä*, from *kieli*/language and *kääntäjä*/translator) on the basis of language competence only, knowledge of technical terms and grammar structures as tested on isolated "text fragments" (Holz-Mänttäri 1984a: 176) – which of course was actually no different from the current practice elsewhere.

In contrast to that Holz-Mänttäri describes her "translatorial action" as follows: "Die translatorische Handlung ist in ein System anderer Handlungen eingebunden und wird von Faktoren gesteuert, die außerhalb ihrer selbst liegen (1984a: 177)." (Translatorial action is integrated into a system of other actions and is controlled by factors lying outside it.) In viewing translation as a complex form of action, or intercultural communication in a social context, and by reducing the status of the source text and of the entire language component, Holz-Mänttäri already has much in common with Vermeer, though both scholars have always insisted that their theories were developed independently of each other, but the common ground led to their close cooperation in later years.

The theory of translatorial action has meanwhile been described in English by Christina Schäffner (1998a), and from today's perspective it appears entirely plausible. At the time however it seemed exotic and eccentric, and I remember that particularly at the Lund conference (of applied linguists!) few people could really understand was Holz-Mänttäri was trying to get at. One reason was that she used completely new terminology. She rejected the traditional German term *Übersetzung* for "translation" because of its association with language exercises in the classroom, and she looked for specialized terminology in keeping with professional standards. For her key-term she used *Translation* in Kade's sense as a generic term for translating and interpreting, with the attendant forms *Translator* for the agent and *translatorisch* as the modifier, and for the envisaged academic discipline providing the theory she used *Translatologie* (see 1.4). She also invented brand-new terms, such as *Botschaftsträger* (literally "message conveyor") to replace had been otherwise called a text (but including additional material such as diagrams), again to avoid inaccurate associations produced by words from everyday language. At the time, we must not forget, a text was still considered in the purely verbal sense as a sequence of sentences, and for Holz-Mänttäri the message was central and not the linguistic items. Her *Bedarfsträger* is in commercial terminology the consumer, and in the context of professional translation simply means the client (at that time not yet visible in the translation debate).

Secondly, she used the style then required in German to qualify as being "scholarly": this applied particularly to her 1984 book, which was submitted as a thesis for the highest academic qualification in Finland (the examining board, as direct recipients, being scholars of German). The result was language popularly dismissed as "jargon", occasionally defended as "technical", but – at least at first – rarely understood. That remained the case for years, although the actual content of Holz-Mänttäri's message is in fact sound common sense and reflects the real-life job of the professional translator.

In concrete terms it could be illustrated as follows: a Finnish client (such as the head of the marketing department of a firm producing electrical equipment) needs an English (or German or Arabic) version of the instructions for use of a washing machine. His aim is of course to market the washing machine in the countries concerned. As he has no command of their languages himself, he commissions a translator with the job,[24] providing him/her with the instructions for use in Finnish. The task of this translator is to produce a text which the English/German/Arabic buyers of the washing machine can understand so that they can really use the machine. To do this s/he may need to check internal details with the marketing manager or, particularly in the case of Arabic, to find out further information about the envisaged user (including cultural implications), about possible market restrictions as regards spare parts, or about legal implications concerning the guarantee. In any case, a good deal of cooperation with the firm (and maybe other specialists) is involved, the translator does not operate in isolation. What is not required is an exact reproduction of the sentences or grammatical structures in the Finnish text, as this may not help the English/German/Arabic user to operate the washing machine[25] – and maybe part of the verbal text is in fact better rendered in the form of a diagram or sketch. If the text eventually enables the user to operate the machine, the immediate purpose of the translation has been reached, and the firm's ultimate purpose will be achieved if such texts help to boost their sales. The aim of the translation therefore lies outside the linguistic content of the source text.

In more abstract terms (and including Holz-Mänttäri's terminology) the process can be described as follows: Translatorial action is not linguistic transcoding,

---

24. How unprofessionally this is often done is shown by Sobotka (2000).

25. I can illustrate this from personal experience: I once bought a Japanese digital clock, but could not use it because I could not understand any of the versions of the instructions for use provided in European languages. These had simply reproduced Japanese language structures, which in English/French/German etc, did not create a coherent text and in part it could not be applied to the product.

but consists of a whole complex of actions (*Handlungsgefüge*) involving team-work among specialists, including the client, or initiator (*Bedarfsträger*) and the translator, who has the role of a professional expert in text-design and as such assumes the responsibility for his/her product (cf. 3.1.1). As in the skopos theory, translation is seen as an act of communication across cultural barriers, the main criteria being determined by the specific function of the translation for its recipi-ent. Translatorial action is a process involving various steps: these begin with the client placing the order, providing the source-language material and presenting the contract with information on the intended target text and its proposed use. The course of the translation project is then mapped out and the translation prod-uct specified. On the basis of source-text analyses and further background infor-mation, a text is produced, where necessary checked with the client or subject specialists and modified accordingly, and translation decisions are explained. The translator then assumes full responsibility for the final product.

With her expert professional translator Holz-Mänttäri effectively does away with the popular image of the translator as the man (or woman) in the street who buys a bilingual dictionary and attempts to transcode texts as in practical classes at school or university (cf. Holz-Mänttäri 1986: 371) – although unfortunately such an image still exists, at least among the general public, today (see Snell-Hornby 2005 and 6. below). It is worth emphasizing that at first Holz-Mänttäri's message was more favourably received by practising translators (Stellbrink 1985, cf. Snell-Hornby 1988: 48) than by academics, her *Translatologen* who taught in the train-ing institutions. Those however who were active in both worlds were quicker to understand the message – one was Douglas Robinson, who declared in 1991:

> My colleague at the University of Tampere, Justa Holz-Mänttäri, has offered what is perhaps the most comprehensive (and increasingly influential) overview of translation, in terms of key terms (…) in her *Translatorisches Handeln*, on transla-tional activity, translation as doing, or, in Burkean terms, translation as drama. By directing attention away from the linguistic conception as abstract correspon-dence between texts to what *happens* in translation, Holz-Mänttäri has opened a potentially dramatistic alternative to translation as conceived by applied linguists. (1991: 128–129)

While Holz-Mänttäri's concept of translatorial action may at first sight seem to be tailor-made for non-literary translation, especially the translator working in industry, case-studies have shown how eminently well it can be applied to the real-life world of interpreting or even of literary translation, in the "dramatistic" sense understood by Robinson: convincing examples are Pöchhacker (1994) on confer-ence interpreting (see 4.1.1), Kaindl (1995) on opera translation (see 3.1.3), Kadrić (2001) on court interpreting (see 4.1.1), Salmhoferova (2002) on legal translation and Framson (2005) on international marketing (see 4.1.2). These studies show how Justa Holz-Mänttäri contributed not only to the cultural turn of the 1980s, but beyond that to further major developments that have since taken place in Translation Studies as a recognized academic discipline.

2.4   Deconstruction, or the "cannibalistic" approach

In 1986, in São Paolo, a small book was published by Rosemary Arrojo with the title *Oficina de tradução* (Translation workshop). With reference to Alexander Tytler's *Essay on the Principles of Translation* (1791) (cf. 1.1) she takes up the question of the source text as the "sacred original", an issue that had been debated in Brazil for some decades.

The discussion was closely bound up with the country's colonial history, and translation was understood as a means of shaking off the fetters of the past, including the domination of European cultural values. In the 1920s the "Anthropophagy Movement" arose in Brazil as a form of political resistance with the aim of rediscovering the indigenous roots that had been repressed by the European influence: the cultural values of the industrialized countries were to be "devoured" and absorbed into the indigenous culture (*anthropophagos* = "man-devouring" or "cannibalistic").[26] During the 1960s two renowned Brazilian poets and translators, the brothers Augusto and Haroldo de Campos, took up these ideas in their work with language, which they saw as material for creative text-production. They developed a "Third World translation model", using the "cannibalistic" metaphor, not in the sense of negating or ignoring the Other, but in the sense of absorbing it and then reproducing it, enriched with indigenous elements. Thus from a political resistance movement, "cannibalism" turned into a metaphor for reaction against cultural domination and then into a "translation philosophy" that was to gain a new meaning in postmodern translation theory (cf. Vieira 1994: 66–67).

In the 1980s the discussion concentrated on the tension between the authority of the original (representing the central culture of the colonizers) on the one hand and the autonomy of the translation (representing the peripheral culture of the colonized) on the other (cf. Wolf 1997: 15–16). The "cannibalistic" interpretation of the text aims at creating a new reading of colonialism, which in translation produces a variety of discourses, challenging the hierarchy of power between "original" and translation. That is the starting point of Rosemary Arrojo. Using the deconstructionist approach of Jacques Derrida (1978), she questions the logocen-

---

26.   For an account of how the Brazilian colonial past was directly absorbed into translation processes see Cruz Romão (2000).

trism of Western philosophical tradition with its fixation on the written word, which was the basis of traditional translation theory (as exemplified in Tytler's Principle of 1791 "that the Translation should give a complete transcript of the ideas of the original work", see Tytler 1978: 17). In Derrida's view a text cannot have a fixed or final "sense", and every new reading results in a translation. The translator himself takes on the role of an author, and concepts such as the "sacred original" or the attempt to reproduce the intentions of its author are "deconstructed" – and with them of course the notion of "faithfulness" to the source-text.

Arrojo aims to show the inadequacy of the traditional translation theories, specifically in Tytler 1791, Catford 1965 or Nida 1964, and later in Steiner 1975 (Arrojo 1992), by taking a story by Jorge Luis Borges as an example (1986: 13 ff.). Its protagonist is Pierre Menard, an early 20th century writer who tries to reconstruct Cervantes' "Don Quijote", and the story shows how the reading of a text varies with cultural values, and also with time and place (cf. 3.3). Arrojo shows that a text is primarily the result of the interpretation of the individual reader. Hence reading does not merely transmit the intended meaning of an author, it rather produces new meanings:

> Ao invés de considerarmos o texto, ou o signo, como um receptáculo em que algum "conteúdo" possa ser depositado e mantido sob controle, proponho que sua imagem exemplar passe a ser a de um *palimpsesto*. Segundo os dicionários, o substantivo masculino *palimpsesto*, do grego *palímpsestos* ("raspado novamente"), refere-se ao "antigo material de escrita, principalmente o pergaminho, usado, em razão de sua escassez ou alto preço, duas ou três vezes (...) mediante raspagem do texto anterior".

> Metaforicamente, em nossa "oficina", o "palimpsesto" passa a ser o texto que se apaga, em cada comunidade cultural e em cada época, para dar lugar a outra escritura (ou interpretação, ou leitura, ou tradução) do "mesmo" texto. (1986: 23–24)

> (Instead of considering the text or sign as a container which can be filled with "content" and hence controlled, I propose using a new metaphor, that of the "palimpsest". The dictionary defines *palimpsest* (from Greek *palimpsestos*) ("rubbed smooth again") as a manuscript (usually old and on parchment) "on which two or more successive texts have been written, each one being erased to make room for the next" (CED).

> Metaphorically, in our "workshop" the "palimpsest" can be seen as a text which in every cultural community and in every epoch can be erased to make place for another "rewrite" (or interpretation, reading or translation) of the "same" text.)

In this interpretation translation, like reading, is no longer an activity that preserves the "original" meanings of an author, but one which sees its task in *producing* meanings. Furthermore, in this view, as reflecting Derrida's deconstructionist approach, if the text is no longer a static vessel containing an author's intended meaning that can supposedly be reproduced in translation, the notion of "original" as well as the relationship between translator and translation must be completely revised. Translation turns into a kind of "transformation", the concept of equivalence is invalid, and the translator becomes a visible and active participant in this transformation. And if there is no "original" and no irrefutable "intended meaning", this implies the death of the author – famously celebrated by Barthes (1977) as the "birth" of the reader (cf. Arrojo 1997a, and see 3.3).[27]

This kind of thinking clearly corresponds with that of Vermeer, particularly with his image of "dethroning" the source text, his rejection of the static concept of equivalence and his concept of the active role of both the translator and the target-text reader. In his Preface to the volume containing essays from Brazil in German translation (Wolf 1997), Vermeer expresses open enthusiasm for Arrojo's work, and explains it as follows:

> Der Grund ist leicht einzusehen: Ich hatte inzwischen meine "Skopostheorie" entwickelt (an deren Weiterführung u.a. auch eine Brasilianerin: Margret Ammann mitgearbeitet hat) und bei einer ersten Begegnung mit Justa Holz-Mänttäri (damals Turku, Finnland) bereits 1983 festgestellt, dass wir auf einer ganz ähnlichen Linie lagen (vgl. Holz-Mänttäris *Theorie über translatorisches Handeln*). 1986 stellte ich nun fest, dass auch Rosemary Arrojo ganz unabhängig von uns als dritte eine parallele strikt funktionale Theorie des Übersetzens geschrieben hatte. Die Schwerpunkte liegen ein wenig anders: Justa Holz-Mänttäris Schwerpunkt ihrer – durchaus allgemein gehaltenen – Theorie liegt im Bereich der Gebrauchstextübersetzung; Rosemary Arrojo geht in ihrem ebenfalls allgemeinen Ansatz zentral auf das literarische Übersetzen ein. (1997a: 9)

> (The reason is easily explained. I had meanwhile worked out my "skopos theory" (among those who helped to continue it was a Brazilian colleague, Margret Ammann), and during a first meeting with Justa Holz-Mänttäri (then at Turku, Finland) in 1983 I had already discovered that we were working along very similar lines (cf. Holz-Mänttäri's *Theory of translatorial action*). Then in 1986 I discovered that Rosemary Arrojo as a third scholar, quite independently of us, had written a corresponding, strictly functional theory of translation. In each case there is a slight difference of emphasis: Justa Holz-Mänttäri's basically general theory concentrates mainly on the translation of pragmatic texts, Rosemary Arrojo's equally general approach focusses on literary translation.)

The common ground between the three approaches could hardly be described more clearly, and they were coordinated and developed, firstly by mutual cooperation (as was the case with the scholars of the Manipulation School), and secondly

---

27. For a semiotic approach to the translation-original relationship see Stecconi (2000).

by joint publications within the German-speaking community (cf. Wolf 1997). The fact that the three approaches had independent and completely different origins is here quite immaterial.

The Brazilian "anthropophagic" or "cannibalistic" approach anticipates later work on postcolonial literature: as a literary metaphor it describes exactly the output of Salman Rushdie or Arundhati Roy, for example, who had totally absorbed the language and culture of their former colonial overlords and then expressed it, enriched with "indigenous" elements, in their own eminently creative English (for the problems in translating this see 3.2.1). As a term for translation it might however, at least in English, evoke unfortunate associations: whereas the Hard Word *anthropophagic* is clinical and opaque, the metaphorical English *frame* "cannibalistic" has an element of brutality and finality that may not express the creative potential inherent in the act of translation.[28] Arrojo's image of the "palimpsest" seems more appropriate. Similarly the deconstructionist metaphor "death" of the author, though long since common currency, is in my opinion unfortunate when applied to literary works, particularly in the context of translation. The *frame* "death" is now not necessarily understood as a preliminary to Resurrection, but all too often implies annihilation. We shall later concern ourselves in more detail with the role of the reader (3.3), whose "birth", particularly for purposes of translation, need not "destroy" an author (or his/her work), but rather creates the potential for a further existence.

2.5   The 1980s in retrospect

The immediate impression produced so far seems to be that during the 1980s there was indeed a change of paradigm in the study of translation, but that there were two separate and different branches: the "Manipulation School" on literary translation with writings in English on the one hand, and the functional schools stimulated by Vermeer, writing mainly in German, on the other.

This picture seems to blur what all the developments described in this chapter have in common: they are all by self-definition target-oriented and functional, they all encountered fierce opposition, but from today's perspective we can say that they all largely overcame the opposition and contributed substantially to the development of Translation Studies as an independent discipline. Conspicuously common elements are the interplay of theory and practice (as in Descriptive

---

28. See however Bassnett and Trivedi (1999a) for a convincing interpretation of this metaphor as against Steiner's (1975) view of translation as involving the "penetration" of the source text (see 1.2).

Translation Studies and Holz-Mänttäri's theory of translatorical action), and the concept of "rewrites" (Lefevere and Arrojo).

However, a close reading of the literature shows that actually the same terms are sometimes used in different ways. One example is the term *culture*, as discussed by Toury (2.1) in the sense of *system*. Another is *function*, which, as Toury later explained, when writing of "the (prospective) position (or function) of a translation within a recipient culture" (1995: 12) he uses in a sense different from that of the skopos theory:

> The term 'function' here is used in its *semiotic* sense, as the 'value' assigned to an item belonging in a certain system by virtue of the network of relations it enters into (…). As such, it is not tantamount to the mere 'use' of the end product, as seems to be the case with the *Skopostheorie* (…) or *Handlungstheorie* (e.g. Holz-Mänttäri 1984). The correlations between the two uses of 'function', which may well exist, still await scholarly processing. (1995: 12).

A third example is the term *norm*, as developed by Toury in Descriptive Translation Studies, but again with a specific meaning of its own (see 3.1.1).

Where their ways really do part is on the issue of "descriptive" vs. "evaluative". The new paradigm of the Manipulation School was based on the vehement rejection of "the normative and source-oriented approaches typical of most traditional thinking about translation" (Hermans 1985: 9), and this extends to the rejection of translation critique in general and basically too of translators' training institutes with their inevitably normative and evaluative approach. The German functional approach was developed within such institutes and naturally included an element of evaluation, but the criteria were shifted from the linguistic components of the source text to the function of the translation in the target culture. That the Manipulation scholars rebelled against the particular normative dogmas of the time is absolutely plausible, but their own dogmatic rejection of any kind of evaluation has never been convincingly explained. It has also resulted in a large quantity of work in Descriptive Translation Studies, some of which, as Hermans was later to admit (1998: 99), does not go beyond a formalistic approach and lacks a clear purpose. That in fact even literary translations can very well be judged in the functional terms of the skopos theory is exemplified in Margret Ammann's model of translation critique (3.3.1).

The second difference lies in the fact that the conception of Translation Studies, as presented by James Holmes and further developed by the Manipulation scholars, was explicitly focussed on literary translation. Against that the skopos theory, within the discipline of *Translationswissenschaft*, set out to be a general theory of translating and interpreting. As described above by Vermeer (2.4), the three "general" streams in the functional approach together covered both literary and non-literary translation. Descriptive Translation Studies, as Hermans later pointed out (1998: 99), has for the most part remained oriented to literary texts, but without considering later developments such as postcolonial theories (3.2.1) or Gender Studies (3.2.2). While the skopos theory laid claim from the outset to being a general theory, in the 1980s and within the context of translator training it was automatically associated with pragmatic texts, but its relevance for literary translation was questioned. As one of the sceptics, I then pointed out that there were various problems to be considered, including the status, situation and function of the source text, and the intricate problems of style (Snell-Hornby 1988 and 1990). Meanwhile, as will be seen below (3.1.3, 3.3.1), I have modified my position, and here Ammann's model of translation critique has played a major part. I am now convinced that the skopos theory can be applied to more areas of the discipline than can Descriptive Translation Studies.

Between the two branches themselves there was little correspondence during the 1980s, although they both arose, albeit independently of each other, at the same time, both were "polemically oriented" against the then linguistic dogmas, and both aimed at creating a new paradigm. In 1995 Toury summed up the situation as follows:

> Interestingly, the first formulations of the *Skopostheorie* by Vermeer (e.g. 1978) almost coincided with the beginnings of my own switch to target-orientedness (Toury 1977) – which sheds interesting light on how changes of scholarly climate occur, especially considering that for quite a while, the two of us were practically unaware of each other's work. To be sure, even now, there is at least one major difference between the interests of the two target-oriented paradigms, which also accounts for the different assumptions each of them proceeds from: whereas mainstream *Skopos*-theorists still see the ultimate justification of their frame of reference in the more 'realistic' way it can deal with problems of an *applied* nature, the main object being to 'improve' (i.e. change!) the world of our experience, my own endeavours have always been geared primarily towards the *descriptive-explanatory* goal of supplying exhaustive accounts of whatever has been regarded as translational within a target culture, on the way to the formulation of some *theoretical* laws. Recent attempts to conduct historical studies of translation within *Skopostheorie* (most notably Vermeer 1992), on the one hand, and to apply some of the basic assumptions of the other target-oriented paradigm to translation didactics (...) on the other, indicate that the gap may be narrowing. This tendency is also manifest in the recent work of some second-generation *Skopos*-theorists, most notably Nord (1991), who has made an interesting attempt to integrate a version of the notion of "translational norms", so central to my own way of reasoning and its evolution (...), into an account which is basically Vermeerian. Unfortunately, while doing so, Nord (re)introduced the concept of 'loyalty', and as an a priori *moral* principle at that, which may well be opening a new gap between the two approaches as the old one seems to have been closing. (1995: 25)

Some of the content of these observations, particularly the question of "translational norms", is taken up below in 3.1.1. What is interesting is the acute awareness of basic differences and similarities. That this awareness is mutual is seen in a discussion by Vermeer, who first criticizes Toury's concept of equivalence (Toury 1980: 39) as retrospective and his early approach in general as "meta-prescriptive (meta-normative)" (Vermeer 1995: 49), and then compares it with the skopos approach as follows:

> The skopos is hierarchically higher than the equivalence postulate. Such a procedure is then not retrospective (as is the case when taking the source-text structure as the highest element in the hierarchy), but prospective in the sense that the skopos demands a full consideration of source-text structures for a given purpose. In such a case, the difference between Toury's approach and that of skopos theory is one of focus; in practice, the result may look the same. (1995: 51)

In a "Postscript" written after Toury's 1995 book had appeared, Vermeer modified his position:

> Toury's functional approach to translation no longer has the 'retrospective' outlook I still believed it had, when I quoted some passages about "equivalence" from previous publications. – Toury uses the term "function" in a semiotic sense, different from the one mentioned above. (1995: 111)

Apart from differences in focus and in usage of terminology, there may be a very clear explanation of why writings from these two outstanding movements in Translation Studies might be mutually misunderstood, and above all sometimes only barely comprehensible to outsiders: the opacity of their academic language and presentation. Firstly, it was still en vogue in the 1980s to garnish one's arguments with mathematical formulae and illustrate them with immensely complicated diagrams, and this certainly explains why Vermeer's 1983 volume and even Holz-Mänttäri's 1986 essay now look like products of another age. Secondly, there is the problem of what Lefevere and Bassnett, with reference to Toury, delicately phrased as "his somewhat more than hermetic style" (1990: 5) and of what has been less delicately phrased with Justa Holz-Mänttäri as "jargon". This problem is connected with academic traditions and cultures and is a serious one for a discipline like Translation Studies whose goal is communication.

As Michael Clyne has established in his study of English and German scholarly texts, English texts tend to be linear, symmetrical, inductive and reader-oriented; it is the author's reponsibility to make him/herself understood. German academic writings on the other hand tend to be digressive, asymmetrical, deductive and author-oriented: it is up to the reader to take the trouble (and to equip him/herself with the knowledge) to understand them (Clyne 1991). Vermeer and Holz-Mänttäri write (or were required to write) in the latter tradition. The English native speakers Bassnett and Holmes adhere to the former tradition, as do bicultural writers like Lefevere and Hermans, who have lived and worked in an English-speaking environment for decades. Many non-native academic writers of English, including Toury, use the language code of English, but tend to a digressive style as in the German tradition. This involves a distinct translation problem (cf. Kussmaul 1998), and it is Christina Schäffner's merit, as another bicultural scholar, that she has meanwhile explained both the skopos theory and the theory of translatorial action (1998b, 1998a) to a global readership in reasonably comprehensible English.[29]

At the end of the 1980s however, there was still a noticeable gap between the varying sub-fields of the newly emerged field of Translation Studies, and no significant attempt has been made to bring them together. I saw a solution in my integrated approach of 1988. This then referred specifically to the linguistic as against the literary orientation, which I thought could be overcome by the culturally oriented approach. This chapter has shown that there were other, and more subtle difficulties to be overcome, and the conclusion of my Warwick paper has proved only too true: "A bridge across the gulf has yet to be built, so that, when two translation scholars from different countries and different backgrounds talk about translation, they may have some common ground". (Snell-Hornby 1990: 85 and 6 below)

---

29. Some of Holz-Mänttäri's terminology is however not entirely convincing in Schäffner's translation: e.g. "message transmitter" (for *Botschaftsträger*), which rather misleadingly implies electronic equipment.

CHAPTER 3

The "interdiscipline" of the 1990s

The political turn of 1989 that changed European history had an immediate effect on the work of European translators and interpreters, and with it on the development of Translation Studies. This was especially noticeable in Vienna, the one-time imperial city which for four decades had occupied a remote position on the most easterly tip of Western Europe, and now found itself, geographically at least, in the centre again. New markets for translators and interpreters suddenly became available, and proficiency in the languages of Hungary, Poland and Czechoslovakia, which for decades had counted as "small" and exotic, was now in great demand. With the disappearance of the Iron Curtain travel was again permitted, and immediately contacts with the colleagues of the neighbouring countries began to flourish again. One of the first Translation Studies conferences to take place in this new constellation was the "Central European Symposium" held in Vienna in November 1991 for colleagues from the new democracies (see Snell-Hornby 1992b).

All in all, it was a favourable climate for the development of Translation Studies. After the paralyzing effects of the Cold War it was a time of dialogue, of rediscovering the value of human contacts, on the personal level, but also internationally, in trade and industry, in culture and politics. Moreover we were aware of living on a continent which had a rich variety of languages and cultures but whose states were at the same time beginning a new phase of cooperation and integration. These seemed ideal conditions for translators and their work, and it seemed the right time to boost their status in society. And after the cultural turn of the 1980s it was a heyday of Translation Studies. Against this background, a group of scholars collected (not unlike those in the Low Countries over a decade before) who met in Vienna for what were dubbed, not without a touch of self-irony, the "Vienna Translation Summits" (see Pöchhacker 2004a). We had spirited and enthusiastic discussions on various aspects of the discipline, on curricular reform and the teaching of translating and interpreting. Kussmaul (2004) writes in retrospect:

> Dass Konferenzen nicht nur wegen der wissenschaftlichen Vorträge, die dort gehalten werden, sondern auch wegen der Geselligkeit beliebt sind, wissen wir alle schon lange und dürfen wir seit David Lodges Roman *Small World* auch zugeben.

> Das Besondere an den Wiener Translationsgipfeln lag aber darin, dass die Gesell-
> igkeit wieder wissenschaftliche Ideen gebar. Im Jugendstilhotel "Cottage" saßen
> wir oft noch lange beim letzten Frühstück zusammen, und eine Idee schälte sich
> immer deutlicher heraus: Die Übersetzungswissenschaft als relativ neue Disziplin
> müsste eigentlich bekannter werden, als sie es bisher war. (2004: 225)

> (We have all known for a long time that conferences are not only popular for their
> academic lectures but also as social occasions, and after David Lodge's *Small World*
> we can now freely admit it. But the special thing about the Vienna Translation
> Summits was that the social exchanges created new ideas for the discipline. In the
> Art-Nouveau "Cottage Hotel" we would often sit for ages over the last breakfast,
> and one idea emerged that increasingly became clearer: Translation Studies as a
> relatively new discipline really ought to get better known than it was up to then.)

The result was the Vienna Translation Studies Congress in September 1992 with
the foundation of the European Society for Translation Studies (EST).

If we can already speak of a Translation Studies "tradition" in Radnitzky's sense,
we might say that in the early 1990s we are still firmly in the domain of the "masters", with Toury (for Descriptive Translation Studies), Bassnett and Lefevere (for
literary translation in general), and Vermeer and Holz-Mänttäri (for the German-
speaking functional approach) clearly leading the way, as was reflected in their
respective journals *Target* (launched in 1989) and *TextConText* (launched in 1986).

However, as we shall see in the next two chapters, during the course of the
decade it was above all the "disciples" who were increasingly to make their mark
on the discipline. Beside them, with the founding of numerous new training institutes and with graduate degree courses in Translation Studies, there also emerged
a whole legion of people eager to jump on the bandwagon of what was becoming a
trendy new subject. It became virtually impossible to keep up with the sheer quantity of publications, which were of varying quality. It would go far beyond the
scope of this volume to try and assess all the diverse trends: my aim is rather to single out those contributions which brought really innovative concepts or fertile
ideas, and which in retrospect could be seen as milestones pointing the way ahead.

3.1   Beyond language

With the cultural turn in Translation Studies, its emancipation from linguistics
and comparative literature and its emergence as an independent discipline, the
question naturally arose as to its disciplinary profile. In 1988 I presented a conception of Translation Studies as an integrated and independent discipline within a
prototypological framework covering all kinds of translation, from literary to
technical (Snell-Hornby 1988: 35). Potentially such a conceptual framework was
designed to include interpreting studies, terminology and machine-aided transla-

tion, and to involve relevant areas of neighbouring disciplines, not only language and literary studies, but also semiotics, ethnology, sociology and psychology. The panorama of Translation Studies has meanwhile been sketched in the *Handbuch Translation* (Snell-Hornby et al. 1998). It was Gideon Toury who first pointed out to me (personal communication) that such a complex field should rather be described, not as a discipline, but an "interdiscipline", which was then adopted as the key-word of the Vienna Translation Studies Congress in 1992 (cf. Snell-Hornby et al. 1994).[30]

Klaus Kaindl (2004) has discussed in detail the issues arising in defining the profile of an academic discipline, along with the phenomenon of interdisciplinarity. In his assessment of the relevant literature, the term "interdiscipline" itself is not quite unproblematic:

> Interdisziplinen stellen keinen eigenen Fachbereich dar, sondern vielmehr ein offenes Forschungsfeld, auf das verschiedene Disziplinen Zugriff nehmen können. Interdisziplin bezeichnet somit genau genommen einen "disziplinlosen" Zustand, oder wie Rintelen es formuliert: "Die *interdisziplinäre Wissenschaft* ist aber nicht eine besondere Disziplin, sondern eine gegenseitige Ergänzung der verschiedenen Fächer" (1974: 235). Verdichtet sich dieses Forschungsfeld zu einem eigenen Fach, indem die bis dahin als Grenzfragen angesehenen Themen des Forschungsfeldes zu einem eigenen Wissenschaftsgegenstand werden, so bedeutet dies, dass damit "eine neue Disziplin als Ausdruck eines neu umschriebenen Bereichs der Wirklichkeit" (Schwarz 1974: 59) entstanden ist. Diese kann sich wiederum in ihrer Arbeit interdisziplinär ausrichten. Im allgemeinen liegt genau darin das Ziel der Translationswissenschaft, auch wenn ein ungenauer Gebrauch des Terminus Interdisziplin dies nicht immer deutlich macht. (Kaindl 2004: 58)

> (Interdisciplines do not constitute a separate area of study but are rather an open field of research to which various disciplines have access. This means that the term 'interdiscipline' strictly speaking describes a state "without a discipline", or as Rintelen put it: "Interdisciplinary science is however not a particular discipline but a mutual supplementing of the various subjects" (1974: 235). If this field of research develops into a subject in its own right because topics hitherto considered peripheral turn into a subject on their own, this means that "a new discipline has emerged as an expression of a newly delineated area of reality" (Schwarz 1974:

---

30. Wilss (2000) has problems with the term "Interdiscipline" as applied to Translation Studies, whereby in his concept interdisciplinary work involves cooperation between the "two cultures" of natural sciences and arts subjects. Any discipline is of course a construct, produced and institutionalized according to the needs of its time, and the (inter-)disciplinary concept represented here obviously does not correlate with the above dichotomony. Meanwhile however Michèle Kaiser-Cooke (2003) has presented a study combining insights from biology with those of Translation Studies, and bridging the gulf between the "arts" and the "sciences".

59). And this new discipline can in turn have an interdisiplinary orientation in its work. Generally speaking, that is precisely the goal of Translation Studies, even if an imprecise usage of the term *interdiscipline* does not make this quite clear.)

It is relevant here that the studies quoted by Kaindl go back to the 1970s, when the classical modes of categorization I tried to overcome (1988) were still dominant. Just as in the holistic way of thinking the whole does not amount to the mere sum of its parts, an "interdiscipline" is in my view not merely a kind of no-man's land between other clearly defined territories. We could rather say that through the varying constellations of its topics and methods, it evolves into something qualitatively different from the ingredients of which it originally consisted. The interdisciplinary case studies later discussed here might show what is meant by this.

Another important point raised by Kaindl is the quality of cooperation between the disciplines and what might be termed the "hierarchy of roles". Kaindl distinguishes here between three successive stages of development, "imperialistic", "importing" and "reciprocal" (2004: 64–65). We can speak of imperialistic interdisciplinarity when one discipline simply imposes its concepts, theories and methods on another, as did linguistics on translation during the 1960s and 1970s. The second stage of "importing" is the one Kaindl diagnoses as that still prevalent in Translation Studies, whereby a lack of adequate tools and methods within a discipline is offset by borrowing from others. Where one discipline simply has the role of tool-supplier for the other, the gain is of course one-sided. The third and highest stage of development is reciprocal interdisciplinarity, which brings gain for both sides: two or more disciplines cooperate on equal terms, jointly developing methods and concepts, resulting in mutual enrichment. Kaindl rightly concludes that if Translation Studies is to consolidate its position as an interdisciplinary field of research, it must get beyond the stage of simply "importing" from other disciplines and aim at projects based on reciprocal cooperation (cf. 5.3).

During the 1990s this stage had certainly not been reached, although some of the interdisciplinary studies carried out at the time were definitely impressive, and will be occupying us later on (3.1.3, 4.1.1, 4.1.2). For the moment, we shall start at the point where the cultural turn set us down, and look at insights developed in Translation Studies since 1990 that actually lie beyond language.

3.1.1   Of norms, memes and ethics

Gideon Toury's work on translational norms goes back to the paper he gave at the Leuven colloquium in 1976 (Toury 1978). It is then developed further in Toury 1980, of which the book *Descriptive Translation Studies and Beyond* (Toury 1995) is intended as a replacement (1995: 3), whereby some issues are are presented again in detail:

> In one case a whole chapter was reproduced, albeit in a highly revised form. This is the programmatic essay on the role of norms in translation, a notion which started my own thinking, back in the seventies, and which is still central to my entire position. (1995: 4)

For our discussion we shall use this revised version of Toury's concept of norms, which meanwhile, at least in the field of Descriptive Translation Studies, has become enormously influential. This is however less so with scholars working in other fields (note the "gap between the approaches" mentioned under 2.5), and it is the aim of this section to try and discover the reason.

Toury makes it clear that, given the cultural significance of translation, the translator plays a social role, for which norms need to be acquired (1995: 54). He then distinguishes between the poles of "relatively absolute *rules*" on the one hand and "pure *idiosyncrasies*" on the other, with "intersubjective factors commonly designated *norms*" occupying the vast middle ground in between:

> The norms themselves form a graded continuum along the scale: some are stronger, and hence more rule-like, others are weaker, and hence more idiosyncratic. The borderlines between the various types of constraints are thus diffuse. Each of the concepts, including the grading itself, is relative too. (1995: 54)

With time, constraints can change, and what may start off as a mere whim can become normative, if not a rule. Toury then offers a definition:

> Sociologists and social psychologists have long regarded norms as the translation of general values or ideas shared by a community – as to what is right or wrong, adequate and inadequate – into performance instructions appropriate for and applicable to particular situations, specifying what is prescribed and forbidden as well as what is tolerated and permitted in a certain behavioural dimension. (1995: 54–55)

Hence a norm implies "regularity of behaviour in recurrent situations of the same type" (1995: 55), and is a key concept in the social order.

Toury then applies the concept of norm to the activity of translating, which involves two languages and cultural traditions, and thus two "sets of norm-systems" (1995: 56). In translation behaviour, definite regularities can be observed.

Firstly, Toury's names the *initial norm*, understood as a basic choice made by the translator: either he/she follows the norms of the source text/culture (determining source-text *adequacy*) or those of the target text/culture (determining target-culture *acceptability*). Translation practice usually involves some compromise between the two extremes.

Then norms are discussed which are involved during the actual translating event, the *preliminary* vs. the *operational* norms. Preliminary norms concern translation *policy* (e.g. why a publisher chooses a particular text or work for translation), and *directness* of translation (e.g. as through a mediating language). Operational norms direct decisions made during the actual act of translating, such as "the modes of distributing linguistic material" (1995: 58), and consist of *matricial* norms (e.g. text segmentation, omissions, additions) and *text-linguistic* norms. Finally, norms determine the type and extent of *equivalence* in translations, a term Toury wishes to retain, but as an historical and not a prescriptive concept. Translational norms all depend on the position held by translation in the target culture. (1995: 61)

There then follow some general comments on translational norms: their *sociocultural specificity* (they need not apply to all sectors of a society, still less across cultures) and their *instability* (they change with time). Furthermore there are *mainstream* norms alongside *previous* and *new* norms on the periphery, explaining how some things are "trendy", others "old-fashioned". (1995: 63)

Let us now look at similar definitions, categorizations and comments on norms from the German functional school. The importance of the concept of norm on the skopos theory is shown in Vermeer's definition of his central concept of culture as "the totality of norms, conventions and opinions that determine the behaviour of the members of a society" (as quoted under 2.2). The distinction between *norm, convention* and *rule* is taken up by Christiane Nord (1991). She takes over Toury's definition of norm (from Toury 1980: 51, but identical with that quoted here from 1995: 54–55), as taking a position between a *rule* – as a regulation set up by a legislative power (e.g. traffic rules) – and a *convention* as defined by Searle (1969), this being regular behaviour following specific expectations:

> Conventions are not explicitly formulated, nor are they binding. They are based on common knowledge and on the expectation of what others expect you to expect them (etc.) to do in a certain situation. Therefore, they are only valid for the group that shares this knowledge. (Nord 1991: 96)

For Reiss and Vermeer rules (not mentioned separately) and norms seem to merge: "Normen sind Vorschriften für rekurrentes Verhalten (Handeln) in Situationstypen. Normen sind kulturspezifisch." (1984: 97). (Norms are regulations for recurrent behaviour (action) in types of situations. Norms are culture-specific.). We do however find a comparison of norms (in their sense) and conventions, though not under the heading of translation theory, but as part of their discussion of text-types (genres):

> Wir ziehen den Terminus "Konvention" dem in manchen Publikationen verwendeten Terminus "Norm" vor, weil er einen weiter gefassten Begriff zu bezeichnen scheint und dadurch dem Umstand Rechnung getragen wird, dass sich die damit erfassten Erscheinungen 'herausgebildet' haben, während sich mit dem Begriff der Norm hier zu stark der Charakter einer 'Vorschrift' verbindet, deren Nichtbefolgung

Sanktionen nach sich zieht. Konventionen können anscheinend leichter durch andere Konventionen ersetzt werden als Normen durch Normen. (1984: 178–179)

(We prefer the term "convention" to the term "norm" as used in a number of publications, because it seems to describe a broader concept, taking into account that the diverse phenomena have evolved with time, whereas the concept of norm is too strongly associated with the character of a regulation that involves sanctions if disobeyed. Conventions can apparently be more easily replaced by other conventions than norms can be by norms.)

There then follows a detailed account of *Textsortenkonventionen* or text-type conventions, in a purely descriptive sense, and as part of text theory, not of translational behaviour.

Let us now see what these two conceptual frameworks have in common and where they diverge. Toury's threefold division, or rather the cline with the two extremes of *rule* and *idiosyncrasy* with *norm* occupying the middle ground, goes back to Coseriu's linguistic cline of *system, norm* and *text/discourse* (see 1.2),[31] although they were intended to refer to literary translation (cf. Toury 1980: 52 ff.). The seemingly similar division in the German functional approach refers to neither language nor literature, but is essentially sociocultural. Nord distinguishes between *rule, norm* and *convention*, taking over Toury's definition of norm and resorting to the speech-act theory (Searle, cf. 1.3) for her definition of convention. For Vermeer the distinction between *rule* and *norm* is blurred, and because the concept of (German) *Norm* is seen as being too prescriptive, the skopos theory preferred the term *Konvention* (for describing text-types, not the act of translation). It is also relevant that Toury's *idiosyncrasy* is individual, while Nord's *Konvention* indicates group behaviour.

As regards Toury's translational norms, we see interesting parallels with the German tradition. His "initial norms" echo Schleiermacher (1.1), who however ruled out the compromise permitted by Toury. The "preliminary norms" as "translation policy" are in the German functional school part of the translation brief or skopos, (for literary translation see 3.3.1), whereas the operational norms are discussed as "translation strategies", e.g. involving "text-type conventions" (Toury's text-linguistic norms).

In both approaches norms are defined as culture-specific, whereas Toury's unstable mainstream norms (vs. previous and new) are treated by Nord as conventions. Otherwise the terminology remains fuzzy, if not confusing. Toury retains the term *equivalence*, but not in a prescriptive sense (Vermeer explicitly rejects it,

---

31.   This is not specifically mentioned in Toury 1995, but cf. 1980: 23.

see 2.2), and uses the terms "acceptability" and "adequacy", the latter also being used in Reiss and Vermeer (1984: 139), but again in a slightly different sense.

As we have seen, while bearing in mind the different priorities and perspectives between Descriptive Translation Studies and the skopos theory, they both actually cover the ground mapped out by Toury's norms. Whereas however Toury has retained a generic, and extremely broad, norm concept with a hierachy of various subdivisions (similar to Holmes' "map" of the discipline), the skopos theory has developed an action concept dealing with the diverse phenomena in different terms. An obvious cause of misunderstanding is the terminology, which yet again illustrates the "illusion of equivalence" (cf. Snell-Hornby 1988: 17). Vermeer's *Norm* is not the same as Toury's *norm,* and the latter is used sometimes in the sense of policy, sometimes to mean strategy, sometimes convention. The use of other terms, such as *adequacy* or *equivalence* remains idiosyncratic and hence opaque. It might indeed be helpful if the common ground evidently existing between the two approaches could be marked by compatible and mutually comprehensible terminology.

The discussion of translational norms, rules and conventions was to continue during the 1990s (especially Hermans 1991 and 1996, Dizdar 1997), with extensions, differentiations and individual variations. One problem is that the three basic terms, as "frames" from everyday language in Fillmore's sense, have an innate degree of fuzziness and evoke varying associations in different communities (hence Vermeer's *Norm* is more "normative" than Toury's *norm*). There is less danger of this with a new coinage that is sharply defined from the outset.

Such should be the case with the term *meme* introduced into the discussion on translation theory in 1997 by both Vermeer (here in English) and Chesterman. As neither scholar refers to the other, we can infer that here again similar innovative ideas were developed at the same time, but independently of each other. In any case, both contributions exemplify what Kaindl described above as "importing" from another discipline. The immediate source of the term *meme*, a concept from sociobiology, is Dawkins, who presented it as a parallel term to *gene* to describe the evolution of cultural phenomena, defining it in 1976 as:

> a unit of cultural transmission, or a unit of *imitation*. (…) Examples of memes are tunes, ideas, catch-phrases, clothes fashions, ways of making pots or building arches. Just as genes propagate themselves in the gene pool by leaping from body to body via sperm or eggs, so memes propagate themselves in the meme pool by leaping from brain to brain via a process which, in the broad sense, can be called imitation. (Dawkins 1976: 206, cit. Chesterman 1997: 5)

Vermeer also quotes Dawkins, but in a later definition from 1982, according to which a meme is a

> unit of information residing in a brain (Cloak's 'i-culture'.) The 'size' or range of memes may vary. Their types as well (e.g. an idea, a habit, a lecture). They may be perceived by the sense organs of other individuals, and they may so imprint themselves on the brains of the receiving individuals so that a copy (not necessarily exact) of the original meme is graven in the receiving brain. (Dawkins 1982: 109, cit. Vermeer 1997: 155)

Vermeer continues his discussion of meme structure and its relevance for translation theory ("Cultures can be considered 'meme pools' where memes are (considered to be) interdependent", 1997:163), and in a later article (1998) he applies it to translation in general ("The translator is a meme-transmitter", 1998: 59) and the skopos theory in particular. For our purposes his approach is compatible with that of Chesterman, who draws some conclusions that are highly relevant for our discussion. These will be outlined here, along with some thoughts as to their implication for future developments in Translation Studies.

Chesterman first introduces five "supermemes" of translation (including source-target, equivalence and free-vs-literal) and then traces the evolution of translation memes (from words, through Word of God, Logos, linguistic science, communication and cognition), which would match the historical development we have traced in Chapter 1. He then takes up the discussion of norms (as already debated in Chesterman 1993), which for him, as with Vermeer, exert "prescriptive pressure" as binding standards (1997: 68).[32] Chesterman then leads the discussion in a direction which is vital for act of translating, for the translator's profession and hence for the discipline of Translation Studies. As a "meme of translation" the concept of norm includes "professional standards of integrity and thoroughness" (1997: 68) which leads on logically to the domain of translation ethics. This complex area had already been implicit in those German functional theories which emphasize the translator's responsibility, but the discussion of translation ethics was only to be systematically pursued in the 1990s (cf. Pym 1997 and 2001). It has become a particular issue in interpreting studies (cf. 4.1.1) although the topic remains a glaring omission in all three reference books on translation published during the decade (Chan and Pollard 1995, Baker 1998 and Snell-Hornby et al. 1998). If the mention of ethical problems in translation is not entirely new, Chesterman's memes do provide a tool for further investigation. One example is the *accountability norm*, formulated by Chesterman as follows:

---

32. This also correlates with the conception of the norm in terminological standardization.

> A translator should act in such a way that the demands of loyalty are appropriately met with regard to the original writer, the commissioner of the translation, the translator himself or herself, the prospective readership and any other relevant parties. (1997: 68).

This is in fact precisely the demand made by Nord :

> The translator is committed bilaterally to the source and the target situations and is responsible to both the ST sender (or the initiator, if he is the one who takes the sender's part) and the TT recipient. This responsibility is what I call loyalty. Loyalty is a *moral* principle indispensable in the relationships between human beings who are partners in a communication process. (Nord 1991: 94)

This concept of loyalty towards all parties involved in the translation event (to replace the old concept of "faithfulness" to the source text, as already suggested in Nord 1989) was in my opinion a valuable contribution towards a framework of translation ethics. It was however explicitly rejected by Toury (1995, as quoted under 2.5), possibly because it contradicts his conviction that "translations are facts of one system only: the target system" (1985: 19). As viewed by the German functionalists and by Chesterman, this is not the case: translation is rather a complex event with a number of participants, specific needs and various expectations.

Chesterman develops the discussion of translation ethics in a later chapter, elaborating on issues such as the *expectancy norms* of the reader (with questions such as clarity and truth), the FIT "translator's code of ethics" (1997:187) and emancipatory translation (cf. 3.2.2). Immediately involved in this complex issue is also the question of power (cf. 3.2.1), likewise central to the debate on Translation Studies during the 1990s. Thus the debate on the ethics of translation was opened: from today's perspective we can say that it should still go on (cf. 6 below. At present it seems that the "ethical turn" in Translation Studies has yet to be taken.

Postscript: In 1998 a meeting on the topic "Translation and Norms", with lectures by Toury and Hermans, was held at Aston University Birmingham and published the following year, along with the ensuing debates and additional responses (Schäffner 1999). What possibly strikes the reader most (beside the clashing views aired during the debates) is again that this is an issue not of content, fact or even perspective, but one of the varying use of concepts. Many disagreements are due to differing use of the basic terms: beside "norms" of varying kinds, we again have "conventions", "agreements", "values", "strategies", "difference", "sameness", and of course "equivalence". One can only emphasize again that some minimal agreement on basic terminology in Translation Studies might be a great help in creating the desired common ground.

3.1.2   Translation and nonverbal communication

Whereas Descriptive Translation Studies and the skopos theory focussed on the text in the target culture, Justa Holz-Mänttäri's 'dramatistic' theory already took translation "beyond language". From text to action: Kaindl (1997) describes this step as a kind of liberation from the "fetishes" of source and target texts, and sees it as a key to the future of the discipline of Translation Studies – with some justification, as we can say today. Of course nobody pretends that translation can dispense with language (or with source and target texts) altogether, but it is now seen as a tool or instrument for translatorial action rather than as the central object of study in itself. With this approach the definition of "text" is also widened considerably: the "communicative occurrence" is by no means only verbal. This section will investigate the role played in the act of translating by nonverbal communication.

This perspective was introduced into the Translation Studies debate by Fernando Poyatos, a Canadian of Spanish descent lecturing in Nonverbal Communication Studies in the Departments of Anthropology, Psychology, and Sociology at the University of New Brunswick. Poyatos therefore approached Translation Studies from without, as it were, "exporting" his methodological ideas and models from his own interdisciplinary research.

Poyatos defines nonverbal communication as follows:

> The emissions of signs by all the nonlexical, artifactual and environmental sensible sign systems contained in a culture, whether individually or in mutual costructuration, and whether or not those emissions constitute behavior or generate personal interaction. (1997: 1)

It concentrates on *paralanguage* (qualities of voice such as timbre, resonance, loudness, tempo, pitch, intonation range, syllabic duraction and rhythm) and *kinesics* (body movements, posture, gestures, facial expression) (Poyatos 1997a: 42–43). The connection with the act of interpreting (including conference interpreting, but especially court or dialogue interpreting, see 4.1.1) may be obvious, but Poyatos also puts nonverbal communication in relation to (literary) translation through what he describes as:

> ...the fascinating experience of reading, bringing to life a whole array of personal and environmental elements. This means, not only the speaking face and body and total appearance of the characters, which include their explicit or implicit between-the-lines paralanguage and kinesics, but the eloquent quasiparalinguistic sounds of people and environment, and their silences and stillness, all knitted together and first funnelled into just a visual medium, the printed page, to be later multisensorially amplified by the reader through a sort of sign countermetamorphosis. But any of these nonverbal systems undergo profound changes through translations, and translators need to become extremely sensitive to all that hap-

> pens or does not happen as they translate a text, for it is well known that transla-
> tion is not only an interlinguistic exercise, but an intercultural one as well.
> (Poyatos 1997a: 17–18)

Such problems are addressed in a collection of essays on literary and audiovisual translation and (conference) interpreting edited by Poyatos (1997), which open up a number of new perspectives for Translation Studies.

In this section we are focussing on the role played by nonverbal communication in translating narrative texts (for audiovisual and drama translation see 3.1.3, for interpreting cf. 4.1.1). The problems vary from the reader's perception of a character through the description of facial expression and gestures, the expression of paralanguage and kinesic behaviour in the text, and the varying implications of this for the source and target cultures, to the varying expressive richness inherent in the languages of source and target text.

The challenges are particularly clear when dealing with societies and cultures which seem "exotic" and distant for a European or "Western" reader, as for example those of the Far East. (Vermeer's frequently cited example is the lack of such a basic word as "Thank you" in Indian languages, because in Indian cultures thanks are "shown" in a gesture.) In Poyatos' volume, Rie Hasada examines aspects of Japanese cultural ethos as embedded in nonverbal behaviour, whereby nonverbal communication is more important for the Japanese than for example in Anglo culture (1997: 87). Not only does kinesic behaviour differ in the two cultures, what may physically be similar behaviour is given different interpretations. A case in point is eye-contact and the different attitudes towards it in Japanese and Anglo culture. While English people have a strong social norm against staring, they place high value on eye-contact to show "politeness" to the other person. Hasada quotes studies showing that Americans feel uneasy because Japanese avoid eye-contact, as these in turn feel uneasy if someone's eyes are fixed on them, this being in conflict with the Japanese custom of 'bowing', where one lowers the head so that the eyes cannot meet. (Hasada 1997: 87–88) Another example is the interpretation of smiling and laughter. In Japan laughter is felt to have the potential of hurting other people's feelings, and only children are allowed to laugh freely. The most agreeable face is the 'smiling' face, whereby the Japanese smile (for Westerners often "inscrutable") can often actually mask negative feelings or signalize a request for a favour (Hasada 1997: 94–96). The differing associations evoked by the semantic field *smile* and the matching items in Japanese would be a basic problem in translation (cf. 1.3).

Yau Shun-chiu investigates what he calls "corporal behavior" as exemplified by gestural images in Chinese literary expressions (Yau 1997). He emphasizes that the

Chinese do not have such a rich "active gestural repertoire" as the Latin people, for historical reasons:

> How could the Chinese, dressed for centuries in long sleeves covering the hands up to the fingertips, develop their gestural expression? Gestures might be discouraged but were not eliminated, since long sleeves only handicap manual gestures but not necessarily other bodily movements. Indeed, gestures practiced in ancient China have left their traces in many written expressions. (1997: 70)

Yau proceeds to cite such gestures, as for example one expressing thanks for serving a drink of tea or wine:

> One taps the table near the cup two or three times with the tips of the middle and index fingers, both of them slightly bent in an imitation of *kowtow*. This gesture was once practiced exclusively in the Guangdong province in Southern China, and only in the past two decades have people in other provinces begun to use it. This gesture is practical because it can be used to express thanks but avoids interrupting the conversation. It should be noted that until recently this gesture was a masculine preserve and to a great extent it still is. (1997: 73)

In *An Encyclopaedia of Translation, Chinese-English, English-Chinese* (Chan and Pollard 1995), there is a an intriguing entry by David Pollard, who discusses the same topic, but calling it "body language", and provides interesting material for comparison. He deals with body language as a highly problematic issue in translation, gives examples of text and then lists possible translation strategies:

> "Xiangwen did not answer. Her shoulders jerked spasmodically. She cried even more bitterly. Li … figured out what had happened. He clenched his fists and bit his lip hard."

> This is a quotation from a respectable Taiwan writer of fiction. To the Chinese reader it is entirely unremarkable, standard fare. It could have come from the pen of any number of authors, from Hong Kong, Taiwan or mainland China. But to the foreigner it marks itself out as typifying a peculiarity of Chinese fiction, namely the great attention that is paid to the outward manifestations of emotions. Add to this the description of bodily sensations that are not apparent and gestures or expressions that convey attitude, and you have a body of vocabulary that presents the translator with problems. (Pollard 1995: 70).

Pollard categorizes the difficulties as arising from three sources: firstly, a specifically Chinese view of body functions; secondly, expressions and gestures specifically Chinese or with different significance from Western ones; and finally descriptions of physical reactions which Western authors normally do not discern. The suggested strategies range from bald translation and omission to elaboration or glossing, and it is clear, as Pollard concludes, that body language may give rise to "headaches rather than pleasure" (1995: 77).

Similar problems arise, even if they are not so immediately obvious, between cultures that seem related, as with English and German. Paralinguistic and kinesic behaviour may vary widely, and the perception and evaluation of such behaviour may be lexicalized quite differently, leading to considerable difficulty for the translator. Based on observations made in translation classes during the 1960s, I identified the "descriptive verb", which "describes" an action rather than merely stating it (Snell-Hornby 1983). More numerous in English than in German, these verbs are morphologically simple (usually monosyllabic) and are frequently used in everyday language, but they usually have a highly complex semantic structure that can make them seem "untranslatable". Such verbs are outstanding examples of what the French linguist Tesnière (1969: 102) described as "un petit drame" (a miniature drama) – fully in keeping with Holz-Mänttäri's "dramatistic" concept of translatorial action. They can for example express a distinct attitude on the part of the speaker or narrator, evaluating the agent of the action, emphasizing specific facets of the action or describing the perception of its results. They are easily arranged according to these components into semantic fields, which in English and German often have a different structure – one such semantic field is that mentioned above in connection with Japanese, smiling and laughter (see too Snell-Hornby 1998). If we concentrate on how "smiling" can be perceived, evaluated and lexicalized in English and German, we note for example that *grin* is by no means always an equivalent of *grinsen*. *Grin* indicates a broad, unrestrained smile expressing some reaction of emotion; it can be cheeky, foolish or malicious, but can equally imply friendly warmth, spontaneity or mirth, hence the evaluation of the speaker varies and emerges from the context. It is matched in German by *grinsen, feixen* and *schmunzeln*. *Grinsen* usually has negative evaluation: the agent is often disagreeable, sometimes even cynical or malicious, and while the facial expression is ostensive and communicative, the agent can reveal a callous disregard for those at whom it is directed. *Feixen* focusses on a play of the facial features, such as a grimace, aimed for effect at a spectator rather than to communicate a message to a partner; as such it is essentially provocative and expressive, as of undisguised pleasure, but it can also be perceived as being complacent or smug. *Schmunzeln* on the other hand clearly has positive evaluation, focussing, not on facial expression or communicative content, but rather on the agent's feeling of amusement, contentment or inner satisfaction, whereby no partner or spectator is presupposed and the action of smiling is extremely subdued. The English verbs *simper* and *smirk* both indicate a silly, fatuous smile, whereby *simper,* typically with a female agent, focusses on an affected or self-righteous primness, and *smirk* shares with *feixen* the element of provocative, often derisive effect; neither *smirk* nor *simper* however indicate a broad grimace, but rather focus on the attitude of the agent, with distinctly negative evaluation by the speaker (see Snell-Hornby 1983: 119).

These were some sample results of what was essentially a linguistic study of the late 1970s (based on the approach of Ernst Leisi, see 1.3), but it was one that already went "beyond language". It easily connects up with the work on nonverbal communication by Fernando Poyatos. Descriptive verbs are a common element of English narrative, and are used frequently as a means of characterization and description, fitting in with the "fascinating experience of reading" as quoted above from Poyatos 1997a. They are used conspicuously often by Charles Dickens, resulting in considerable problems for the translator (cf. Poyatos 1993, Kurth 1995), but also by other types of novelist ranging from Malcolm Bradbury to Carson McCullers and Salman Rushdie. Examples from novels by a number of authors using them are discussed in Poyatos 1997a.

Descriptive verbs, especially numerous in the area of sound-perception, abound in the subsection on audible kinesics and environmental sounds (Poyatos 1997a: 28–33), and Poyatos implicitly refers to them, in comparison with matching lexemes in Spanish, in his discussion of the "expressive richness of a language":

> It is inevitable to recognize the extraordinary richness of sound verbs in English, and, above all, the gamut of acoustic effects to differentiate more or less similar sounds that cannot be evoked with just one word, as we would try to do in Spanish with, for instance 'tintinear' to refer to the 'tintín' or 'jingling' of a small bell (the 'tintín' of a small bell, according to the dictionary), the clinking of glasses, etc. when in English we say 'Jingle bells, jingle bells!'. 'The bell (door bell) rang insistently', 'The cigarette vendor in Istanbul jingles his coins to attract our attention', 'The two lovers clinked their glasses gently while looking at each other', etc. In the last example we clearly see an acoustic evocation which, in this specific case – without thinking here also of its literary value – we simply cannot achieve writing 'Los dos amantes hicieron chocar sus copas suavemente', as in "chocaron las copas, expresando con igual calor su afecto a la simpática familia" (Galdós Miau, VII) – since 'chocar' does not contain the onomatopoeic etymological element we see in 'to clink'. (1997a: 34–35)

It is such richness going "beyond language" that presents a (hitherto largely neglected) challenge in literary translation, and it is remarkable that the topic was raised, neither by a linguist nor by a translation scholar, but by one doing interdisciplinary work from outside.

In interpreting, the question of nonverbal communication is far more apparent than in translation, and an impressive survey of the manifold components of the basic communicative sign systems is given in his volume by Poyatos himself (1997b: 251). Support is then forthcoming from the professional conference interpreters Sergio Viaggio, who writes on the topic of kinesics in simultaneous interpretation, and Edna Weale, whose essay – entitled "From Babel to Brussels" – concentrates on messages "scrambled to the point of becoming almost completely lost" (1997: 295) by misunderstandings in the nonverbal field. These include cultural and emotional elements such as pride, honour, anger and humour, the latter being "the ultimate in communication and yet it is the most difficult to translate. British humour is usually subtle and based on understatement and will seldom make a Spaniard laugh. Likewise Spanish jokes, spontaneous, vociferous and rather loud will usually be considered slightly over-stated and vulgar by an Englishman" (1997: 300).[33] Weale's comments on the three cultures involved in her work might well be taken to heart by all translation scholars, and they are quintessential for the basic message of this book (cf. 6. below):

> I have the greatest respect for the three cultures I am involved with in my work – and in my life generally – English, French and Spanish. I admire the Englishman's dignity and respect for others' privacy, the Frenchman's inimitable talent for style and quality, and the Spaniard's warmth and spontaneity. But they have different perceptions of the world. Through their tradition and educational system they have a different hierarchy in their order of values and therefore a different vision of themselves vis-à-vis others. (1997: 304)

3.1.3   Translating multimodal texts

It was Katharina Reiss back in 1971 who realized, in discussing her text-typology for translators as based on Bühler's organon model (see 2.2), that the three basic types (informative, expressive and operative) were incomplete. She then suggested a fourth type which she called "audio-medial": such texts have been written to be spoken or sung (1971: 34) and are hence dependent on a non-linguistic (technical) medium or on other audio-visual forms of expression for their full realization; language is only part of a broad complex of elements (1971: 49). These observations gave rise to a heated debate among translation scholars in Germany, and after some time Reiss modified her position. Following a suggestion by Bernd Spillner (1980: 75) she changed the term *audio-medial* to *multi-medial* to include texts (such as comics) which have visual but not acoustic elements, and in 1990 she conceded that such texts do not form a fourth text-type in her original sense, but contain elements belonging to any of her other three text-types. Examples of multi-medial texts in this sense would be songs, stage-plays, film-scripts and opera libretti, as well as comics and advertising material that includes audiovisual elements.

Then however the term *multimedia* was used to refer to the combined use of media (as of television and slides in teaching), and during the 1990s it was extended to the media of information technology. At the same time it was gradu-

---

33. For other studies of humour as a problem in translation see Mateo (1995) and Vandaele (2002).

ally realized in Translation Studies that the range of texts as listed by Reiss in 1990 was so varied that a good deal of confusion existed and further subdivisions were necessary. Today there are four standard terms for four different classes of text that all depend on elements other than the verbal:

1. *Multimedial* texts (in English usually *audiovisual*) are conveyed by technical and/or electronic media involving both sight and sound (e.g. material for film or television, sub-/surtitling),
2. *Multimodal* texts involve different modes of verbal and nonverbal expression, comprising both sight and sound, as in drama and opera,
3. *Multisemiotic* texts use different graphic sign systems, verbal and non-verbal (e.g. comics or print advertisements, cf. 4.2.2),
4. *Audiomedial* texts are those written to be spoken, hence reach their ultimate recipient by means of the human voice and not from the printed page (e.g. political speeches, academic papers).

All these texts go "beyond language", and for the most part beyond the aspect of nonverbal language we have been considering in 3.1.2. In Translation Studies they are all texts which until well into the 1980s were hardly investigated as a specific challenge for translation (cf. Snell-Hornby 1988: 33).

The audiomedial text centres round issues already introduced by Poyatos, particularly those of paralanguage. Two basic factors are *rhetoric* and *speakability*. It is a feature of the audiomedial text, as against spontaneous spoken discourse, that such elements are planned and contrived. The rules of rhetoric vary from one culture to another and this should be considered when translating a text for spoken presentation. English favours the classical devices of oppositions (theses/antithesis), metaphor, alliteration, rhythm, building up towards a climax (often with nouns or verbs in groups of three or four) with end-focus and end-weight (cf. Snell-Hornby 1997a for an analysis of Churchill's 1946 Zurich address to the "academic youth of the world", and Snell-Hornby 1998a/Pöchhacker 1997 for an analysis of Clinton's 1993 address in Berlin). Rhythm is another important factor for speakability, usually involving linear and symmetrical syntactic progression (parataxis), end-weight by means of postmodification and the avoidance of heavy consonant clusters (cf. Snell-Hornby 1998a). As we have seen in 2.5, this can be crucial for German academic papers translated to be read in English: the German academic culture favours a digressive, asymmetrical structure, along with a strictly nominal style, complex premodification and hypotactic syntax. If taken over in the English translation, all this, especially for a scholar with less than perfect competence in English, can amount to a text that is literally "unspeakable".

Multisemiotic texts such as comics present their own brand of problems, which have been discussed in detail by Kaindl (2004). What turned out to be of special interest during the 1990s was the highly specialized area of screen translation (both subtitling and dubbing as the ultimate form of "constrained translation") and translation for the stage. The two forms of screen translation were dealt with extensively during the decade (Luyken et al. 1991, Ivarsson 1992, Gottlieb 1994, Pisek 1994, Manhart 1996, Gambier and Gottlieb 2001). Not quite so extensive is the research on multimodal or stage translation, which has its own fascination as an area "beyond language".

In traditional translation theory, the discussion on drama translation revolved round the question of the faithful "scholarly" translation on the one hand, and the "actable" or "performable" stage text on the other, parallel to the "supermeme" of literal vs. free. Within modern Translation Studies an early contribution is Susan Bassnett's paper held at the Leuven Colloquium of 1976 (Bassnett-McGuire 1978), followed by her essay in the anthology *The Manipulation of Literature* (Bassnett-McGuire 1985). Up to that time it was unanimously pointed out that stage translation was an area previously ignored by translation theory, though the deficit was to some extent corrected during the course of the 1980s.

During this time there were two basic approaches, the semiotic and the holistic. The concept of theatre semiotics, represented by Fischer-Lichte (1983), uses both the Peircean trichotomy of *icon, index* and *symbol* and the notions of *paralanguage* and *kinesics* (as discussed under 3.1.2) and *proxemics*, involving the relationship of a figure to the stage environment, as with varying distance to other characters or objects on stage (see Snell-Hornby 1997: 190–191 for an application of this to Macbeth's "dagger monologue"). The problem for stage translation is that the interpretation of the theatrical signs can vary radically from one culture to another (particularly with symbolic signs), and much depends on the acting style and conventions of the cultural community concerned.

The holistic approach sees the stage text, like the musical score in a concert, as a basis for the dramatic performance (see Snell-Hornby 1993), the key words being *actability/performability,* also *speakability* (as discussed above), and in the case of the musical or opera, *singability* – these criteria again depending on the varying theatrical traditions and acting styles. The basic components of the stage text, with criteria for performability, could be summed up as follows:

1. Theatre dialogue is an *artificial* language, written to be performed, highly sophisticated and with special dynamics of deictic interaction.
2. It is characterized by an interplay of *multiple perspectives* resulting from the simultaneous interaction of different factors and their effect on the audience (e.g. irony, metaphor, word-play, allusion).
3. Language can be seen as *potential action in rhythmical progression,* including the inner rhythm of intensity as the plot or action progresses.

4. For the actor his/her lines combine to form a kind of idiolect, a *"mask of language"*, as a means of expressing emotion through voice, gesture and movement.
5. For the spectator in the audience, language and the action on stage are perceived *sensuously*, as a *personal experience* to which s/he can respond. (cf. Snell-Hornby 1984 and 1996 for a more detailed discussion).

Given the necessary expertise required for stage translation, the translator should cooperate with actors and producers before and during rehearsals, in other words s/he should be integrated into the production team (cf. Hörmanseder 2002). Aaltonen makes a clear distinction between the "powerless" translators who only work with the script, and those who work within the theatre (e.g. as dramaturges), who exercise more power and are free to make adjustments to the text where necessary (1997: 92).

While these hypotheses had been formulated during the 1980s, they were applied and tested in several empirical studies carried out at the University of Vienna during the 1990s – with interesting results. Susanne Zajic, for example, investigated the criteria of actability, performability and "breathability" (*Atembarkeit*) introduced by the German stage director Ansgar Haag (1984) as shown in two German translations of Oscar Wilde's *The Importance of Being Earnest,* one by a literary translator and one by a group of actors (Zajic 1994). One of her examples (Lady Bracknell's "accusation" scene with Miss Prism in Act III), clearly showing the "performability" criteria favoured by the actors, is presented in Snell-Hornby 1997: 195–198. Claudia Lisa investigated the genesis of two versions of the musical *Les Misérables* – in English (London/New York) and in German (Vienna). She interviewed the two translators, who were both integrated into the production team, which enabled them to contribute towards the success of both productions (Lisa 1993). And Klaus Kaindl, working with Holz-Mänttäri's concept of translatorial action, has sketched modalities of interaction for opera translation (1995). In his interdisciplinary study he combines insights from theatre studies, literary studies and musicology, viewing the opera text holistically as a synthesis of the libretto, music and performance (both vocal and scenic). One of several examples of the interplay of music, performance and language is the "champagne aria" "Fin ch'han dal vino" from *Don Giovanni,* as shown in various renderings through the centuries, where it becomes clear that in opera, to an even more drastic extent than in spoken drama, the verbal text is only one of a whole complex of elements simultaneously at work.

A question frequently raised is whether the creative, actable, singable foreign language version of a theatre text is actually a translation at all. It is probably the low prestige and the lack of influence associated with the work of the translator that anyone working creatively would rather call himself or herself a poet, a writer or a librettist. Such was the case with Herbert Kretzmer, creator of the English version of *Les Misérables,* who in his interview with Claudia Lisa, was quite vehement in his refusal to see his work as a translation:

> The work that I did for *Les Misérables* can be described in any terms other than translation. It is a term that I absolutely reject. About a third of the piece might be described as translation of a kind, a rough translation following the line of the story, which was of course important to the project. Another third might be described as rough adaptation and the other third might be described as original material because there are at least six or seven songs in the show that did not exist in the original French production at all. (Lisa 1993: 62).

These words may be partially explained by the fact that Kretzmer – following common practice in stage translation – was provided with an interlinear translation of the French text along with English material from James Fenton, the first translator engaged for the project, and he did add new material of his own, again as is frequently the case in stage productions. However, on being asked the reasons why he so vehemently rejected the term "translation" for his work, he replied:

> I resist and resent the word 'translator' because it is an academic function and I bring more to the work than an academic function. (…) I like to think that I brought somethng original to the project, that I was not a secretary to the project or a functionary, that I was as much a writer of *Les Misérables* than (sic!) Boublil and Schönberg[34] and anyone else. So that is why I reject the term 'translator'. It is a soulless function. You do not have to bring intelligence, you do not have to bring passion to the job of translation, you only have to bring a meticulous understanding of at least another language. You do not bring yourself, you just bring knowledge and skill. (Lisa 1993: 62)

Against that Heinz Rudolf Kuntze, a rock singer and graduate in German literature, who created the Vienna version of *Les Misérables,* did not pretend to do anything other than translate, but he sees this absolutely as a creative and poetic activity which aims at evoking a "similar effect" in the target language, and not as merely reproducing individual linguistic items (Lisa 1993: 76). Kunze expresses complete disdain for those producers in London and the USA who, in the early stages of the venture, gave him no scope for creativity, but "...sich nicht nur Zeile für Zeile, sondern Silbe für Silbe alles haben übersetzen lassen" ("...had everything translated, not only line for line, but even syllable for syllable"). (Lisa 1993: 75)

---

34. Alain Boublil, librettist, and Claude Michel Schönberg, composer of the French version of *Les Misérables.*

As indicated above, interlinear versions such as these are common in theatre practice, reducing the translator's contribution even more to hack-work which is then refined and improved by the "creative" expert who produces the final version. This is especially the case when the expert concerned is not familiar with the language of the source version. As outstanding example is Tom Stoppard, who, with the help of literal transcripts provided by linguists, has created English versions of plays by Slawomir Mrozek, García Lorca, Arthur Schnitzler and even Johann Nestroy (see Snell-Hornby 1993). Of his "adaptation" of *Undiscovered Country* (Schnitzler's *Das weite Land)* he writes:

> So the text here published, though largely faithful to Schnitzler's play in word and, I trust, more so in spirit, departs from it sufficiently to make one cautious about offering it as a 'translation': it is a record of what was performed at the National Theatre. (Stoppard 1986: x)

One can only recall – and warmly endorse – Susan Bassnett's discussion of 1985 where she deplores the futile discussion about whether a stage translation is a "version" or "adaptation" or even a "collage": "The disinction between a 'version' of an SL text and an 'adaptation' of that text seems to me to be a complete red herring. It is time the misleading use of these terms were set aside." (Bassnett-McGuire 1985: 93)

A serious problem can however be seen in the practice of using translators simply to produce a rough literal version, with correspondingly meagre pay, which merely provides raw material for the "real" text then created by the artist. In film dubbing it is standard practice to get such a rough version (produced under extreme time pressure and without any access to the film material), which is then finalized by those responsible for the foreign-language version (see Manhart 1996). Such abuse of translators as against the "specialist" was in fact freely admitted by Matthias Münterfering, head of the dubbing department at the Berlin company Deutsche Sychron, in a special issue of *Language International* (14/2, 2002) , as can be seen from these three statements taken from his article "Dubbing in Deutschland":

1. "Today there is more competition in the dubbing industry. This has resulted in lower prices and greater time pressure, but higher quality. Consequently all companies are desperately looking for ways to cut costs. The first victim is usually the translator. Translators are powerless, and there are many of them. What they create is not the final product. It is transformed by the dubbing writer into lip-sync dialog. People therefore don't treat them particularly well, and I have to admit, neither do I". (2002: 15)
2. "The translators prepare the text for the dubbing writers, who, if they are lucky, find the lip-sync words with the same meaning. Dubbing writers don't really offer any scope for our cost cutting. (...) They are one of the deciding

factors in the dubbing process and have to be chosen very carefully for each project." (2002: 15)

3. "If we have to dub highly realistic programs like *Emergency Room*, we obviously need to get in specialist advice. We therefore employ two surgeons, who first check the translation and then the dubbing script" (2002: 16).

The obvious solution – especially for companies desperate to cut costs – might be to employ one carefully chosen person with the expertise of both dubber and translator and who would know which questions to ask the subject specialists. This applies precisely to the subtitler Alan Wildblood, who in the same volume describes a "day in his life". As such he does not see himself however as a translator: "Subtitling is not translating. It's a lot harder, but it's a lot more fun". (2002: 43)

Such abuse of translators is another facet of ethics in translation, here from the opposite angle (cf. 3.1.1). Translations for stage and screen are highly complex activities for which only trained experts should be employed, and as multi-facetted manifestations of a cultural transfer both within and beyond language, they will remain a vital issue of the interdiscipline of Translation Studies.

3.2   "Imperial eyes"

In 1992 – coinciding with the Columbian quincentennial – there appeared an interdisciplinary book by Mary Louise Pratt with the title *Imperial Eyes. Travel Writing and Transculturation*. It shows, as the comment on the back cover informs us, "how travel writing goes about creating the domestic subject of European imperialism, and how reading publics have been engaged with expansionist enterprises." In a decade like the 1990s that witnessed a surge of interest in postcolonial translation, Pratt's study offers a number of concepts, parallels and insights that are relevant for Translation Studies in general and for our topic in particular, and which will hence be presented here.

Among the translation scholars who have emphasized the connection between translators and travel writers is Susan Bassnett:

> Translation can be seen as a kind of journey, from one point in time and space to another, a textual journey that a traveller may undertake in reality. Moreover, both translation and travel writing are hermeneutic activities that involve different kinds of cross-cultural contact. Travel necessarily involves some form of translation, and many early travel accounts detail attempts to render in the language of the explorers the undiscovered, the unknown, the new and unfamiliar. (2000: 106, see too Cronin 2002))

Similarly Michael Cronin sees both travellers and translators as people engaged in a dialogue between languages and with other cultures:

> The translator and the interpreter, moving between disciplines, between the allu-sive language of general culture and the hermetic sublanguages of specialisms, are practitioners in a sense of the encyclopedic culture of travel, or a *third culture* that is inclusive not only of the classic polarities of the humanities and sciences but of many other areas of human enquiry. In an era of disciplinary parochialism, the third wo/man as translator or travel writer is valuable as a nomad bringing us the news from elsewhere. (2000: 150)

Bearing this comparison between travellers and translators in mind, let us now look at some terms and concepts introduced by Pratt in their relevance to Transla-tion Studies, in particular to postcolonial translation.

The relevance of the term *transculturation,* taken from ethnography and used in the title of her book, seems immediately evident. It was coined in the 1940s by the Cuban sociologist Fernando Ortiz in a description of Afro-Cuban culture, and was intended to replace the two concepts of *acculturation* and *deculturation.* (Pratt 1992: 228) In ethnography it is used to describe how subordinated or marginal groups select and invent from materials transmitted to them by a dominant or metropolitan culture (Pratt 1992: 6).

A key concept in Pratt's book is *contact zone,* which she defines as

> social spaces where *disparate cultures meet, clash and grapple* with each other, often in highly *assymetrical* relations of *domination* and *subordination* – like colo-nialism, slavery, or their aftermaths as they are lived out across the globe today. (1992: 4. emphasis added)

and later:

> the space of *colonial encounters,* the space in which peoples *geographically and his-torically separated* come into contact with each other and establish *ongoing rela-tions,* usually involving conditions of *coercion, radical inequality, and intractable conflict.* (1992: 6, emphasis added)

Pratt emphasizes that the term "contact" is used to foreground the "interactive, improvisational dimensions of colonial encounters" which in many accounts are frequently ignored (1992: 7). The term *contact zone* has already been applied in Translation Studies (cf. Simon 1999).

Another significant term used by Pratt is *autoethnography* (or *autoethno-graphic expression*), which refers to

> instances in which colonized subjects undertake to represent themselves in ways that *engage with* the colonizer's own terms. If ethnographic texts are a means by which Europeans represent to themselves their (usually subjugated) others, auto-

> ethnographic texts are those the others construct in response to or in dialogue
> with those metropolitan representations. (Pratt 1992: 7)

Finally, there is what Pratt refers to as the European *planetary consciousness*, or
Europe's conception of itself and its global relations. Pratt's starting point is the
mid-18th century with two momentous developments: the emergence of natural
history as a structure of knowledge, and the movement toward interior, as
opposed to maritime, exploration. These are exemplified by two events occurring
in the year 1735: the former by the publication of Carl Linné's *The System of
Nature*, which presented a classificatory system designed to categorize all plant
forms on the planet, and the latter by the La Condamine expedition in Spanish
America. For Pratt, these two developments register a shift in the European planetary consciousness:

> …a shift that coincides with many others including the consolidation of bourgeois
> forms of subjectivity and power, the inauguration of a new territorial phase of cap-
> italism propelled by searches for raw materials, the attempt to extend coastal trade
> inland, and national imperatives to seize overseas territory in order to prevent its
> being seized by rival European powers. (1992: 9)

It is this "planetary consciousness", this view of nature, the world, of the self and
others that constitute the "Imperial eyes" that were to dominate the next two centuries. Pratt's book reviews the writings and experiences of European explorers
and travellers – from John Stedman and Alexander von Humboldt[35] to Flora
Tristan and Richard Burton – mainly in Africa and South America. Particularly
for translation scholars it presents a thought-provoking panorama of the world, of
cultural phenomena and above all of human interaction, as seen from the perspective of the "Imperial eyes". It provides our starting-point for the time when towards
the end of the millennium, the Empire starting "writing back", as Salman Rushdie
put it, both in postcolonial writings and in translation.

3.2.1   Postcolonial translation

One of the most thought-provoking papers at the Warwick conference in 1988 was
presented by the Indian scholar Mahasweta Sengupta with the title "Translation,
colonialism and poetics: Rabindranath Tagore in two worlds" (Sengupta 1990). At
a time when we were already beginning to celebrate the cultural turn and were
stressing the function of the translation in the target culture, she gave the chilling
counter-example of the autotranslations of the Bengali poet Rabindranath Tagore

---

35.   (1769–1859), brother of Wilhelm von Humboldt (see 1.1).

(1861–1941). Her example is taken from Tagore's collection of poems *Gitanjali: Song Offering*, for which in 1913 – as the first non-European – he was awarded the Nobel Prize for Literature. Sengupta first cites Tagore's (prizewinning) English version (1990: 56), then gives her own literal translation from the original Bengali (1990: 57), which in several respects is very different. As she points out:

> One can notice clearly that Tagore changes not only the style of the original, but also the imagery and tone of the lyric, not to mention the register of language which is made to match the target-language poetics of Edwardian English. These changes are conscious and deliberately adopted to suit the poetics of the target system, which Tagore does by altering tone, imagery and diction, and as a result, none of the lyrical qualities of the originals are carried over into the English translations. (Sengupta 1990: 57)

Sengupta assumes that the reason why Tagore made his own poems in English so different from what they were in Bengali lay in his understanding of English language and literature as it was disseminated in India at the time. That was, in Pratt's terminology, the contact zone, and he translated his own poems to suit the aesthetic ideology of the dominating culture. Sengupta maintains:

> Tagore inhabits two different worlds when he translates from the originals; in his source language, he is independent and free of the trappings of an alien culture and vocabulary, and writes in the colloquial diction of the actually spoken word. When he translates, he enters another context, a context in which his colonial self finds expression. (1990: 59)

This is autoethnography translated into ethnography, a "colonial self" which harmonized exactly with the image Europeans had constructed of "Orientals", as had already been described by Edward Said in 1980 and as Sengupta puts it:

> He fits perfectly into the stereotypical role that was familiar to the colonizer, a voice that not only spoke of the peace and tranquillity of a distant world, but also offered an escape from the materialism of the contemporary Western world. (1990: 58)

As we can see from this world-view, colonialism, and with it "colonial translation" was characterized by sharp divisions and dichotomies: colonizers/colonized, Occident (West)/Orient (East), own/Other. Tagore sought to cross the divide, and after translating his poems to reach a wider – English-speaking – audience (a motive equally familiar to us nearly a hundred years later), he immediately became fashionable in the West, and was even hailed as a 'saint' and mystic. Ironically, he was awarded the Nobel prize, although he hailed from what in the planetary consciousness of the Nobel committee was such a "distant location", for the spiritual support his poetry was thought to give the Christian missionaries. Here the committee's appraisal:

> More especially, the preaching of the Christian religion has provided in many places the first definite impulse toward a revival and regeneration of the vernacular language, i.e. its liberation from the bondage of an artificial tradition, and consequently also toward a development of its capacity for nurturing and sustaining a vein of living and natural poetry. (Frenz 1969: 129, cit. Sengupta 1990: 61).

When European aesthetic ideology changed with the First World War, and when Tagore outgrew the straitjacket the West had made for him and became the innovator in Bengali literature known to Indians today, he was discarded and soon forgotten. For translation scholars he remains startling evidence of how "Imperial eyes" can invent their own realities.

There are many other examples in translation history of similar phenomena, ethnographic texts in Pratt's sense, one of the best known probably being *The Rubaiyat of Omar Khayyam* (1859) in the version of Edward Fitzgerald (1809–1863) (cf. Bassnett 2000), also the work of Richard Burton (1821–1890), one of Pratt's most intrepid travellers – she emphasizes his "monarch-of-all-I-survey" perspective (1992: 205) – and translator of the *Arabian Nights* (1885–1888), *Kama Sutram* (1883) and other Oriental erotica (cf. Carbonell 1996: 80–81).

During the 1990s the relationship between colonialism, language and translation became a popular topic for research. A milestone in this field is a book by another Indian-born scholar, Tejaswini Niranjana. In *Siting Translation. History, Post-structuralism, and the Colonial Context* (1992) she shows how both language and translation were used to enforce and perpetuate unequal relations of power, prejudice and domination. This applies particularly where Indian texts were translated into English for the benefit of the British colonizers. A striking example is the work of Sir William Jones (1746–1794), the orientalist and jurist who arrived in India in 1783 and sought to use translation "to domesticate the Orient and thereby turn it into a province of European learning" (1992: 12). Jones's work has had a lasting impact on generations of scholars up to the present day, and Niranjana maintains that it has helped construct a powerful but falsified image of a submissive and indolent nation of "Hindus" taken over wholesale by later writers. She diagnoses the basic factors underlying Jones's work as follows: firstly, the need for translation by a European translator, because the natives were considered unreliable interpreters of their own laws and culture; secondly, the desire as colonial overlord to be a lawgiver, to give the Indians their "own" laws (i.e. as seen by the colonizers after translation by a colonizer), and thirdly, the desire to "purify" Indian culture and speak on its behalf. Particularly this third factor is confirmed in the case of the poet Tagore.

When after the end of colonialism the Empire started "writing back" in the form of what was at first, rather misleadingly, classified as "Commonwealth literature" (cf. Schäfer 1981: 7), there developed the phenomenon of the "hybrid text". This fits in exactly with the anthropophagic conception of "devouring" the once dominant culture and language (as described in 2.4). In memorable words, the Nigerian writer Chinua Achebe describes the language suitable for use by the African writer as a vehicle of expression in postcolonial English literature (cf. 4.2.3):

> Can he ever learn to use it like a native speaker? I should say, I hope not. It is neither necessary nor desirable for him to do so. The price a world language must be prepared to pay is submission to many different kinds of use…The African should aim at fashioning out an English which is at once universal and able to carry his peculiar experience. It will have to be a new English, still in full communion with its ancestral home, but altered to suit its new surroundings. (cit. Villareal 1994: 62)

A similar situation developed in countries with former French domination, particularly in the Maghreb area of Northern Africa. A further significant contribution published in 1992 was Samia Mehrez' essay "Translation and the colonial experience" devoted to the francophone North African text, in which she describes in detail the new phenomenon of the "hybrid text":

> Indeed, the emergence and continuing growth on the world literary scene of postcolonial anglophone and francophone literatures from the ex-colonies as well as the increasing ethnic minorities in the First World metropoles are bound to change and redefine many accepted notions in translation theory which continue to be debated and elaborated within the longstanding traditions of western 'humanism' and 'universalism'. These postcolonial texts, frequently referred to as **'hybrid'** or **'métissés'** because of the **culturo-linguistic layering which exists within them**, have succeeded in **forging a new language** that defies the very notion of a 'foreign' text that can be readily translatable into another language. With this literature we can no longer merely concern ourselves with conventional notions of linguistic equivalence, or ideas of loss and gain which have long been a consideration in translation theory. For these texts written by postcolonial bilingual subjects create a **language 'in between'** and therefore come to occupy a **space 'in between'.** In most cases, the challenge of such space 'in between' has been double: these texts seek to decolonize themselves from two oppressors at once, namely the western ex-colonizer who naively boasts of their existence and ultimately recuperates them and the 'traditional', 'national' cultures which shortsightedly deny their importance and consequently marginalize them. (Mehrez 1992: 121, emphasis added)

The key phrase here is the "space 'in between'", also known, in Homi Bhabha's wording, as the "Third Space" (1994: 36), and it can be interpreted as a repository of those cultural and linguistic phenomena that constitute hybridity. For Translation Studies these literary contact zones are fertile territory, and various analyses and case studies were to appear during the course of the 1990s: some of many examples are Villareal (1994) for a view of translation "from Filipino eyes", Carbonell (1997) for a panoramic view from a Spanish perspective and the collection of essays edited by Dingwaney and Maier (1995) on diverse "cross-cultural texts" varying from Arabic to Spanish American.

From these studies the extent becomes clear of the asymmetrical power relationship that was behind translation during and after colonial times. In 1999 a collection of essays appeared, edited by Susan Bassnett and Harish Trivedi, with the title *Post-colonial Translation. Theory and practice*, which was to take stock of the situation. As the editors put it in their introduction:

> At this point in time, post-colonial theorists are increasingly turning to translation and both reappropriating and reassessing the term itself. The close relationship between colonization and translation has come under scrutiny; we can now perceive the extent to which translation was for centuries a one-way process, with texts being translated *into* European languages for European consumption, rather than as part of a reciprocal process of exchange. European norms have dominated literary production, and those norms have ensured that only certain kinds of text, those that will not prove alien to the receiving culture, come to be translated. As Anuradha Dingwaney and Carol Maier point out, translation is often a form of violence. (1999a: 5)

As an antidote, Bassnett and Trivedi argue for "a new politics of in-betweenness, for a reassessment of the creative potentialities of liminal space" (1999a: 6), completely in the sense of hybridity and the "space in between" as detailed above. The essays in the volume focus largely on India and provide a counter-balance to the case of Rabindranath Tagore. G.J.V Prasad's contribution "Writing translation: the strange case of the Indian English novel" is a case in point. He echoes Chinua Achebe's views on the "new English" by quoting Salman Rushdie's dictum: "all of us share the view that we can't simply use the language the way the British did; and that it needs remaking for our own purposes" (Rushdie 1991: 17, cit. Prasad 1999: 41). Rushdie, who famously described British Indians as "translated men", had a positive view of both "hybrid" language and translation, believing that much could be gained by it rather than, as is usually believed, lost. Prasad rightly comments: "This gain is mirrored in the pollinated and enriched language (and culture) that results from the act of translation – this act not just of bearing across but of fertile coming together" (1999: 41). The essay then details strategies for creating such language – by approximating thought-structures and speech patterns or by translating local speech rhythms, idioms and culture-specificities from Indian languages into English. As an example of such a text Prasad takes a passage from Rushdie's *Midnight's Children*, of which the first paragraph is quoted here:

Padma's story (given in her own words, and read back to her for eye-rolling, high-wailing, mammary-thumping confirmation): "It was my own foolish pride and vanity, Saleem baba, from which cause I did run from you, although the job here is good, and you so much needing a looker-after! But in a short time only I was dying to return." (cit. Prasad 1999: 52)

For the European reader this seems to be typical Rushdie language, from the complex adjectival phrases ("eye-rolling, high-wailing, mammary-thumping"), to the mix of formal and familiar registers ("confirmation, "foolish pride", beside "dying to return") and the creation of new words ("looker-after"). The scholar proficient in Indian languages can recognize various kinds of signals and deviations in their relationship to the Indian setting, from the form of address "Saleem baba" ('baba' as used by servants for young boys of higher social status, also as a term of affection) to the phrase "from which cause I did run from you", recognizable as a structure literally transcoded from Hindustani/Urdu. The author thus locates his character "in terms of region, class and gender through the construction of a specific English using the strategies and resources of a translator" (Prasad 1999: 53). It is devices such as these, Mehrez' "culturo-linguistic layering", that characterize the postcolonial Indian hybrid text (cf. too Snell-Hornby 2003).

As a world bestseller and winner of the Booker Prize (1981), *Midnight's Children* was naturally translated into various European languages, including German, with the aim of making the novel accessible to a German-speaking readership and repeating the commercial success on the German market. There are however fundamental problems involved in translating a hybrid English postcolonial text for another European target culture. In the case of German one difficulty lies in the lack of a comparable colonial past with the corresponding plurality of associations, language usages and cultural backgrounds. The envisaged reader may be cultivated and well-informed, but detailed knowledge of the kind of people figuring in the novel cannot be presupposed (cf. 3.3). Above all, the multi-layered nature of the source-text language sometimes proves to be an insurmountable problem. Here is the passage quoted above in Karin Graf's German version:

Padmas Geschichte (in ihren eigenen Worten erzählt und ihr wieder vorgelesen, damit sie augenrollend, laut jammernd, brustschlagend bestätige): "Mein eigner dummer Stolz und meine Eitelkeit, Saleem Baba, sind der Grund, dass ich von dir weggelaufen bin, obwohl die Arbeit hier gut ist und du so dringend jemand brauchst, der auf dich aufpasst! Aber schon nach kurzer Zeit wollte ich unbedingt wieder zurückkommen." (Rushdie, *Mitternachtskinder* 1983: 253)

In his discussion of the English version, Prasad refers to the "layered nature of otherness" and diagnoses the spoken language as "a transcript of a speech made by an illiterate woman" (1999: 52), but neither is recognizable in the German text.

Padma's language is grammatically correct, formal German; there is no sign whatsoever of any transcoding from Urdu, nor of the coinage "looker-after", and the signals in the form of address identified by Prasad (despite limited explanations in the Glossary at the end of the novel) will surely be unrecognizable for a non-specialist German reader. In other words, the language has been neutralized into a linguistically correct and stylistically unified formal German statement (cf. 3.3.1).

A completely different kind of problem is posed by postcolonial literature written in a local language, and afterwards (as was once the case with Tagore) translated into English in order to reach a wider market (autoethnography in the sense of Mary Louise Pratt). Nowadays English translations of these texts, often short stories, are usually sponsored and/or published locally. One such series is "Modern Indian Novels in Translation", sponsored by an Indian industrial house published by Macmillan India. Concept, strategy and method are described by the project editor Mini Krishnan in his General Preface as follows:

> Whatever our quarrels and shifting factions, all Indians know that they have a complex, stable system of values, belief and practices which – though forged long ago – has never really been interrupted. It still underlies the surface differences and makes them comprehensible. Our programme of translations is an exploration of this Indian tradition which is one of humankind's most enduring attempts to create an order of existence that would make life both tolerable and meaningful.

> The method we have adopted is to translate selections from the corpus of fiction Indians have created after their Independence (1947). It is our hope that these novels will express most of the customs, unquestioned assumptions and the persistent doubts that have characterised Indian life for at least a thousand years, and, more recently, after the impact of western ways of thinking on it. (Krishnan in Sethumadhavan 1995: v)

With this last sentence Krishnan characterizes the series as postcolonial literature, but the English versions are clearly seen as translations in the classical sense and not as hybrid texts. With his final remark "Some of the footnotes may seem excessive, but they have been prepared with non-Indian readers in mind" (1995: v), Krishnan also identifies the envisaged reader as someone unfamiliar with Indian daily life and culture. One typical example of this series is the story *Pandavapuram* written in Malayalam by the well-known Keralan novelist Sethu (the pen-name of A. Sethumadhavan, born in 1942), translated by Prema Jayakumar (1995). The story is set in rural Kerala, blending fantasy and narrative with veiled social criticism and minute description of local culture. The English text reveals various translation strategies, one being the above-mentioned frequent use of footnotes, usually concerning culture-bound items such as *pottu* and *pujari*, but not so much of the glossing usually typical of postcolonial translations (cf. Snell-Hornby 1997c:

50).[36] Another strategy concerns the variations of Malayalam forms of address in dialogue:

> "Shyamaledathi is greedy. Whatever she sees, she wants", Raghu said. "Amma is always scolding her for that."
>
> "Why do you call her 'edathi'? She is your aunt, isn't she?"
>
> "She doesn't like me calling her 'aunt'. She says she prefers to be called 'edathi'."
>
> He could hear voices from inside. Devi was probably scolding Shyamala. (p.43)

In a previous footnote the reader has been informed that *edathi* means 'elder sister', which can be added as a suffix to the name (Shyamala) as here. The same applies to numerous kinship terms with diverse variations, which are typically left untranslated in the text, after an initial footnote explanation. The result is a text, describing a South Indian setting, which basically observes the norms of Standard British English, but at the same time is interspersed with untranslated forms of address and constantly changing names, sometimes to the cost of intratextual coherence (cf. 3.3.1).

Such "classical" translations with footnotes and glosses form a remarkable contrast to the hybrid texts of postcolonial literature. What Friedrich Schleiermacher – against the historical background of his age – had once disdainfully dismissed as *Blendlinge* (1.1) has meanwhile transformed itself into a genre in its own right. After the demise of the British Empire, this "remade English" developed in former colonies and dominions all over the world, resulting in high-quality literature which has enriched the language beyond measure, providing a welcome contrast to the reduced *lingua franca* form of International English arising from globalization (4.2.3). And as we have seen here, with the new literature there arose new challenges for translation and new perspectives for Translation Studies.

However, it should be pointed out that literary hybridity is by no means limited to the classical colonial scenario with its vertical divide of conquerors and conquered – it is a phenomenon of any multicultural society and in fact of European literature. Taking up Homi Bhabha's concept of "double vision" (1994: 50), Michaela Wolf (2000) has investigated the cosmopolitan scene of Trieste at the beginning of the 20th century, when it was still the vibrant port of the Austro-Hungarian Empire where Italian, German and Slovenian cultures flourished alongside each other (albeit in that hierarchical order). These "three worlds" merge symbiotically in the literature of the time. An outstanding example is the

---

36. The typical example discussed in the essay cited is also taken from an English translation (by K.M.George) of Malayalam stories, whereby key culture-bound items are left untranslated in the text and then paraphrased with a broad generic term, e.g. "He was the *karanavar*, the chief of the house (or *taravad*, as it is called)".

work of Scipio Slataper (1888–1915), whose autobiographical novel *Il Mio Carso* ("My Karst") is examined by Wolf as a hybrid text reflecting all three elements of the author's linguistic and cultural identity (cf. 4.2). In her comparison of two German translations of the novel we can see that, despite the apparent closeness of the cultures concerned, similar features can be identified and similar problems arise as with the prototypical postcolonial texts from the distant Indian subcontinent.

3.2.2   Gender-based Translation Studies

Like postcolonial studies, the subject of Gender Studies, of which feminist Translation Studies forms part, developed in reaction to asymmetrical power relationships, as caused by patriarchal hegemony. We are again, but in another sense, under the gaze of "Imperial Eyes", whereby the active, creative and structuring subject with its all-pervading planetary consciousness, is male.

One of the early figures on the interface of Empire and feminism – and one of Mary Louise Pratt's few women travellers – was the French writer and pioneer socialist Flora Tristan (1803–1844). Her book *Pérégrinations d'une Paria* (1838), describing her adventuresome travels to and in Peru in 1833–34, is cited by Pratt in the English version *Peregrinations of a Pariah*,[37] and it is quite an extraordinary document of the time. Tristan, who on the one hand has the planetary consciousness of a European colonialist not above expressing distaste at the "negroes" in Cap Verde, is at the same time a vehement opponent of the slave trade and an equally ardent fighter for women's rights. From the postcolonial viewpoint her book is ethnographic, but as one of the early feminist manifestos it is autoethnographic. Her "contact zones" are similarly complex: on the one hand she mainly has contact with her fellow Europeans (such as the ship's captain and crew) or her aristocratic relatives, but on the other she delivers intriguing descriptions and thoroughly feminist insights on the "local" members of the society, in particular the women of Lima. These had been dismissed by male European travellers as people who are "slovenly and dirty", "smoke cigars" and "never wear stays" (Charles Brand, cit. Pratt 1992: 151), but Tristan is fascinated by their independence:

> "There is no place on earth", she exults, "where women are so *free* and exercise so much power as in Lima". (…) The *Limeñas* are taller than the men, mature early, have easy pregnancies, are "irresistibly attractive" without being beautiful, and are far above the men in intelligence and will-power. They come and go as they please, keep their names after marriage, wear men's jewelry, gamble, smoke, ride

---

37.   I have here used the German translation *Meine Reise nach Peru. Fahrten einer Paria* (Tristan 1983).

in breeches, swim, and play the guitar. They lack education however, and are very ignorant." (cit. Pratt 1992: 167)

In the climate of the early 1990s, such a rousing topic might have been seen to invite intense exploration, but whereas postcolonial studies flourished during the course of the decade and was soon "imported" into research on translation, interest in feminist perspectives largely remained limited to those (feminists) immediately concerned, and in European Translation Studies this field of research was for years more or less ignored. There is a conspicuous lack of contributions on feminist aspects of the discipline in the journals *TextConText, Target,* and *The Translator,* and there is no relevant entry in the *Routledge Encyclopedia of Translation Studies.* The article in the *Handbuch Translation* on "Feministische Aspekte" reveals, both in its content and through the affiliation of the author (Flotow 1998), where feminist Translation Studies partially originated and really did flourish – in Canada. Here too the origins go back to the colonial past.

This is evident from another contribution to the Warwick conference of 1988, the paper on "Theorizing Feminist Discourse/Translation" by Barbara Godard, who mentions parallels between the colonized position of Quebec and the linguistic alienation of women (Godard 1990: 87).[38] Again rejecting notions (such as equivalence) still prevalent at the time, she depicts a concept of feminist discourse that involves the transfer of a cultural reality into a new context, thus harmonizing both with the functional approach of Vermeer and with the deconstructionist approach of Arrojo. Referring to the work of Canadian scholars, she describes the new approach as follows:

> Translation, in this theory of feminist discourse, is production, not reproduction, the *mimesis* which is 'in the realm of music' and which, by an 'effect of playful repetition' (…) makes visible the place of women's exploitation by discourse. Pretensions to the production of a singular truth and meaning are suspended. This theory focusses on feminist discourse in its transtextual or hypertextual relations, as palimpsest working on the problematic notions of identity, dependency and equivalence. It is mimicry, repetition which redoubles as it crosses back and forth through the mirror, a logic of disruptive excess in which nothing is ever posited that is not also reversed. Linear meaning is no longer possible in a situation caught up in the supplementarity of this reversal. In this, feminist discourse presents transformation as performance as a model for translation. Transformation of the text is conceived within the axioms of topology. However, this is at odds with the long dominant theory of translation as equivalence grounded in a poetics of transparence. (1990: 91).

---

38. Flotow (2001: 51–52) mentions other origins in the Anglo-American area, including Bible translations of the late 1970s.

In this concept the feminist translator is a manipulator, a rewriter (absolutely in the sense of André Lefevere) who delights in exploiting the potential of playing with language, "womanhandling" the text, as it is described in Godard's article (1990: 94). Work in this area of feminist discourse flourished in Canada during the decade, and similar wordplay proliferated, most famously recorded in the "Re-Belle et Infidèle" of Susanne de Lotbinière-Harwood, who sees translation as a political instrument for women:

> My translation is a political activity aimed at making language speak for women. So my signature on a translation means: this translation has used every possible feminist strategy to make the feminine visible in language. Because making the feminine visible in language means making women seen and heard in the real world. Which is what feminism is all about. (Lotbinière-Harwood 1991, cit. Flotow 1998: 131)

The kind of patriarchal metaphor used for translations and translators (such as the *belles infidèles* in fact, or biological terms like "reproduction") became a basic issue in the debate (see Chamberlain 1992), and even gave rise to one of the few critical discussions of the problem in a Europe-based international journal (Resch 1998).

In Europe scholarly interest in feminist translation resulted from movements in sociology and linguistics during the late 1970s and early 1980s. 1984 witnessed the publication, beside the volumes by Holz-Mänttäri and Reiss and Vermeer, of similarly revolutionary books by the linguists Luise Pusch – *Das Deutsche als Männersprache. Aufsätze und Glossen zur feministischen Linguistik* ("German as a man's language. Essays and glosses on feminist linguistics") – and Senta Trömel-Plötz *Gewalt durch Sprache. Die Vergewaltigung von Frauen in Gesprächen* ("Violence through language. The rape of women in conversations"). The latter title clearly recalled the book published in 1978 by the two sociologists Cheryl Benard and Edit Schlaffer *Die ganz gewöhnliche Gewalt in der Ehe. Texte zu einer Soziologie von Macht und Liebe* ("The quite ordinary violence in marriage. Texts on a sociology of power and love"). The issue of discriminating language depicted by Trömel-Plötz and Pusch suddenly became a cause of heated debate in language subjects, and meanwhile efforts have been made to counteract it (cf. Grbić and Wolf 1998).[39]

Within the discipline of Translation Studies however, it was only during the 1990s that attempts were made to broach topics of feminist issues in Europe (as

---

39. It is remarkable that James Holmes managed this problem very elegantly, even with wry wit, in his Vienna paper given in that same year 1984: "And the literary translator is still reimbursed accordingly. He, or more often she, works hours per day…" (1988: 103), and elsewhere: "Even twenty years ago, the university-based researcher who focused on translating or translations as phenomena deserving of his (or, all too rarely, her) unswerving attention as objects for research was generally deemed a wrong-headed if harmless eccentric." (1988: 105)

against the Canadian scientific community, with publications like Flotow 1997 and Simon 1996). At the University of Vienna three doctoral dissertations were devoted to different aspects of gender in translation: in an interdisciplinary study based on ethnological insights, Plecher (1998) combines postcolonial and feminist aspects in her investigation of Jamaican novels in translation, showing how in the German versions the descriptions of women are "distorted by the patriarchal mirror". Beuren (2005) investigates the life and works of the writer Carson McCullers and of her German translator Elisabeth Schnack, and she shows how in the same stories the fictional female figures are differently "constructed" by the American author on the one hand and the German translator on the other. Gibbels (2004) compares four German translations of Mary Wollstonecraft's manifesto "A Vindication of the Rights of Woman" (1792) – the versions by Georg F.C. Weissenborn (1794), Bertha Pappenheim (1898), Edith Schotte (1989) and Irmgard Hölscher (1999) – and, with reference to the unusual biographies of each of the translators, she investigates the reasons for the fundamental differences in their texts.

In June 2000 an international conference on feminist Translation Studies was held at the University of Graz, where attention was focussed on an important aspect of the field (barely included in our discussion so far): the role of female translators in history. Of the contributions published in Messner and Wolf (2001) two of the most interesting (Walter 2001 and El-Akramy 2001) describe the life and works of the two translators Louise Gottsched (1713–1762), wife of Johann Christoph Gottsched, literary theorist and André Lefevere's pioneer of traditional German translation theory (see 1. above), and Caroline Schlegel-Schelling (1763–1809), wife of August Wilhelm Schlegel, the Shakespeare translator and one of Lefevere's masters of the German tradition (see 1.1). Numerous volumes have been written about the two illustrious husbands, but little is known of their wives, whose biographies sound, even for feminists of today, sadly familiar. Both were highly cultivated, intelligent, creative and industrious, both became disillusioned by marriage. Both wrote and translated as diligently as their husbands, for whom they acted as helpmates and secretaries, but who of course took the fees and the fame. Caroline Schlegel even had a large share in the Shakespeare translations attributed to her husband (in 1797 she wrote her own translation of *Romeo and Juliet*), and in 1828 A.W. Schlegel felt obliged to mention in the Preface of his "Critical Writings" that they came "zum Teil von der Hand einer geistreichen Frau, welche alle Talente besaß, um als Schriftstellerin zu glänzen, deren Ehrgeiz aber nicht darauf gerichtet war" (…in part from the hand of an intelligent woman, who had all the talents to shine as a writer, but whose ambitions were not thus engaged). (El-Akramy 201: 76).

3.3   The positions of the reader

One of the features of our "interdiscipline" during the 1990s is that it did not only "import" from outside, but integrated and coordinated the various new strands of knowledge from within. One invariable factor, at least for translation, is the reader, whether this is the translator as reader or the reader of the translation. In the light of what we have seen in this chapter so far, we should now consider the various positions of the reader in their relevance for Translation Studies.

In her early volume *Translation Studies* (Bassnett-McGuire 1980, 2002[3]), Susan Bassnett pointed out a typical failure of translators to understand that a literary text is made up of "a complex set of systems existing in a dialectical relationship with other sets outside its boundaries" (2002[3]: 80), and they focus on particular aspects of a text at the expense of others. She then quoted four essential positions of the reader as determined by the Soviet semiotician Juri Lotman:[40]

1. Where the reader focusses on the **content as matter**, i.e. picks out the prose argument or poetic paraphrase.
2. Where the reader grasps the complexity of the structure of a work and the way in which the **various levels interact.**
3. Where the reader deliberately **extrapolates one level** of the work for a specific purpose.
4. Where the reader discovers elements **not basic to the genesis** of the text and uses the text for his own purposes. (2002[3]: 80, emphasis added)

For our present purpose, the third and fourth positions are less relevant: the fourth concerns texts belonging to "a cultural system distanced in time and space" (2002[3]: 81) with specific elements that have evolved since its genesis (Hamlet's "fatness" is an example), whereas the third characterizes those typical text-fragments criticized by Holz-Mänttäri which are chosen for translation classes (and examinations) because of specific linguistic problems.

The first two positions deserve more attention, because they reveal a problem of many translators, especially of novels, who focus on content at the expense of the inner structuring of the text. Bassnett's excellent example is the opening of Thomas Mann's *The Magic Mountain* in the translation by Helen Lowe-Porter:

> An unassuming young man was travelling in midsummer, from his native city of Hamburg to Davos-Platz in the Canton of Grisons, on a three weeks' visit.
>
> From Hamburg to Davos is a long journey – too long indeed, for so brief a stay. It crosses all sorts of country; goes up hill and down dale, descends from the pla-

---

40.   She quotes the Italian version *La struttura del testo poetico* (Milan: Musia, 1972) of Lotman's Russian original published in Moscow in 1970.

teaus of Southern Germany to the shores of Lake Constance, over its bounding waves and on across marshes once thought to be bottomless. (2002³: 111)

This fast-moving, strongly descriptive and completely realistic passage reads like a geographical account – and the distance between source and target text becomes clear when one reads the opening of *Der Zauberberg* in German:

> Ein einfacher junger Mensch reiste im Hochsommer von Hamburg, seiner Vater-stadt, nach Davos-Platz im Graubündischen. Er fuhr auf Besuch für drei Wochen.
>
> Von Hamburg bis dorthinauf, das ist aber eine weite Reise; zu weit eigentlich im Verhältnis zu einem so kurzen Aufenthalt. Es geht durch mehrerer Herren Länder, bergauf und bergab, von der süddeutschen Hochebene hinunter zum Gestade des Schwäbischen Meeres und zu Schiff über seine springenden Wellen hin, dahin über Schlünde, die früher für unergründlich galten. (cit. Bassnett 2002³: 111–2)

As Bassnett points out in detail, the reader is here given clues to various codes operating through the novel,[41] and the journey functions on different levels (the young man's actual journey, the symbolic journey across a nation, the journey as a metaphor for the reader's quest in the novel). This emerges from some quite definite devices, such as antiquated literary terms: *Gestade* for *Ufer* (shore), *Graubündischen* for *Graubünden* (Grisons), *Schwäbisches Meer* for *Bodensee* (Lake Constance). The English version has been shortened by compressed syntax and deliberate omissions, and the highly evocative ambiguous metaphor, the *Schlünde*[42] (ravines, gorges) which are *unergründlich* (unfathomable) are misunderstood as *Sümpfe*, "bottomless marshes", a phenomenon which not only gives false clues to the reader but is in non-existent in that mountainous region.[43]

However, this brings us back to our discussion of text and reader, of the "sacred original" and of "re-reading" in the German skopos theory (2.2) and in the deconstructionist, "cannibalistic" approach (2.4). Vermeer emphasizes that a text is not a static object in a vacuum, but "is" as it is received by the reader, Arrojo echoes the principle that the text is not a "vessel" with content, but could be seen as a "palimpsest" with various readings. Derrida maintained that the reader no longer "preserves" the author's meaning but produces new ones, involving the "death" of

---

41. This is frequently the case with the opening passage of a novel (and is often ignored in translation). Cf. a similar discussion of the opening lines of Rushdie's *The Moor's Last Sigh* in Snell-Hornby 2001.

42. *Schlund*, a dated literary term for *throat, gullet* is here used metaphorically in the sense of *gorge, ravine, abyss*.

43. This is not an isolated example but tends rather to be typical of this phenomenon in Lowe-Porter's translations of Thomas Mann. See too the discussion of *Das Wunderkind/The Infant Prodigy* in Snell-Hornby 1997b: 78–82.

the author and the "birth" of the reader. The matter has been intensely debated, again creating an issue that has led to dichotomies and polarities. My own position is an intermediary one. I still believe (as in Snell-Hornby 1988) that the status of the literary source text is not identical with that of, for example, the instructions for use of a digital watch, but this by no means turns the literary text into a static container of meanings – on the contrary, it is highly dependent on reader activation (cf. Snell-Hornby 1988/1995²: 114–115). What has evolved since I wrote those lines in the mid-1980s is the reflection process with scholars adhering to the skopos theory.

On the one hand Nord's concept of loyalty as quoted under 3.1.1 has made it possible to extend functional principles to literary translation. A good example of what can happen when such loyalty does not exist was given by Piotr Kuhiwczak in his contribution to the Warwick conference of 1988. He takes up the problem of the cultural transfer at a time when Europe was still divided into the two colliding worlds of "East" and "West", and discusses the English 1969 translation of Milan Kundera's early novel *The Joke* (which appeared in Czechoslovakia in 1967), or rather its rewriting, in this case used negatively as "appropriation", implying the original sense of "dispossessing, without compensation". In our own days of an enlarged Europe with translation going on within the daily routine of EU institutions,[44] it may be difficult to understand the cultural problems then seen to be at stake in translating a Czech novel into English. Central Europe, historically a "melting pot of nations, religions and ideologies" (Kuhiwczak 1990: 119), has always been a region of immense complexity, and the paper focusses on the extreme simplification and even elimination of complex elements in the narrative structure and themes of the novel in its first, highly criticized, English version. One of the two translators admitted in a letter to the *Times Literary Supplement* that

> ...he found the lack of strict chronological order in the book misleading, and even bewildering. With the prospective reader anxiously in mind, he decided to introduce chronology by cutting, 'pasting' and shifting the chapters around. His decision must have been accepted by the publisher, since the editor responsible for the final shape of *The Joke* provided the following justification: 'It is an editor's responsibility to suggest anything that, in his view, might help to clarify things for the reader'. (Kuhiwczak 1990: 125)

The theme eliminated from this English translation was that of Moravian folk music, significant in the novel for the preservation of cultural tradition, specifically against the background of a Marxist political system. But the translators

---

44. Cf. Chapter 6 for a discussion of "culture" versus "discourse system".

found the theme "redundant". As Kuhiwczak points out, with these and other alterations stripping layers of meaning from the narrative and leaving only a 'flat' story, the translators "have trespassed across the magical line beyond which simplification can be taken for reality" (1990: 128). There is small wonder that Kundera himself complained that his novels have been misinterpreted, mistranslated, and misunderstood, and that "for some years, he spent more time correcting translations of his novels and chasing the journalists who misrepresented his views than in writing the original works" (Kuhiwczak 1990: 122–3). In the case of *The Joke* he solved the problem by forcing the publishers to produce a complete version of the novel in 1970 and then asking for a new translation (which appeared thirteen years later). This may be an extreme case, but for translation scholars it raises important questions, not only about the cultural transfer as such, but particularly about translation ethics, and the responsibility of translator, editor and publishers towards both author and readers.

A further breakthrough in the skopos theory came with Margret Ammann's functional model of translation critique (as based on Vermeer) of 1990 (see 3.3.1). A crucial component of this is the concept of the "model reader" as presented by Umberto Eco (1985). Eco describes the text as a "meccanismo pigro" (an "inert mechanism") (1985: 52) only realized as a text when activated by the reader, who follows a strategy "di cui fan parte le previsioni delle mosse altrui" ("which involves foreseeing moves made by another") (1985: 66). These "foreseen moves" may concern the reader's background knowledge or his/her reading habits and preferences, but in any case it involves active participation, as in filling in spaces (resulting from presuppositions or allusions), and the author of a text assumes that these can indeed be filled (1985: 52). For Eco the model reader is one who is in a position to do this, and, in interpreting the text, to recognize as many of its multiple layers as possible (cf. Lotman's second position of the reader as discussed by Bassnett).

With this concept we can see that an author, and a translator as author, can envisage (and write for) a particular readership or target group. Translation is seen by Eco as "cooperazione interpretativa messo in publico" (interpretative cooperation made public), and the translator is "un lettore empirico che si è comportato come un Lettore Modello" (an empirical reader who behaves like a Model Reader) (1985: 186). For translation purposes Ammann rightly considers this over-simplified, and, with reference to the scenes-and-frames concept (see 1.3), she offers her own definition of the model reader:

> Der Modell-Leser ist somit für mich jener Leser, der aufgrund einer Lesestrategie zu einem bestimmten Textverständnis kommt. Seine Lesestrategie zielt auf ein Gesamtscene (als Gesamtverständnis) eines Texts, die sich zum einen aus dem von ihm vorgenommenen kulturspezifischen Aufbau von Einzelscenes ergibt,

darüber hinaus jedoch durch Vorwissen und Erwartungen des Lesers entschei-
dend beeinflusst werden kann. (1990: 225)

(So for me the model reader is one who achieves a particular understanding of the
text as based on a reading strategy. This strategy aims at creating a complete *scene*
(complete understanding) of a text, which partly results from his/her own activation of individual culture-specific *scenes*, but can also be triggered by previous
expectations.)

Ammann's model of translation critique, including this conception of the model
reader will be applied under 3.3.1.

Meanwhile however I would like to return to Helen Lowe-Porter's Mann
translations and, in the light of our discussion of the "model reader", cite an example of an academic debate that would have gained in quality if this concept had
been known and applied. On 13th October 1995 *The Times Literary Supplement*
published an article by the Germanist Timothy Buck with the title "Neither the letter nor the spirit", discussing the deficiencies of Helen Lowe-Porter's translations
of Thomas Mann (above all *Der Zauberberg* and *Death in Venice*). The main reason for the poor quality is diagnosed as her deficient competence in German,
which led her to misunderstand Mann's highly complex language, as illustrated by
copious examples (mainly words and phrases, largely given without context). Buck
then comments as follows:

> For Lowe-Porter who once wrote, revealingly, of "the promise I made to myself of
> never sending a translation to the publisher unless I felt as though I had written
> the book myself' – translation work offered a large measure of "the pleasures of
> creative authorship". The dangers of her kind of "creative" translation – with, at
> times, scant regard for the author's text or intentions – are clearly shown in the
> examples above. (1995: 17)

This, along with another highly criticized retranslation of *Buddenbrooks* by John
Woods, is then placed in contrast to the translation of *Death in Venice* by David
Luke (1988), which Buck describes as "a model translation, faithful to the original,
yet fluent" (1995: 17).

On 24th November 1995 the *TLS* then published a letter from Lawrence
Venuti (1995a) on "Timothy Buck's screed" which "raises to new heights of
thoughtlessness the typical academic condescension toward translation". Venuti
(apparently without having read the texts themselves) defends the translations on
various grounds. Firstly, "neither Lowe-Porter nor Woods adopted contemporary
academic canons of translation accuracy, which require extreme precision, not to
mention the inscription (somehow) of whatever interpretation of the German
texts currently prevails among academic specialists." (1995: 17) And secondly:

Buck's "model" translation is "faithful to the original, yet fluent". But canons of accuracy are always fitted to the audience for which the translation is made, and they change over time (…). And what seemed fluent at one moment can't be expected to seem so at another. Buck's attack on Lowe-Porter's "imprecision – in which the translator reinterprets the author's words" – naively assumes that translation can be a simple communication of the foreign text, uncomplicated by the translator's reinterpretation of it according to domestic values. (1995a: 17)

On 8th December 1995 the *TLS* then published a reply by David Luke, who wrote that Venuti "wilfully misses the main point of Timothy Buck's recent criticism", emphasizing that what is at stake is not "reinterpretation" but "the type of mistranslation that used to be called schoolboy howlers", and that neither translator understood enough German to be able to translate Thomas Mann (1995: 15).

Various points emerge here. Firstly, there is the truism that a translator needs proficiency in the languages concerned, and as "model reader" must be able to adopt a position capable of "filling in gaps" and recognizing multiple layers and structures. Helen Lowe-Porter's deficits in that respect have been frequently pointed out (cf. Snell-Hornby 1995, 1997b) and partly emerge from the opening lines of *The Magic Mountain* quoted above. On the other hand however, the two scholars of German do treat translation as a linguistic exercise that must demonstrate faithfulness to a static "sacred original", whereby Thomas Mann's works are acclaimed prototypes of canonized German literature. It is unfortunate that Venuti adopted such an aggressive tone (and seems unfamiliar with the texts at stake) because behind his slings and arrows he is in principle quite right: a translation is not a simple communication of the foreign text, not even one by Thomas Mann, and if Lowe-Porter had had the necessary expertise, she might have been able to read the texts actively (in Eco's sense) and have been in a rightful position to enjoy "the pleasures of creative authorship" as understood by Translation Studies at the end of her century.[45]

3.3.1   Applying a functional model of translation critique

Descriptive Translation Studies, particularly as represented by Toury, takes an approach which is essentially descriptive and not evaluative, which places theory above its "applied extensions" and sees translations as "facts of one system only: the target system" (Toury 1985: 19) – without recourse to the source text author. It is my aim here to show that translation critique (evaluation) based on an adequate

---

45. The issue is taken up again later by Venuti (1998: 32–33), but again without going beyond evaluative generalizations on the one hand and comparison of lexical items on the other.

theoretical model (applied extension) is not only desirable but necessary, and that even literary translation needs to consider all the participants involved, including the author of the source text.

Our starting point is the concept of "scenes-and-frames" as presented by Charles Fillmore (1.3). Rarely has a linguistic concept proved so fruitful for the practice of translation irrespective of specific languages or language-pairs. Mia Vannerem, a teacher in an Antwerp translation school, applied it in her translation classes in the early 1980s and gave papers on the topic at local conferences. The results were then made available to a wider public (Vannerem and Snell-Hornby 1986 and Snell-Hornby 1988) and inspired further work in Germany on 'scenes' and 'frames', especially Vermeer and Witte 1990 (which includes the concept of 'channel' as introduced by Fernando Poyatos) and Margret Ammann's model of translation critique, as based on a draft by Vermeer (Ammann 1990). The latter has proved to be an invaluable frame of reference for many masters' theses on translation critique over the past decade, as will be illustrated here in a recent example.

First however we should explain the theory of scenes and frames in its specific relevance for translation. In the scenes-and-frames approach, translation can be described as a complex act of communication involving interaction between the author of the source text, the translator as both source text reader and target text author, and then the reader of the source text. The translator starts from a presented frame (the source text and its linguistic components), which was produced by an author who drew from his/her own repertoire of partly prototypical scenes. Based on the frame(s) of the source text, the translator-reader builds up his/her own scenes as activated by personal experience and internalized knowledge of the material concerned. Depending on his/her proficiency in and knowledge of the source language and culture, the translator might well activate scenes that diverge from the author's intentions (as with Helen Lowe-Porter's "bottomless marshes" in the Swiss canton of Grisons) or deviate from those naturally activated by a native speaker of the source language (as with *Schlünde* meaning "gorge" or "ravine" in the same example). Based on the scenes s/he has activated, the translator must now find suitable frames in the target language; this involves a constant process of decision-making, depending on his/her proficiency in and knowledge of the target language and culture.

This approach was developed in the 1980s, and was taken a step further in Ammann's functional model of translation critique. This involves five steps of analysis, whereby the starting point is not the source text as in other models (e.g. Reiss 1971), but the translation. With this in mind, the model sets out to establish (1) the function of the translation in the target culture, (2) the intratextual coherence of the translation, (3) the function of the source text in the source culture, (4) the intratextual coherence of the source text and (5) the intertextual coherence between target and source texts. Ammann utilizes both the concept of scenes-and-frames and Umberto Eco's notion of the "model reader".

In her recent master's thesis (2004), Tzu-Ann Chen applied Ammann's model to Amy Tan's first novel *The Joy Luck Club* in Sabine Lohmann's German translation with the title *Töchter des Himmels*. This is a book which fits in well with the basic themes of the present chapter, postcolonialism and gender, and before embarking on the translation critique we need to clarify some points about the content and narrative technique of the novel.

The protagonists are four women, who fled from Red China to America during the Second World War, and their four daughters, who were born and raised in the USA and show no interest in the culture and traditional thinking of their mothers. During the course of the novel however each one recognizes her "true" identity as well as the possibility of living in two worlds and two cultures. The basic problems in the novel are the mother-daughter relationship, the search for identity and the compatability of two distant cultures.

The novel consists of four parts, each with four short stories, written from the differing perspectives of the four mothers and four daughters. It opens in San Francisco in the post-war years, with a scene where Jing-mei, one of the daughters, takes the place of her deceased mother Suyuan at the mah-jong table of the Joy Luck Club. Suyuan had founded the club in Guilin, South China during the war, to keep up the spirits of her three friends and herself while they were hiding from the Japanese. After a traumatic escape she reaches the USA, where many years later she starts a new Joy Luck Club with three new friends, the "mothers" in the novel. In Part 1 each mother describes her relationship to her own mother in China; in Part 2 the four daughters recall their childhood and their relationship to their mother, Part 3 shows the problems of the adult daughters in work and marriage, and in Part 4 the mothers try to provide solutions by telling their daughters the story of their own life. In the final chapter, Jing-mei travels to China with her father to meet her two half-sisters who were left behind there, and only now is she able to understand her mother – and she realizes that the Chinese culture is part of her identity.

In this novel the linguistic 'frames' are used as a device for showing and establishing cultural identity. The language deficits, both on the part of the mothers, who know Chinese but only speak broken English, and on the part of the daughters, who speak perfect American English but only a little Chinese, reflect the mutually inadequate knowledge of the other culture. The mothers read too much into what the daughters say, and the daughters understand too little: communication problems are inevitable. The mothers want to pass on part of themselves and their Chinese culture to their daughters, but have great difficulty in "translating"

Chinese mentality and cultural concepts. And in our target text all that has to be expressed in German.

Tzu-Ann Chen, herself of Chinese origin, analyzed the novel using Ammann's five-step model. For those dealing with intratextual coherence (2 and 4), a suitable passage of text will be presented by way of illustration.[46]

The *target-text function* is (ideally) defined by the publishers, and it is evident from factors like the cover design, blurb or translator's notes (or preface). The German text was published by Goldmann in 1990 (only a year after the English version), first as a hardback and then as a paperback, indicating that a wide general market was envisaged. A preface about the book and its author indicates that the German version focusses mainly on the mother-daughter topos, but it also mentions the cultural impact and literary quality. On the back cover we read that this is a "jewel of a book" whose "poetry and tender magic touch the heart", and the brightly coloured front cover highlights the title *Töchter des Himmels* ("Daughters of Heaven"), all of these 'frames' suggesting a light novel for mainly female readers.

To establish the *intratextual coherence of the translation* let us look at a short passage at the beginning of the novel where Jing-mei recalls diverse communication problems with her mother. She thinks her mother's clumsy English is one of the causes of their difficult relationship.

> "Was ist der Unterschied zwischen jüdischem und chinesischem Mah-Jongg?" habe ich meine Mutter einmal gefragt. Doch ihrer Antwort war nicht zu entnehmen, ob nun die Spiele verschieden waren oder das alles mit ihrer Einstellung gegenüber Juden zu tun hatte.
>
> "Vollkommen andere Art zu spielen", sagte sie in dem Tonfall, den sie immer annahm, wenn sie etwas auf englisch erklärte. "Jüdisches Mah-Jongg, da achtet man nur auf die eigenen Steine, spielt nur mit den Augen."
>
> Dann sprach sie auf chinesisch weiter: "Beim chinesischen Mah-Jongg muss man seinen Kopf anstrengen und sehr geschickt vorgehen. Man muss aufpassen, was für Steine die anderen ablegen, und alles im Gedächtnis behalten. Wenn keine gut spielt, ist es wie beim jüdischen Mah-Jongg. Wozu denn überhaupt spielen, ohne Strategie? Da sieht man die Leute nur Fehler machen."
>
> Solche Erklärungen machten mir immer bewusst, dass die Sprache meiner Mutter von der meinen grundverschieden war, was ja auch stimmte. Wenn ich etwas auf englisch sagte, antwortete sie auf chinesisch. (cit. Chen 2004: 43–4)

---

46. Usually up to about 20 passages of text are analyzed in a translation critique of this kind: due to limitations of space only one can be considered here.

The reader can clearly imagine the mother's clumsy English: in German this is expressed by loosely connected items without any basic syntax (hence 'frames' deviating from the standard norm and evoking the 'scene' "foreigner"), whereas the part intended to be spoken in Chinese is rendered in coherent, syntactically well-formed sentences (standard norm in formal German). The difference comes across clearly and the text is in that respect coherent.

The third step analyzes the *function of the source text*. Amy Tan's *Joy Luck Club* was published in 1989 by Heinemann, after some of the stories had been printed in literary journals. The envisaged reader was therefore cultivated and critical and was not likely to expect "light reading". The title evokes a group of people looking for joy and luck, 'frames' in this wording reminiscent of the 'scene' "China". In 1998 the novel was published as a paperback by Random House (Vintage): the cover text mentions the particular problems of Chinese-American immigrants: "two generations of women struggling to come to terms with their cultural identity". In 1989 this was already a topical issue in the USA and today the book is compulsory reading in many high schools and university departments.

To establish the *intratextual coherence of the source text* let us take the corresponding English version of the passage analyzed above:

> "What's the difference between Jewish and Chinese mah jong?" I once asked my mother. I couldn't tell by her answer if the games were different or just her attitude toward Chinese and Jewish people.
>
> "Entirely different kind of playing", she said in her English explanation voice. "Jewish mah jong, they only watch for their own tile, play only with their eyes."
>
> Then she switched to Chinese. "Chinese mah jong, you must play using your head, very tricky. You must watch what everybody else throws away and keep that in your head as well. And if nobody plays well, then the game becomes like Jewish mah jong. Why play? There's no strategy. Your're just watching people making mistakes."
>
> These kind of explanations made me feel my mother and I spoke two different languages, which we did. I talked to her in English, she answered back in Chinese. (cit. Chen 2004: 61–2)

There is a marked contrast between Suyuan's awkward English (evoking the 'scene' "foreigner") and her manner of speaking Chinese, which is syntactically more complex, but not identical with idiomatic American English. Amy Tan describes the language she uses as "…what I imagined to be (my mother's) translation of her Chinese if she could speak in perfect English, her internal language, and for that I preserve the essence, but neither an English nor a Chinese structure." (Tan 1996: 44). These are then 'frames' intending to evoke the scene "foreigner translating".

In the fifth and final step of Ammann's model the target and source text are compared to establish the *intertextual coherence* between them. In the short passage we have quoted, the most striking aspect is the part intended to be spoken by the mother in Chinese.[47] Whereas Amy Tan created a language of her own within the code of English, making it quite clear that the mother is speaking a foreign language, the corresponding German text is linguistically so correct that one gets the impression that the speaker is not Chinese but German, evoking a different 'scene' of narrative. Similar observations can be made thoughout the book, leading us to the conclusion that linguistic idiosyncrasies made to characterize the Chinese mothers are suppressed: broken American English with the odd slang phrase or bizarre metaphor is turned into cultivated, sometimes even stiff and old-fashioned Standard German where the humorous content is preserved but the multi-layered wit in the language usage is lost – a conclusion which echoes precisely our comments on the German translation of Rushdie's *Midnight's Children* (3.2.1).

Margret Ammann presented her model as a tool for analyzing literary texts, but it is also eminently suitable for non-fiction, such as biographies, historical surveys or life-style counselling, as has been shown in a several master's theses in Vienna – as for example a study by Elisabeth Vogt (2002) analyzing the German translation of Robert McNamara's book *In Retrospect. The Tragedy and Lessons of Vietnam* (see too Snell-Hornby 2005a) and one by Sonja Limbeck (2005) analyzing the German version of Thomas Gordon's *Parent Effectiveness Training*.

In general we can say that such translation critique is not only illuminating for the translation scholar, it would seem urgently necessary for giving the general public an idea of what literary translation involves. As Katharina Reiss rightly pointed out in 1971, newspaper reviews of translated works rarely indicate that a translator has been at work at all – and the situation has hardly changed today (cf. Snell-Hornby 2003a). The translator's achievement is not deemed worthy of mention, let alone appreciated: Margret Ammann's model might well be recommended to literary journalists to make them aware of what they are writing about when reviewing translated literature.

---

47. An oversight in the German text deserves mention: in line 3 the phrase "ihre Einstellung gegenüber Juden", whereby the 'frame' *Juden* used alone evokes anti-Semitic associations, as against the English text, where "Chinese and Jewish people" are compared.

CHAPTER 4

The turns of the 1990s

Apart from looking outward to neighbouring fields, during the last decade of the last century the "interdiscipline" of Translation Studies was also undergoing crucial developments from within. In interpreting studies major changes were to take place regarding both content and method, and at the end of the decade it had developed from being a kind of sideline, either ignored or "automatically included" in translation theory, into a fully fledged branch of the discipline on equal terms with the study of (literary and non-literary) translation. During the 1990s interpreting scholars developed their own scientific community, their own objects of research and their own basic reference works, and there are now few translation scholars (excluding the "general theorists") who can rightfully claim to be specialists in interpreting studies at the same time.

From today's perspective, there seem to have been two basic "turns" in the discipline as a whole. The first is a methodical one, resulting from the call for more empirical studies in both translation and interpreting. The second was caused from without, by the breathtaking developments in technology and in the globalization process, which together radically changed the job profile of translators (4.2.1) and, in part, of interpreters too (4.1.1). Here again, studies in areas like terminology and computer-aided translation have meanwhile come to occupy a world of their own, beyond the expertise of the scholar in "ordinary" or literary translation. This chapter attempts an overview of these developments, and it sets out to summarize and assess the translator's (and to a more limited extent the interpreter's) "turns of the 1990s".

4.1 The empirical turn

After a long history of philosophizing and theorizing, and after decades of linguistic factorizing, the call for more case studies and empirical investigations was overdue in Translation Studies. Part of the programme of the "Manipulation School" in 1985, as stated by Hermans in his introduction (2.1) was "ongoing practical research" and the "continual interplay between theoretical models and practical case studies" (1985: 11). During the 1990s such intentions were to be realized in the form of empirical surveys which themselves helped to change the profile of the discipline. This section will outline the developments and give an account of some examples.

4.1.1   New fields of interpreting studies

During the 1980s the main centre of Interpreting Studies in (West) Europe was the Paris School under Danica Seleskovitch (see 1.2), whose "théorie du sens" was a basic doctrine. Among those "polemically oriented" on this tradition was Daniel Gile, who in a lecture given at the Vienna Translation Studies Congress in 1992 with the title "Opening up in Interpretation Studies" formulated a new manifesto, as it were, with a "raw programme" (in Radnitzky's sense) for the coming years (Gile 1994). This involved making information widely available in what had been a "closed circle" of scholars, sensitizing young researchers to the potential value of this information, cooperating in interdisciplinary projects, especially with cognitive scientists (1994: 153–154), and heeding the "increasing calls for more empirical studies" (1994:151).

In fact, a seminal empirical study in the field of conference interpreting had already been published in 1986, Hildegund Bühler's survey on acceptance criteria for the performance of conference interpreters, which was to be a much-quoted starting point for future work. Beyond that, Daniel Gile's appeal seems to have been heeded, for during the 1990s there was to be no lack of empirical and interdisciplinary studies on various aspects of interpreting. Birgit Strolz (1992) investigated German simultaneous interpretations of the speeches broadcast on the occasion of signing of the Austrian State Treaty on 15th May 1955 (see too Strolz 2000), Ingrid Kurz, in cooperation with the Institute of Neurophysiology of the University of Vienna, looked inside the interpreter's "black box" (1994, 1996), and Franz Pöchhacker applied Holz-Mänttäri's theory of translatorial action to the interpreters' performance at a Vienna business conference (1994). These were only some of a number of similar studies carried out by researchers who were themselves practising interpreters.

But perhaps the most exciting development of the decade was the discovery of new fields of interpreting (or in some cases an awakening awareness of their existence). These fall into two main groups: firstly, interpreting activities arising through new technologies, and secondly, what became known collectively as dialogue interpreting (including Community Interpreting).

Simultaneous interpreting had already taken its own "technological turn" in the first half of the 20th century, first with the invention of suitable equipment, and then with the particular constellation created by the Nuremberg war trials of 1947. Both technology and equipment became increasingly sophisticated over the years, and in 1998 Pöchhacker was to conclude that:

...die Simultandolmetscher einem Prozess der Anonymisierung und Technisierung unterliegen, der sie im Lauf von fünf Jahrzehnten sozusagen von bewunderten Akrobaten zu notwendigen Technokraten der internationalen Kommunikation hat werden lassen. (1998: 303)

(Simultaneous interpreters have undergone a process of anonymizing and mechanizing that during the course of five decades has, as it were, turned them from admired acrobats into necessary technocrats of international communication.)

Spectacular new fields in simultaneous interpreting, made possible by advanced technology, are media interpreting and videoconferencing. The former has been described by Kurz (1997), herself a television interpreter, who provides convincing details of the particular constraints and stresses of interpreting live material (whether interviews, reports or speeches), often via monitor, for a national or even world-wide TV audience, and Pöchhacker presents an example of such a performance (Clinton's speech at the Brandenburg Gate in 1993, cf. 3.1.3) with a detailed analysis of the German interpretation (Pöchhacker 1997).

Even more complex are the variants of audiovisual communication made available for conference interpreting via satellite. Christian Heynold (1998) has described the technical and organisational details of such a "brave new world". Four distinctions are made in a *Code for the use of new technologies in conference interpretation*, published in 1997 by the International Association for Conference Interpreters (AIIC), with an Appendix listing set terms with their definitions:

- *'Tele-conference'*: any form of communication between two or several participants in two or several different places and relying on the transmission of one or several audio signals between those places.
- *'Video-conference'*: a tele-conference comprising one or several video signals which convey the images of some or all the participants.
- *'Multilingual video-conference'*: a video-conference in two or several languages with interpretation (consecutive or simultaneous).
- *'Tele-interpreting'*: interpretation of a multilingual video-conference by interpreters who have a direct view of neither the speaker nor their audience. (1997: 24)

Kurz, who describes some illuminating case-studies (2000: 299–300), stresses that this last category, where interpreters are not physically present at the conference venue but only receive information via monitor, is explicitly rejected as professionally unacceptable. A possible alternative would be video conferences with both participants and interpreters at the one conference venue and a simultaneous transmission to other locations. Contributions from "outside" are then interpreted via screen or monitor (2000: 293–294).

Other new fields in interpreting studies may be less spectacular, but they concern basic aspects of our daily lives and society that have frequently gone unnoticed. The term *Community Interpreting*, along with its conceptualization as an area of interpreting, is of Anglo-Saxon origin (although this too is strongly reminiscent of Schleiermacher's concept of *Dolmetschen* discussed under 1.1). It was introduced by the Institute of Linguists in London during the early 1980s (Longley 1984) and refers to the individual interpreting provided for individuals or small groups (such as families), usually immigrants, refugees or migrant workers, for communication with government authorities, in schools or hospitals or social institutions (Bowen 1998: 319). In times marked by regional wars or by a sharp economic divide between rich and poor countries, resulting in waves of refugees and asylum-seekers, community interpreting turns into a dire necessity. In some countries, such as Canada, Australia or Sweden, community interpreting services are well developed, but the occupation has nowhere reached the professional status of conference interpreting. In their early study of the history of interpreting, Thieme, Hermann and Glässer (1956, see Snell-Hornby 1996: 15) discussed the "vertical" as against the "horizontal" perspectives of interpretation according to the status of the partners involved. The "horizontal" perspective implies partners of equal status, as in diplomatic meetings, business negotiations or conference interpreting. The "vertical" perspective implies unequal status, as with conquerors or colonizers versus those defeated or colonized, or in the case of immigrants and refugees versus government authorities. In such situations interpreting is regarded either as a mere necessity or as a kind of social service, and in those countries which have not developed an awareness for the needs involved, and hence lack viable professional structures, the interpreters are not highly trained professionals as in the video conference or the international organization, but quite often native speakers who happen to be available, cleaning staff or even children.

One reason for this lies in the languages involved. Simultaneous interpreting at conferences or international meetings works with international languages like English, French or Arabic (where necessary with relays into languages of lesser diffusion). Community interpreting works with the native languages of the immigrants or refugees, usually those of limited diffusion and varying according to the origin of the people concerned, and the language of the host country.

In 1996 Pöchhacker carried out a large-scale empirical survey of Hospital Interpreting Needs in Vienna (Pöchhacker 1997a: 2000). According to information given by the hospital authorities, there were no less than 27 languages involved apart from German: by far the most frequently used were Bosnian/Croatian/Serbian and Turkish, followed by English (largely regional varieties), Polish, Arabic and Czech. Other languages mentioned were (in descending order of frequency): Hungarian, French, Russian, Chinese, Indian languages, Romanian, Italian, Albanian, Filipino, Spanish and Persian.

As part of a comprehensive study of community interpreting practices in healthcare and social service institutions in Vienna, including both a staff questionnaire and case studies, Pöchhacker's work was a pioneer project. The aim of the survey was to establish the need for mediated communication between service providers and non-German-speaking patients. The responses of 508 doctors, nurses and therapists demonstrate a substantial need for interpreting services, which are most often rendered by family members (especially children) and "bilingual" hospital employees, particularly cleaners. Most of the respondents were well aware of the shortcomings of current *ad hoc* interpreting arrangements and voiced a clear preference and demand for the establishment of an interpreting service within the hospital.

Two case studies recorded, transcribed and discussed in detail by Pöchhacker show how urgently such an interpreting service is needed. They concern the two languages most frequently used in the hospital with non-German-speaking patients. The first is a speech therapy session for a 10-year-old Bosnian boy "Emir", with two therapists (Tanja and Tina), in the presence of both parents and a Serbian interpreter (in her mid-forties), who is employed as a hospital cleaner and was called from her usual duties to "help out with language problems". From the transcribed passages it becomes clear how the tone and content of the therapists' utterances are manipulated by the interpreter, as in this simple example from the beginning of the session (here translated literally into English)[48]:

> *Tina* (to Emir): Look, today we're not going to sit, we're going to lie down, just like sleeping.
>
> *Interpreter* (from behind to Emir): You're to lie down here.
>
> (…)
>
> *Tina*: OK. Can you understand me? Tell him he…
>
> *Interpreter*: Do you understand? The lady says you've got to lie down. Down there (*pointing to the mat*), you lie down there. (Pöchhacker 2000: 192)

The session continues with similar communicative imperfections, and with additional problems regarding medical terminology, instructions for exercises at home, and unsolicited value-judgements from the interpreter – such as her remark to the child's parents, "They're really super to him here" (2000: 207).

---

48. For the authentic dialogue (in Serbian and German) with English translations of the individual utterances, see Pöchhacker and Kadrić 1999: 164–165.

The second case study centres round a 2-year-old Turkish child "Sefanur" with retarded language development, the therapist Tanja, the child's parents and the interpreter, who is the mother's 16-year-old niece. The problems start right away with the questions on the case history (here again translated literally into English):

> *Tanja (to the mother)*: How was the pregnancy?
>
> *Interpreter*: Auntie, what was your birth like?
>
> *Mother (shrugging her shoulders)*: OK, normal..
>
> *Tanja*: Normal. Hm. And the birth?
>
> *Mother (looks questioningly at the interpreter)*.
>
> *Interpreter (in a low voice)*: Your birth. (*Louder*) Your birth.
>
> *Mother*: What do you mean, my birth?
>
> *Tanja*: Forceps, suction, Caesarian?
>
> *Interpreter*: Your birth. (Pöchhacker 2000: 216–217)

The dialogue continues in this way, and although it may sound like a successful piece of Absurd Theatre, it is sad reality. Further confusion arises through the extreme reserve of the interpreter: whether though embarrassment, ignorance, linguistic incompetence or her own perception of her lowly position within the family, much is left uninterpreted or unclear, even the sex of the child, whom the therapist takes for a boy (it is a girl), and even the nature of the child's malady, which the family insists on seeing as organic and not cognitive. There could hardly be a better demonstration of the need for professional interpreting in such sensitive areas as the health service than this chilling case study.

Another new field of interpreting studies which made headway during this time is signed language interpreting for the deaf and hard of hearing. This area too is better developed in Anglo-American countries (see Isham 1998) than in some countries of Central Europe (see Grbić 1998), although generally one can say that public awareness and respect for this special form of communication and the needs of its varying communities are on the increase, as can be seen from its presence in the media (a varying number of television programmes), and from new training programmes: during the decade a special curriculum was developed at the Translation Studies Institute of the University of Graz, and a full degree course is meanwhile in progress.

Court interpreting, an old field of interpreting discovered over the last decade as a new field of Interpreting Studies, is in some countries, such as Sweden, counted as part of community interpreting, but in most European countries it is seen as a completely separate area, if not a profession in itself, and has its own professional associations. Canada, with its bilingual colonial history, has a long tradition in this field, as do countries in Continental Europe: Driesen (1998) traces the institutionalization of this profession back to the beginning of the 19th century. From an Anglo-Saxon perspective, Gamal (1998: 53) sees official court interpreting as starting only around 1946 with the war trials in Nuremberg and Tokyo – these can in any case be seen as key events in its history.

The English term "court interpreting" can be used to refer to any kind of legal interpreting, such as interviews in police departments or with immigration authorities, as against the more prestigious "courtroom interpreting". In German the first kind of activity is classed separately as *Behördendolmetschen*, as against *Gerichtsdolmetschen* in the courtroom. It is in this latter sense that we are using the English term "court interpreting" here (bearing in mind that court interpreters often also work as translators of legal documents, cf. 4.1.2).

The concept of court interpreting is based on the Declaration of Human Rights issued by the United Nations, in which democratic countries commit themselves to protecting basic rights, in this case equality before the law, whereby no one shall be put at a disadvantage because of his/her language. This means that anyone participating in legal proceedings has a right to an interpreter.

As with any kind of legal communication, the entire complex of court interpreting is dependent on the legal system involved. In an empirical study comparable to the one by Pöchhacker on hospital interpreting, Mira Kadrić investigated the phenomenon of court interpreting in the Austrian legal system (2001). As her theoretical starting point she used Holz-Mänttäri's concept of the courtroom as a "field of translatorial action", and she too carried out both a survey (a questionnaire sent to over 200 magistrates working in district courts in Vienna) and a case study (based on the recording and transcription of a court hearing in 1997). The questionnaire concerned the role and status of the interpreter in court as seen by the magistrates, and it produced some illuminating results. For those cases needing an interpreter, the most commonly used languages were here again Bosnian/Croatian/Serbian and Turkish, mainly involving migrant workers in Austria. The interpreter was viewed by 65% of the respondents as a kind of lowly assistant, by 39% as a language specialist, by 30% as a specialist in language and culture, but by only 8% as a specialist in intercultural communication (Kadrić 2001: 119). Important criteria for selecting an interpreter were linguistic and communicative competence (but not necessarily legal knowledge), trustworthiness, impartiality, discretion, easy availability and a self-confident manner (2001: 112–117). The tasks expected of the interpreter vary: the most important duty seems to be drawing attention to misunderstandings (95%), explaining (underworld) slang expressions on the one hand (90%) and legal terminology (72%) on the other, but also clarifying problematic statements independently by checking with the person concerned (63%) and explaining where a certain choice of words is due to the person's cultural background (85%) (2001: 122–124).

The case study analyzed by Kadrić involves two labourers (from Poland and ex-Yugoslavia) on a building site, who started fighting after a quarrel, during which the Pole was injured and now demands compensation. For the legal proceedings the 33-year-old defendant has a Serbo-Croat interpreter, while the 43-year-old Pole speaks German. The interpreter has had only 6 months experience, she is poorly prepared and not even aware of what the case is all about. She and the magistrate both agree to the hearing being recorded and analyzed (all participants remaining anonymous). (Kadrić 2001: 148) The transcribed text reveals various sources of miscommunication. Whereas the magistrate expects the interpreter to elicit the introductory personal information from the two parties on her own initiative, the interpreter only does what she is explicitly told to do. Further difficulty is created by the incoherent and distorted language of the defendant on the one hand, and the constant "interruptions" of the magistrate on the other, who requires more precise information. This is however in itself problematic, due to the interpreter's lack of competence and background knowledge (2001: 194). All in all, Kadrić concludes that the performance would have been better if the interpreter had had an adequate training in court interpreting – which in Austria is still barely existent. Elsewhere too, the work of the legal interpreter as an intercultural mediator is grossly underrated, the profession has low status, little public support and is poorly funded (cf. Morris 1995 and Barsky 1996).

In his definition of interpreting (*Dolmetschen*) of 1968 (1.2), Otto Kade was evidently thinking only of his own work in conference interpreting: "a source-language text is presented *only once* (usually orally) and rendered as a target-language text which can only be checked to a limited extent and which *due to lack of time can hardly be corrected*" (emphasis added). That certainly still applies for simultaneous interpreting, but not entirely for the fields of dialogue interpreting as illustrated here, where questions can be repeated and answers checked and revised.

All in all, one can conclude that, especially with the (re-)discovery of new fields of activity, Interpreting Studies has expanded beyond measure over the last fifteen years. What in James Holmes' vision of the discipline back in 1972 was merely a part of one of the partial theories of the "Pure" branch of Translation Studies (a small "twig" in the tree diagram in Holmes 1987: 21) has now blossomed into an independent area on its own for research, training and practice, for which the term "oral translation" is as inappropriate as "written interpreting" would be for translating. (See too Pöchhacker and Shlesinger 2002.)

4.1.2   Empirical studies in translation

As with Interpreting Studies, the empirical turn of the 1990s in translation goes back to seminal work in the mid-1980s. In 1986 Hans-Peter Krings, a lecturer in French at the University of Bochum, published a study which aimed at looking into the translator's mind. While Kurz (4.1.1) used methods of neurophysiology for her study of how the simultaneous interpreter's "black box" works, Krings applied the method of "think-aloud" protocols (TAPs) from psychology. In this case, subjects were asked to "think aloud" and verbalize what went on in their minds as they were translating, while their performance was recorded and then transcribed. The result was a sizeable volume with the promising title *Was in den Köpfen von Übersetzern vorgeht. Eine empirische Untersuchung zur Struktur des Übersetzungsprozesses an fortgeschrittenen Französischlernern* (What goes on in the heads of translators. An empirical investigation of the structure of the translation process with advanced learners of French). The blemish of the study is clear from the last words of the subtitle: the "translators" are students of French language and literature, and they are translating into the foreign language. So what is actually being tested is not the work of the professional translator, but the student "transcoder" required to show his/her proficiency in vocabulary and grammar structures. Although the professional translators were quick to rise in protest, the foundation stone for a new area of research (TAPs in Translation Studies) had been laid.

Apart from the nature of the subjects, protests were made against the type of text being used. These were of the kind customary in translation classes for future teachers, but which, as Hönig and Kussmaul had already pointed out in 1982, are rarely translated in professional practice, typically feature articles on topics of current or local interest and full of subtle stylistic devices, texts which:

> ... sich durch eine beachtliche Vielzahl sprachlicher Erscheinungen insbesondere im stilistischen Bereich auszeichnen. So enthalten beide Texte metaphorische Ausdrucksweisen, Wortspiele u.a. Eine große Bandbreite von sprachlichen Merkmalen des Textes sollte für eine entsprechend große Bandbreite von Übersetzungsproblemen sorgen und so die Aussagekraft der Prozessanalyse erhöhen. (Krings 1986: 53)

> (... are characterized by a considerable number of linguistic devices, particularly as regards style. Both texts contain metaphorical expressions, puns etc. A large range of linguistic features in the text should ensure a correspondingly large range of translation problems and increase the significance of the process analysis.)

Krings soon responded to criticism by applying his methods to professional translators, and at the AILA Translation Symposium in Hildesheim in April 1987 he presented a paper with the title "Blick in die 'Black Box' – Eine Fallstudie zum

Übersetzungsprozess bei Berufsübersetzern" (Looking inside the 'black 'box' – A case study on the translation process with professional translators) (Krings 1988). In this case there were two minor blemishes: firstly, for the conference paper a study with only one translator was presented – due to the immense amount of work involved in collecting and analyzing the data, as the author pointed out (Krings 1988: 395) – and secondly, a similar kind of text was used as before, a brief ironical passage from the French satirical weekly "Le Canard Enchaîné" of April 1983. The author was aware that this text "is rather untypical of professional practice", being actually part of the corpus for his first analysis with university students (1988: 396), but precisely for that reason he thought it a good basis for comparison. The analysis then presented was indeed extremely thorough and detailed, and from the methodological viewpoint it provided a good deal of material for future studies using professional translators.

One insight gained from Krings' comparison was that professionals use holistic strategies involving the text as a whole, whereas non-professionals follow linear strategies involving small translation units such as words and structures. These findings were confirmed by later TAP-studies from Finland (Jääskeläinen 1989, Tirkkonen-Condit 1989), which show that professionals activate their general knowledge and experience and focus on the sense of a text, whereas learners concentrate on words and formal elements. Professionals work more efficiently by applying conscious strategies and theoretical criteria, and they have more self-confidence and curiosity and a greater sense of responsibility.

During the 1990s the question of the mental processes behind translation triggered off a lively debate, particularly in European countries. Hönig took up the issue at the James Holmes Symposium in 1990 with reference to Holmes' "Mapping Theory"[49] (Hönig 1991), and Kussmaul carried out extensive studies (explained in detail in the first chapter of Kussmaul 1995), which provided valuable insights for translation teaching, as for error analysis, or studies in creativity (Kussmaul 2000). Critical voices were raised about the methods generally used: TAPs were usually in monologue form, whereby subjects talked aloud to themselves while translating, clearly an artificial situation, which other researchers

---

49. As explained at the FIT Congress in Montreal in May 1978 (cf. 1.4): "I have suggested that actually the translation process is a multi-level process; while we are translating sentences, we have a map of the original text in our minds and at the same time a map of the kind of text we want to produce in the target language. Even as we translated serially, we have this structural concept so that each sentence in our translation is determined not only by the sentence in the original but by the two maps of the original text and of the translated text which we are carrying along as we translate." (1988: 96)

sought to correct by using more than one subject, providing dialogue or even group protocols (Schmid 1994).

Another kind of empirical research in Translation Studies launched during the 1990s went back to methods of corpus linguistics. These had been successfully demonstrated during the 1970s and 1980s for major language projects in Britain, which made use of large-scale computerized corpora such as the Brown and LOB corpora or the British National Corpus. Successful projects included those in monolingual lexicography. One of these was the COBUILD[50] project directed by John Sinclair (as described in Sinclair 1987), which resulted in such major publications as the *Collins Dictionary of the English Language* (Hanks et al. 1979) and the *COBUILD Learner's Dictionary* (1986). While lexicographical projects naturally centre round lexical items (the COBUILD corpus contained 40 million words, 20 million from special language texts and 20 million from general language (cf. Sinclair 1987: vii and Snell-Hornby 1988a: 84), a corpus can of course consist of any kind of language material. The possible application for corpus linguistics in Translation Studies was described by Mona Baker (1993) in her contribution to a *Festschrift* for John Sinclair, and in 1995 she elaborated further ideas on the potential for corpus-based research in translation. She proposes three types of text corpora, parallel, multilingual and comparable. The use of parallel texts as a translation aid is undisputed (see 4.2.1, also Göpferich 1998). Multilingual corpora were to be used to change research methodology (within the linguistic approach still widely prevalent in the UK):

> What I am suggesting is that we need to effect a shift in the focus of theoretical research in the discipline, a shift away from comparing either ST with TT or language A with language B to comparing text production per se with translation. In other words, we need to explore how text produced in relative freedom from an individual script differs from text produced under the normal conditions which pertain in translation, where a fully developed and coherent text exists in language A and requires recoding in language B. (Baker 1995: 233)

This view of translation reflects precisely the linguistic approach described in 1.3 (against which the hermeneutic, functional and culture-based approaches of the 1980s had been rebelling), and will be considered further in 5.1.

Baker suggests that her envisaged shift of focus may be facilitated by access to comparable corpora, which she understands as "a cross between parallel and multilingual corpora" (1995: 234). Such corpora apparently did not exist at the time of

---

50. This was a joint dictionary project run by the University of Birmingham and Collins Publishers. COBUILD is an acronym for **CO**llins **B**irmingham **U**niversity **I**nternational **L**anguage **D**atabase. The COBUILD corpus was later developed into the Bank of English (BoE).

writing, but Baker advocated setting them up, and later Dorothy Kenny was to describe them as "a collection of texts originally written in a language, say English, alongside a collection of texts translated (from one or more languages) into English." (1998: 52) The aim of such comparable corpora would be "to identify patterning which is specific to translated texts, irrespective of the source or target languages involved" (Baker 1995: 234).

In all, the purpose of such corpora, apart from the information provided for the translator by parallel texts, would be to provide extensive data for descriptive work in translation studies, either for machine translation or computer-aided translation, or else for research into translation phenomena. These would range from the frequency of certain items, type-token ratio and lexical density to the possibility of translation universals (see 5.2). There are however problems, as emerges from this conclusion by Kenny:

> Perhaps the greatest challenge that faces corpus-based research into translation stems from the fact that corpus linguistics has always been data driven: it has proceeded from the bottom up, using concrete facts to make generalizations about particular languages. Much current translation scholarship, however, proceeds top down: theorists are interested in finding evidence to support abstract hypotheses. Translation studies thus makes very particular demands on corpora, and ongoing research in translation studies may lead to new ways of looking at corpora, just as corpora are already leading to new ways of looking at translation. (1998: 53)

One close encounter between corpus-based linguistics and Translation Studies had actually already taken place during the 1980s, with discussions between translation scholars on the one hand and COBUILD lexicographers on the other, about how their data could be used to create bilingual reference works for the translator (see Snell-Hornby and Pöhl 1989). Conceptual problems might have been overcome, such as the real needs of the professional translator on the one hand and the lexicographers' assumption on the other that translators needed the same kind of bilingual dictionary as tourists and language students, which provided the "equivalent" for a "slot" in the text. What (above all literary) translators and translation scholars envisaged was a bilingual thesaurus based on semantic fields (Birkenhauer and Birkenhauer 1989, Snell-Hornby 1996b): the lexicographers as language scholars were delighted and theoretically saw great potential. From the commercial viewpoint the publishers were however sceptical: the costs of such a project, so they felt, would never be offset by such a "limited market". For this reason the project was never realized, and James Holmes' lament at the end of his Vienna paper in 1984 was to remain bleak reality: "Our bilingual dictionaries and grammars are still a disgrace and a despair" (Holmes 1988: 110, cf. 5.1).

Another fertile field for empirical studies in translation during the 1990s was legal translation, and this will be taken up here to follow up the account on court interpreting in 4.1.1. On the European Continent legal translation has a long and distinguished history: during the 18th century, at the court of the Empress Maria Theresia in Vienna, there were highly respected officials known as "Hoftranslatoren"[51] (Court Translators in another sense of the word) to deal with all matters of state and administration (for a detailed account see Petioky 1997).[52]

A legacy of the Austro-Hungarian Empire still noticeable in Central European countries today is a legal and administrative system with many common elements. In 1998 Aga Pluta submitted an interdisciplinary master's thesis at the University of Vienna, comparing what is known in Austria as a *Baubescheid* in German, English and Polish. In Austria a *Bescheid* is an official document drawn up by an administrative or legal body with information on a definite decision (usually in answer to an application). It has a prescribed basic structure, consisting of three main parts, the *Spruch* (ruling), the *Begründung* (reasons for the decision), and the *Rechtsmittelbelehrung* (information on the right to appeal), and it is legally binding. Given these basic characteristics, it is a text genre which does not exist as such in Anglo-Saxon countries (cf. Snell-Hornby 2002a: 146–149). There are however parallel texts produced in comparable legal situations and hence offering counterparts, even if these cannot be described as "equivalents". A *Baubescheid* for example is a *Bescheid* issued in answer to someone who has applied for building permission, a situation as common in Britain as it is in Austria. The British counterpart is a "decision notice", which however has the form of a letter and, being part of the Anglo-Saxon legal system, does not have the same legal implications as its Austrian counterpart. In Poland, during the years of communism, the legalities of building permission were in themselves quite different from those in capitalist countries, and, one might assume, the language is in any case so difficult that the corresponding document granting permission must be in a class on its own. In actual fact, as Pluta convincingly demonstrates on the basis of her trilingual corpus, the Polish and the Austrian documents are amazingly similar, in structure, language and, since the political turn of 1989, in legal implications, whereas the British decision notices

---

51. It is significant that the German term *Translator*, which created so much controversy between theorists and practitioners at the end of the 20th century, was already common currency over two hundred years before.

52. Meanwhile Michaela Wolf has presented an extensive account of translation and interpreting in the later Habsburg monarchy (Wolf 2005). In the account of the "German tradition" in the *Routledge Encyclopedia of Translation Studies* (Baker 1998) there is no reference to this long-established practice in non-literary translation. The only mention of the Austrian contribution under "History and Traditions" (Part II) misleadingly appears under the "Hungarian tradition".

turned out to be the "exotic" text-type with various idiosyncrasies. As this example shows, comparing legal texts in the context of translation in fact implies comparing legal systems (cf. Arntz 1986: 291–292 and Stolze 1999).

Interesting work in legal translation was carried out during the course of the 1990s by Susan Šarčević, particularly from an interdisciplinary perspective (1994) and from the viewpoint of lesser known languages (1990). The collection of essays edited by Peter Sandrini (1999) gives an overview of work done in legal translation during the course of the decade (for an interdisciplinary approach see the contribution by Reiner Arntz). Particular mention should be made of the corpus of German-Italian legal texts determined by the political situation in South Tyrol and its ensuing bilingual status. At the European Academy in Bolzano a special project on "Language and Law" directed by Arntz was dedicated to the topic of legal translation in the area (see Arntz 1996), and a critical study of the German translation of the Italian Civil Code in South Tyrol (as a workable frame of reference for court interpreters) was presented by Andrea Bernardini in 2002.

Another valuable empirical study was carried out by Nadezda Salmhoferova among legal translators in the Czech Republic (2002). Based on Holz-Mänttäri's theory of translatorial action, Salmhoferova launched a survey investigating the background, status, self-definition and strategies of 174 translators of legal texts in a country that was still undergoing radical social changes. It turned out that the status quo was very different from the ideal job profile required by the new post-communist society, and the survey proved instrumental in defining new areas of responsibility, in launching programmes for further training of present translators and for the basic training of legal translators in the future.

4.2   The globalization turn

> Just beyond the horizon of current events lie two possible political futures – both bleak, neither democratic. The first is a retribalization of large swaths of humankind by war and bloodshed: a threatened Lebanonization of national states in which culture is pitted against culture, people against people, tribe against tribe – a Jihad in the name of a hundred narrowly conceived faiths against every kind of interdependence, every kind of artificial social cooperation and civic mutuality. The second is being borne in on us by the onrush of economic and ecological forces that demand integration and uniformity and that mesmerize the world with fast music, fast computers, and fast food – with MTV, Macintosh, and McDonald's, pressing nations into one commercially homogeneous global network: one McWorld tied together by technology, ecology, communications and commerce. The planet is falling precipitantly apart *and* coming reluctantly together at the very same moment. (Barber 1992: 53)

Those were the opening words of a sobering article published by Benjamin Barber in *The Atlantic Monthly* in 1992, the year of the Columbian quincentennial (cf. 3.2). In the title "Jihad vs. McWorld" he gave names to the phenomena of tribalism on the one hand and globalism on the other, which he described as "the two axial principles of our age". From today's viewpoint his words assume prophetic dimensions: during the 1990s tribalism was to create tragic areas of conflict (ex-Yugoslavia and Ruanda are striking examples), and globalism – or rather globalization[53] – turned into the key-word to describe the developments of the decade. It applies directly to technology and commerce, but also to communication and language, to international discourse, and hence to translation. Unlike technology and commerce however (and counterbalancing Barber's sombre vision of a future driven on the one hand by "parochial hatreds" and on the other by "universalizing markets"), the phenomenon of language as the means of expression of individual cultural communities, leads on to a third, and more constructive notion, that of *cultural identity*, indicating a self-awareness marked by its own unmistakable features, but able to exist in harmony with and to communicate with other, neighbouring identities in the world around.[54]

The term "cultural identity" was used in a moving contribution by the Nicaraguan poet and political activist Gioconda Belli to a symposium "500 Years Resistance in Latin America", jointly organized by the Universities of Managua and Graz in March 1992 (König et al. 1994). This cooperation project was an answer to what in the European planetary consciousness had long been known as the "discovery of America" by Christopher Columbus, and Belli's contribution – with the title "America in Memory" – mourns the destruction of the indigenous peoples and cultures of what was later Latin America:

> Im Laufe der Jahrhunderte hat dieses halbkoloniale und halbfeudale System Lateinamerika in eine privilegierte Elite und eine besitzlose Mehrheit geteilt. Im Kampf gegen dieses System und die nordamerikanische imperiale Beherrrschung, die die spanische ersetzt hatte, formten sich die Wesenszüge der kulturellen Identität Lateinamerikas. (1994: 16)[55]

---

53. Framson (2005: 47–48) discusses the imprecise usage of these terms: *globalism* refers to the ideology of global marketing, *globalization* the process of global networking along with the ensuing conflicts.

54. This concept of cultural identity is not identical with the same term used by Venuti (1994: 202 and 1998), which refers to *stereotypes* or "representations of foreign cultures" constructed by translation (as described in 3.2.1).

55. The Spanish text read by Belli (and translated into German for the publication) is unfortunately no longer available.

(In the course of the centuries this half colonial and half feudal system turned Latin America into a privileged elite and an impoverished majority. In the struggle against this system and the North American imperial domination, which had replaced the Spanish one, there were formed the basic features of the cultural identity of Latin America.)

For Belli it is thanks to a stubborn resistance to colonization that the Latin American cultural identity "has not entirely disappeared" (1994: 15), but, with reference to Barber's essay in *The Atlantic* Monthly, she sees it (and the future of "Third World" countries worldwide) endangered by globalization and above all by the phenomenon he called "McWorld":

> Angesichts dieser "McWorld"-Kultur, die sich als westlich, als entwickelt, als einzig mögliche zivilisierte Existenzform gibt, befinden wir uns alle in Gefahr. Wir laufen Gefahr, uns in der Mittelmäßigkeit zu verlieren und von einer Kultur der Albernheit kolonisiert und niedergewalzt zu werden.

> Ich habe den Eindruck, dass dadurch die Nationalismen angeheizt werden. Die Menschen suchen Zuflucht in ihrer Identität, in ihrer Volkszugehörigkeit, in ihrer Gemeinschaft – und gleiten dabei auch in Separatismus, Bruderkriege und gefährliche Fremdenfeindlichkeit ab. (1994:18)

> (In view of this "McWorld" culture, which presents itself as western, as advanced, as the only possible civilized form of existence, we are all in danger. We are in danger of losing ourselves in mediocrity and of being colonized and crushed by a culture of stupidity.

> I have the impression that this aggravates nationalisms. People are seeking refuge in their identity, in their ethnic origin, in their community – and in doing so they are sliding down into separatism, fraticidal wars and dangerous xenophobia.)

Considering the further developments since 1992 and after 2000 these words too read today like a prophecy. The parallels Belli draws are easily recognizable in the world of language and translation, and here we shall be investigating how translation – and what came to be called the "language industry" – has become inextricably involved with the phenomena of nationalism, cultural identity and especially globalization.

4.2.1   Technology and the translator

> Allow me to introduce myself. My name is Jack, and I am a translator in the United States, although I share many traits and characteristics with colleagues all over the world. Jacks such as myself may be staffers at international organisations, multinational corporations, government agencies, private concerns, or we may be self-employed. We wade through documents that are often highly technical (sometimes barely legible) and translate them into other languages. One day it

might be environmental regulations and the next day the specifications for a desalinator. (Violante-Cassetta 1996: 199)

With those lines Patricia Violante-Cassetta introduced the paper she gave at an international conference on "Problems and Trends in the Teaching of Interpreting and Translation" held in Misano Adriatico in September 1994. With the harmless sounding title "Jack in the Year 2000", this described how, in the mid-1990s, she imagined the daily life of a translator would be at the turn of the millennium (and how student translators should be trained for it). At the time of the conference, her description of "Jack" surrounded by his sophisticated "high-tech" (computer, data banks for terminology, e-mail, internet and MT-systems) sounded like grim science fiction. Reading her contribution ten years later, one can say all this is routine, if not long since outdated (cf. Schmitt 1998: 193 and Stoll 2000). The status quo in the field of technology has been a constantly recurring theme in the translation profession (as shown in many issues of the news magazine *Language International*),[56] it is also excessively ephemeral, and it is not my aim to try and describe it in its relevance for translation at the time of writing. The only statement that I feel can truthfully be made is that the rapid developments in information technology that took place during the 1990s (and are still continuing today) have, again as documented in many publications, radically changed the daily life of the translator and interpreter (cf. 4.1.1).

What is more interesting for our topic is how such developments are perceived and how they affect the study of translation. One crucial aspect is the perception of language itself. The "latest developments" of the late 1990s were drastically described in the German news-magazine *Der Spiegel* on 14th December 1998. "Kommunikation total" could be seen in bold letters on the magazine cover, and the title of the corresponding article was "Der siebte Kontinent" (The seventh continent), though the subject was not geographical or environmental, but the electronic world of the outgoing 20th century: multimedia, Internet, power-books and swatch-talk. The prototype of the age was a software manager seen pedalling away at his keep-fit bike in the local gym, while surfing in the Internet via a monitor attached to the handle-bars. After ten theoretical kilometres he had glanced through three newspapers online, studied the latest stock market prices and read over a dozen e-mails. Instant information, presented in unlimited quantities through various channels and all at the same time – that was seen as communication in the global village of the time, and it still holds today. The sheer amount of the material, the speed with which it must be processed, the remote or virtual

---

56. E.g. 9/1, 9/3 and 9.6 (1997), 10/4 (1998), 12/6 (2000) etc.

character of the participants in the communication act, all of this has changed the way we produce and perceive language and interact with the world around us.

This is the "McWorld" of Benjamin Barber as applied to language and communication. And here there are three main areas that underwent major changes during the 1990s: the nature of the material the consumer has to process, the language in which it is presented, and the concept of text.

For the first two of these areas we can continue Barber's metaphor: our linguistic McWorld presents its own intellectual "fast food", via the Internet, for example. For the translator this means a virtually unlimited quantity of parallel texts as a potential aid in translation (cf. 4.1.2), along with sophisticated websites for information, but at the same time a massive quantity of language which twenty years ago would have been dismissed as defective. This "McLanguage" is to a great extent a particular brand of American English, reduced in stylistic range and subject matter, and – with the aid of abbreviations, icons, acronyms and graphic design – it is tailor-made for fast consumption (cf. 4.2.3). No less drastic however are the changes caused by multimedia in our concept of text and text-types: at one time the products of the communication act over long distances could be neatly classified into spoken and written, into business correspondence (often governed by rigid culture-specific conventions), telegrams, phone calls, memos, reports, and so forth. Multimedia, with their blend of word, image and sound, and the endless possibilities of telecommunication have produced a "homo communicator" used to e-mailing, SMSing, faxing, speaking, listening, reading and viewing (typically with several of these activities going on at the same time), but often without absorbing or ordering the endless snippets of information or the flood of images into a coherent message.

But our present existence does not consist only of such a Brave New McWorld: at the other end of the scale there emerged a brand of "linguistic retribalization" during the 1990s, as in areas of Central and Eastern Europe. With the emergence of new national identities after the demise of communism, individual ethnic groups began rediscovering their cultural heritage and with it the significance of their own mother tongue, particularly if they were in conflict with other groups. A striking example was the emergence of Bosnian, Serbian and Croatian as separate languages (from what had – artificially – developed as Serbo-Croat), despite minimal, again often artificially created linguistic differences. The definition of "language" (as against "language variety") is here not objectively linguistic, and it does not depend on mutual intelligibility: seen in this light, a language (similar to Toury's definition of "translation", see 2.1) is simply what is accepted (and officially recognized) as such, whether from political, ethnic or religious motives. With the languages of "lesser diffusion", and with the particular kind of cultural identity they represent, there arise completely different translation problems and potential,

but they remain as much part of our world today as the "McLanguage" of globalization (cf. Grosman et al. 2000).

In general, we can say that during the 1990s new developments in technology
brought radical changes in the "language material" (formerly understood globally
as "text") with which the translator works. These can be summarized as follows:

1. Due to the vast amount of material transmitted by telecommunication, the
    speech with which it is processed, the increasing use of colloquial forms and
    the tolerance of what were traditionally viewed as language mistakes or typ-
    ing errors, some communication relies simply on basic mutual intelligibility,
    and here translation has to some extent been made obsolete (much commu-
    nication is carried out in lingua franca English, cf. 4.2.3). Formal business
    correspondence has partly been replaced by informal e-mail correspondence,
    much is dealt with by fax and mobile phone.
2. The same necessity for speedy processing and the tolerance of less than
    impeccable language forms, along with the levelling of culture-specific differ-
    ences within the technological "lingua franca", mean a potentially greater role
    for machine translation (e.g. as "gisting", or rough versions of insider infor-
    mation for internal use within a concern).
3. Multimedia communication creates new text types (the audio museum guide
    is one example), some of them multisemiotic, with the verbal signs interact-
    ing with icons, layout tricks, pictorial images and sounds (as can increasingly
    be seen in advertising techniques (cf. 4.2.2).
4. In the area of intercultural communication, requiring not only language
    mediation but heightened cultural expertise, the (human) translator (and
    interpreter) plays an increasingly important role, whereby he/she will take the
    full responsibility for the "final product" (cf. 3.1.1).

In particular the last point will occupy us in the next section. Meanwhile the dominance of technology in our lives has meant that technical texts have come to
occupy over 75% of professional translators, and new areas of work, such as technical writing, content management, multilingual documentation and software
localization have been created (see Gebhardt 1998 and Schmitt 1999, also Göpferich 2002). The basic work profile of the translator has also radically changed: this
has been vividly described, for example, by Stoll, who contrasts the "grey mice in
the back room functioning as walking dictionaries" of former times, with the successful translators of today, "die mit allen verfügbaren Computer-Tools die Verarbeitung riesiger Textmengen Software-Lokalisierung und E-Commerce managen",
(who, with all the available computer tools, manage the processing of vast amounts
of text as software localization and e-commerce) (2000: 258). At the same time
areas like terminology, language technology (with translation memory systems)

and machine translation have continued their own independent rapid development, largely however through neighbouring disciplines like linguistics and computer science and alongside, rather than actually within, Translation Studies. Among all these fleeting variables there is however, as Stoll freely admits, one aspect that has remained constant: the fundamental components of translatorial competence. These can still be specified as proficiency in the language(s) concerned, basic knowledge of the relevant theoretical approaches in Translation Studies, subject area expertise, and cultural competence (cf. Snell-Hornby 1992).

4.2.2   Translation and advertising

In September 1990 I went on a tour of Polish universities to take up contact with colleagues in the new democracies. In Kraków, in the gloomy Soviet-style hotel where I was staying, I found a small leaflet in English and German advertising some offers of a local travel agency. On the cover there was a logo with the information: "'ORBIS' Kraków invites you" and inside there was a text, of which this is the English version:

"ORBIS" Kraków

1.05.- 15.10.90

offers specially prepared programme of regular local excursions:

- – everyday sighseeings – including visits to: Wawel-former residence of Polish kings: Kings' Chambers, Cathedral, Old City, former Jewish district – Kazimierz.
- – excursions to Wieliczka – one of the oldest Salt Mines in Europe on Tue, Wed, Fri, Sun.
- – excursions to Martyrdom Museum in Oswiecim-former concentration camp Auschwitz-Birkenau on Mou, Thu, Sat. (sic!)

Having been "invited" by Orbis to a programme of local excursions, including what must have been meant as "daily sightseeing tours" to monuments of a rich cultural history, the reader is full of positive expectations, and then the eye rests on "Martyrdom Museum". This English phrase is puzzling, and the alliteration seems at first to be a comic device indicating something rather like a Chamber of Horrors at a fair, or maybe like the "London Dungeon". Reading on, one discovers with dismay that what is meant is the former concentration camp of Auschwitz. This disastrously misleading effect is however not merely due to a stylistic device, it was caused by a primitive translation error. From the Polish name "Muzeum Męczeństwa i Martyrologii Oświęcim-Brenzinka" the words "Muzeum ... Martyrologii" were thoughtlessly transcoded into English. What is meant in the Polish name is however not a museum (as a building exhibiting objects of cultural interest). Neither are we concerned with "martyrdom": the Polish word connotes the history of suffering and self-sacrifice that characterized Poland for centuries. What is left (and shown) of the concentration camp in Auschwitz is in English usually called a memorial (in German it is known as *Mahn- und Gedenkstätte*). After I drew attention to the unfortunate effect of the English text in the leaflet, it was immediately withdrawn.

In 1997 I was back in Kraków for a TEMPUS programme, this time staying in a new hotel in Western style. Orbis was still advertising, now with posters and brightly coloured, lavishly illustrated brochures, one offering tours "Round and about Kraków", including the town of Oświęcim – with its "State Museum of Martyrdom". The additional information on what this exactly referred to was virtually useless. The luring advertising methods together with the misleading translation once again created an effect totally different from the grim reality involved. The translator trainers who attended the TEMPUS seminar were appalled, and as one of their assignments produced their own (German) text encouraging foreigners to visit Auschwitz: it was simple, without any advertising gags, and largely informative – the bare facts being considered motivation enough.[57]

Advertising has become an ubiquitous feature of modern life, particularly since the Second World War and particularly in richer capitalist countries. With globalization, with international markets, multinational concerns and mass tourism it also became an important translation issue, albeit one that has still been given inadequate attention by many companies involved (cf. Framson 2005). The basic issue at stake is the clash of interests already addressed by Benjamin Barber: on the one hand the global conformity of "McWorld" trying to reach consumers worldwide, and on the other hand culture-specific interests, religious, ethical and legal differences, not to mention the problems of language and cultural identity, which all complicate communication.

During the course of the 1990s there developed an increased awareness for the problems of advertising and its potential both for Translation Studies and for the development of new job profiles. In 1994 Candace Séguinot pointed out the multiple issues involved in the translation of advertisements and the varied fields of competence demanded of the translator:

> In translating advertising, translators are expected to take responsibility for the final form of an advertisement. Globalization of the translation business sometimes means providing full marketing services in addition to translation and interpreting. Therefore, in the marketing of goods and services across cultural boundaries, an understanding of culture and semiotics that goes well beyond both

---

57.   This text is reproduced in Snell-Hornby 2003b: 92.

> language and design is involved. Translators need to understand the basics of mar-
> keting; they need to know the legal jurisdictions of the market; they must know
> how cultural differences affect marketing; they must be aware of constraints
> placed by the form and functions of the source text, and they must be able to inter-
> pret the visual elements which are of key importance in advertising. Going global
> successfully means taking control of the final product, researching the cultural
> and marketing aspects, and making sure the translation conforms to legal con-
> straints. All this shows that the range of knowledge and skills needed by the pro-
> fession of the translator is changing. (Séguinot 1994: 249)

Smith and Klein-Braley (1997) emphasize the range of theoretical and practical
issues involved in translating advertising texts, which provides material both for
research and translator training:

> For translation studies, the translation of advertisements provides us with a
> microcosm of almost all the prosodic, pragmatic, syntactic, textual, semiotic and
> even ludic difficulties to be encountered in translating. By analysing such short
> but complex and structurally complete texts we can derive valuable insights into
> possible strategies and methods for dealing with these phenomena in other longer
> texts, whether literary or non-literary. (1997: 173)

On the basis of a corpus of translated print advertisements, they then identify five
main strategies for translation:

1. No change: retain both graphics and text.
2. Export advertisement: retain logo, slogan in original, play on positive stereotypes of source culture, where necessary add copy in target language.
3. Straight translation.
4. Adaptation: keep visuals, change text slightly or significantly.
5. Revision: keep visuals, write new text. (1997: 182–183)

The strategies depend on diverse variables, such as target group, brand name and
the product involved. Strategies (1) and (2) are used for items like perfumes or soft
drinks with strong brand names, the main target groups being young people and
businessmen. Straight translation (3) is the least preferred strategy at the level of
international marketing, because it fails to adjust to the cultural demands of a new
market, whereas adaptation (4) is described as the dominant strategy used by
international advertisers. Revision (5) was described in the analysis as "problemat-
ical". (1997: 183)

    It is significant however that precisely the third strategy of straight translation
is the one found in lower level texts such as hotel brochures or tourist information,
usually by non-professionals and with the type of linguistic inadequacy shown in
the Polish example above. The fact that with menus or hotel brochures the result

can often be seen as hilarious (see examples from Spain and Brazil in Snell-Hornby 1999) does nothing to detract from the harm such shoddy work causes the repute of the translating profession. A simple solution would be better training and better pay for the translator – and more attention from Translation Studies. In an early study (see 1992a) I analyzed a corpus of written advertising texts in German and English to identify linguistic and cultural differences. In both languages clear, terse, rhythmical prose was predominant, with simple syntax, whether in the form of complete sentences or block language (cf. Quirk and Greenbaum (1973: 205). However, the actual devices used to achieve this end differed: in German block language, nominal forms dominated, whereas English favoured verb phrases. Both however favoured unmarked forms of the verb, in English the imperative ("Save time and money"), in German the infinitive ("Jetzt unverbindlich anfordern...").[58] This means that in English advertisements the reader or user was more often implicitly addressed than in German. In both language communities common use was made of devices such as wordplay, metaphor and fixed idioms, while in their concrete realization such devices are of course language-specific, ruling out a "straight translation". Finally, in both language communities local and cultural associations were frequent, and as these are culture-specific in their concrete realization, they too provide a problem for the translator. We could add to that further differences in advertising conventions: the part played by humour, irony or sentiment, the portrayal of social stereotypes or the use of "aggressive" techniques – all of which are culture-specific and change with time and place.

The lack of advertisements – whether TV commercials or billboards on the streets – used to be a conspicuous feature of communist countries, but the years after 1989 brought changes, as the early attempt of the Polish travel agency indicated. During the 1990s we could then witness the development of a completely new genre of text, alongside new markets for translation, in the countries of what was once called Eastern Europe. The former vacuum was filled, not only by linguistic innovations but by the influence of Western values and models – again the "McWorld culture" described in 4.2. Zuzana Jettmarova, Maria Piotrowska and Ieva Zauberga (1997) investigated and compared corpus data of print advertisements and television commercials translated during the early 1990s from and into Czech, Polish and Latvian. As a major obstacle for efficient translation they identified not only language problems, but primarily what they called "cross-cultural

---

58. Since then however imperative forms have become increasingly common in German operative texts, though they are still not as frequent as in (British) English.

unawareness" (1997: 185), whereby literal translation (as in the Polish example) played a major part. They summarize the situation in the 1990s as follows:

> The present decade – a period of incredible expansion of the advertising industry in the East European markets – is a scene of obvious foreign (i.e. West European and American) impact. As a genre representing very strong correlation between the text and culture, as consumer-oriented and overtly persuasive texts recommending not only goods for sale but also attitudes, advertisements produce and are themselves the result of cultural stereotyping. Translated advertisements import social values and often unrecognised beliefs, as well as linguistic patterns. New text type conventions are being created through the adoption of foreign textual features, partly mediated by literal translations, which sometimes cause a clash of linguistic and cultural norms. (1997: 186)

Even in the long-standing consumer societies of the West however, cultural stereotyping is a conspicuous feature, particularly of advertising material, but also of attitudes towards other cultural communities in general. Resch (2000) investigates developments in advertising in the globalized world of the 1990s, emphasizing the viewpoint of the recipient, who meanwhile often finds the surfeit of advertisements a nuisance and will only respond to those felt to be original or of very high quality. Resch discusses the issue as being intertextual and multisemiotic, citing the "iconic turn" and the "fragmentary text reception" (described in 4.2.1) as crucial elements in our perception and acceptance of advertising material today (whether in print or via multimedia).

The reception of advertising is not only culture-specific but also essentially holistic:

> Die einzelnen Gestaltungselemente (Bild, Sprache, Ton etc.) verschmelzen erst bei Betrachtung des Gesamttextes zu einer sinnhaften Werbebotschaft, das Verstehen ist zu einem sehr großen Maß von der von den TextverwenderInnen geleisteten Integration der multisemiotischen Textelemente zu einem Ganzen abhängig. (2000: 183)

> (The individual components (image, language, sound etc.) only merge into a meaningful message when the text is perceived in its entirety, understanding is to a great extent dependent on the users' ability to integrate the multisemiotic components into a complete whole.)

The interaction of visual elements and verbal text, including the culture-specific perception of layout and typography, has already been described by Jürgen Schopp (1994, 1998, 2005), and this is especially crucial in advertising. Even more decisive is often the interaction of slogan and visual material, especially in the form of pictures. Resch (2000: 188–189) describes an advertisement of a well-known telecommunications company in a glossy publicity brochure as a drastic example of how even expensive material can misfire if its producers lack basic linguistic and cultural competence. A young man (a "stereotypical" Austrian in traditional Alpine costume) is shown standing in front of the Tower of London, using his mobile phone. The slogan runs "My home is where my handy is". The various cultural stereotypes juxtaposed here may be interesting (e.g. the allusion to the phrase "My home is my castle", frequently cited by Austrians with reference to the English), but they are not so eye-catching as elements of the body language. The young man's hand, the one not used for phoning, is conspicuously placed in his trouser pocket close to the private parts of his anatomy, where, one could read from the advertisement, he has his home. The producers of this material must have been native speakers of German, where "Handy" means "mobile phone", and they were obviously unaware that it does not have that sense in English. From the failed efforts of the Polish travel agency to the unintentional comic effect of the sophisticated multinational telecommunications company, we have come, so it seems, full circle.[59]

4.2.3   The empire of English

An empire, in the definition of Charles Tilly, is "a large composite polity linked to a central power by indirect rule" (1997: 3). Standard examples are the Roman, Habsburg and Chinese Empires, and for our purposes the already mentioned British Empire – but also all those areas of the world such as Latin America, the Maghreb and Indo-China that were once under colonial rule. Tilly emphasizes in his account the military and fiscal control exercised by the central power. However, there is another element, common to all the above examples: one of the most deep-seated elements of colonial rule that remains long after the empires have gone, is the cultural component with the legacy of language. Within this context I have distinguished between a *dominant language,* which is forced on the subjugated people along with the foreign world-view and culture (cf. 3.2.1), and a *lingua franca,* which is more or less freely accepted as a system of communication for mutual understanding (Snell-Hornby 1997c). In the case of newly formed nations after independence, the former dominant language was usually established either as a lingua franca or even as an official language. At the same time however the new communities see their indigenous language as a means of expressing their individual cultural identity, an essential factor one cannot ignore as a natural reaction to any form of foreign domination, and an important factor for Translation Studies.. Examples

---

59. From the publishers of the volume I was informed that the telecommunications company concerned, on being informed of Resch's comments, refused permission to have the advertisement reproduced in her article or for their identity to be revealed.

of this development are India, and more recently South Africa, with numerous local or regional languages co-existing with English as an official language.

During the course of the 1990s it soon became a truism that within the context of global discourse, English, for better or for worse, had assumed the key position: this phenomenon has been frequently described, especially by British scholars (e.g. Crystal 1997). The omnipresence of English as a consequence of "McWorld" has meanwhile reached such proportions that, from the role of the freely accepted lingua franca, one might say it has reverted to being a dominant language (analogous to the "McWorld culture" bemoaned by Gioconda Belli) used nolens volens by people and institutions in various parts of the globe for economic or political survival (or profit). This is the "indirect rule" of our Empire of English, and it has had deep-seated consequences for translation.

As with French, Spanish and the languages of other former colonial powers, the role of English as a world language originated in its former role as the dominant language of the British Empire, but standard British English, far more so than other former colonial languages, has diversified into numerous regional and local varieties or "new Englishes" (cf. 3.2.1). Its role as the leading international language however, is due on the one hand to the world-wide domination of North American technology and culture (cf. 4.2) and on the other to the fact that its basic grammar and core vocabulary can be relatively easily acquired for everyday conversation as needed for superficial communication by speakers of other languages. This latter factor is coupled with a structural flexibility in the language itself and a general policy of non-puristic openness among the English-speaking cultural institutions. This has not only encouraged the development of the many regional varieties, but has paved the way for the use of English as a less than impeccable common denominator for communication (maybe comprehensible but often full of local interferences) by native speakers of other languages world-wide – "McLanguage", as discussed above (cf. 4.2.1). A counter-example to prove the point is French: despite massive government-sponsored promotion for the French language, the puristic, normative policy of French institutions and academies have helped the language to preserve much of its characteristic correctness (and hence its identity as a language of culture, despite the often reluctantly accepted Anglicisms), but its role as a world language has dwindled, a process that was already in progress in the 1990s. In the *Financial Times* of 9th February 1998, Dominique Moisi, Deputy Director of the Paris-based *Institut Français des Relations Internationales*, made this admission:

> The French should admit they have lost the language battle to 'American English', a less sophisticated version of the language of Shakespeare. To keep the content (if not the language) and the message (if not the medium), the French must learn

from the vital US qualities of openness and flexibility. (Quote of the month in *Language International* 10:2, 1998: 8)

In 1997, in an article entitled "Which is the world's most important language?", Fernando Navarro cited some vital statistics of the time, whereby English was the official language of 52 countries, with a total population of more than 1700 million. Not the number of native speakers is decisive – Chinese has twice as many of these (cf. Stoll 2000: 235) – but above all the number of those with English as a second or working language.

Another crucial factor for the role of languages in the globalized world of today is their economic power (calculated by multiplying the number of speakers in a given country by the per capita GNP, then adding together the results for all countries where the language is spoken). According to Navarro:

> ... the world's most economically powerful languages are those of the world's three leading economic powers: the United States, Japan and Germany, respectively. More than 60% of the world economic production is accounted for by speakers of English, Japanese and German; if we add Spanish and French, this percentage increases to 75%. It is very noticeable that of the six economically most important languages in the world, five are European languages. (1997: 6)

As far as English is concerned, it is important to note that one half of the world's native speakers of English (and three-quarters of the economic power attributed to the English language) are concentrated in a single country, the United States of America. While the statistics may have meanwhile shifted, the proportions remain basically similar, and this too, in a metaphorical sense, constitutes the "Empire of English" (see too Stoll 2000: 236–239).

In Europe however the scene is somewhat different. Europe is essentially multilingual, and the individual languages – especially those of "lesser diffusion", cf. Grosman et al 2000 – are proud hallmarks of cultural identity. The language with the most native speakers in Europe is German,[60] which in Navarro's article was also Europe's language with the most economic power. However, in Europe the issue of language goes far beyond questions of economic power or numbers of speakers; it is also a geopolitical issue and one fraught with historical complica-

---

60. This is still the case at the time of writing. A diagram published in the Austrian daily newspaper *Der Standard* of 22.11.2004 shows the following EU statistics (native speakers in millions): German 88.1, English 58.0, French 55.2, Italian 63.0, Polish 37.3, Spanish 28.6, Dutch 19.5 (with Greek, Portuguese, Hungarian, Czech, Swedish and others together amounting to 52.6). Second languages show a marked difference between the former EU (15 member-states), with 14% speaking English, 19% French, 10% German and 7% Spanish, and the enlarged EU since May 2004 with 23% speaking Russian, 21% English, 17% German and 3% French.

tions, including the historic rivalry between English and French, the proud ambitions of the Spanish, and the longstanding reluctance to accept any kind of dominance of German (despite its historical role as the major lingua franca of Central Europe). At the same time Europe, in the guise of the European Union, is emerging as one of the world's major economic entities, one with the largest translation service in the world and a declared policy of democratic multilingualism (for an account of the practical consequences of this see Dollerup 1996). For internal purposes however, French (for historical reasons), English (for practical reasons, cf. Dollerup 2000) and German (despite the reluctance) are already used as working languages and as the chief means of communication.

Nevertheless, whether within the institutions of the European Union, through business transactions, mass tourism, cultural exchanges or whatever, in Europe both languages and cultures are constantly in contact. This intensive intercultural communication has led to what Schäffner and Adab (1997) defined as the hybrid text. This is not identical with the postcolonial hybrid text discussed under 3.2.1 (although there are common features). In Schäffner and Adab's definition, hybrid texts result from a (deliberate) translation process and show features "that somehow seem 'out of place'/'strange'/'unusual' for the receiving culture" (1997: 325). They are characterized by features (vocabulary, syntax, style etc.) which clash with target language conventions and are "somehow contrary to the norms of the target language and culture" (1997:327). They also include EU texts however, which do not necessarily involve (intended) translation:

> In the process of establishing political unity, linguistic expressions are levelled to a common (low) denominator. Eurotexts reflect a Eurojargon, i.e. a reduced vocabulary, meanings that tend to be universal, reduced inventory of grammatical forms (…)

> Acceptance is due to the limited communicative functions of the texts. EU texts, for example, function within the Community within which they are created (e.g. for the staff, or for meetings pf the respective bodies). This means that there are clearly defined user needs. The multinational EU institutions as such are the target culture, hybrid texts are formative elements in creating a (truly) supranational culture.[61] (1997: 327–328)

This creation of a supranational "culture" through "Eurojargon" mainly affects all three working languages, but especially texts in English. It is reminiscent of the global and rootless "McLanguage" described above, likewise reduced in stylistic and lexical range and open to all kinds of interference features. Like the postcolo-

---

61. Compare this with the concept of 'discourse system' later suggested by Koskinen and discussed in 6.

nial hybrid texts, "Eurotexts" blend features of different languages, but unlike the postcolonial (literary) texts they are a reduction rather than an exploitation of language potential (cf. discussion of Coseriu in 1.2).

The same phenomenon can be observed in other international organizations, as for example the United Nations. As head of the Arabic Section of the UN Translations Service in Vienna, Mohammed Didaoui investigated the role of translators within the organization and the communication interferences that arose (Didaoui 1996). A major problem with UN source texts is that they are usually compiled jointly by a number of authors who are not native speakers and are often, strictly speaking, linguistically defective. Here is a typical example:

> *Note on Morocco's Power Programme*
>
> Organisation structures for implementation of nuclear programme
>
> 1. *The National Electricity Board (ONE)*
>
> The National Electricity Board, being a public industrial and trade authority, has the monopoly of electricity generation and transmission in Morocco. In this connection it is designated as the owner and future operator of any nuclear power-stations to be set up. This is the framework within which ONE, within the assistance of IAEA, has prepared the first planning studies, which will be examined and taken further under the agreement with France, and has also started to collect information and data on site choices. A special study has also been made of present population distribution in the area where a nuclear power-station may be built.

This text is based on material in French, as can be seen from the syntactic interference, it is a hybrid text in the sense of Schäffner and Adab, "McLanguage" in our metaphorical use, and it shows what happens to English as "world property" beyond the "control of native speakers" (cf. Widdowson 1994). In the opinion of some English-speaking translators I have consulted, it should be transedited before it can be translated. (See Snell-Hornby 2000a: 19 for one such version.). Some Spanish colleagues on the other hand saw no linguistic problems in translating it, as the Spanish grammar structures concerned are very similar to the French and can be easily transcoded. Despite that however, the text still has its problems that lie beyond language: it requires some degree of subject-area competence and insider knowledge on the part of the translator, under the circumstances probably available through the cooperation with colleagues in the United Nations department (cf. 2.3).

Connected with all this is a development of the 1990s that cannot be ignored when discussing translation: the vast increase in the quantity of translation work, especially in non-literary fields, and not only as regards English (cf Schmitt 1999: 15). According to Stoll (2000: 247), between 1994 and 1997 the language industries in Europe increased their output by 55%, whereas the number of translators employed only rose by 18%, indicating a rapid increase in productivity by using electronic aids – a trend that has meanwhile continued.

Another observable trend is the increase of publications and conferences entirely in English – even within the discipline of Translation Studies. Using one internationally known language to reduce organization work and costs makes economic sense, but unlike congresses in, for example, medicine or physics, language in Translation Studies is not merely a neutral means of communication but also part of the problem under discussion. Conferences on translation conducted solely in English favour those participants with English as mother tongue or working language (whether in Departments of English or translation institutes), who will tend to talk either about English material with English examples or else those from foreign languages contrasted to English, whereas those scholars working in language pairs without English have other fields of interest and are quite often reluctant to join in the debate at all. Similarly, scholarly journals accepting only contributions in English tend to consist largely of material (even where not presented by Anglo-American authors) with at least a significant relation to English-language problems. The result is that what is generalized as "the discipline" may well be one area of Translation Studies as viewed from a "global" Anglo-American perspective – another facet of the "Empire of English".

It may help at least to be sensitized to the problem and to be aware that English is a multi-facetted phenomenon. Summarizing our conclusions so far, we can make a basic distinction between three broad domains. Firstly, there is International English, the free-floating lingua franca that has lost track of its original cultural identity, its idioms, its hidden connotations, its grammatical subtleties, and has become a reduced standardized form of language for supra-national communication – whether this is the "McLanguage" of a globalized "McWorld" or the "Eurospeak" of a multilingual continent. This has led to the "indirect rule" of our "Empire of English" with the ever-expanding language industry, and here technological aids will continue to play a central part (4.2.1). This is the language every professional translator should know at least passively if s/he is to survive in the competive international market of today, but in the knowledge that it is merely a lingua franca. Secondly, there is still the rich language of culture with its great literary potential (in the sense of Coseriu, cf. 1.3), both in its "standard" form and in the many regional varieties, each an expression of a specific cultural identity with its own idioms, metaphors and cultural allusions. The "regional forms" have already been referred to in the area of dialogue interpreting, but they are equally significant for any translation involving cross-cultural communication as a whole. And finally, there are those literary hybrid forms as we have already discussed in postcolonial literature (3.2.1), forging a new language "in between", but altered to suit their new surroundings. These are a more recent phenomenon, "striking back" at the "Empire of English" and steadily gaining territory of their own.

4.3   Venuti's foreignization: a new paradigm?

The topic of the global domination of English today links up with a notion that developed into a household word in literary Translation Studies during the 1990s, and at the same time it takes us back full circle to our point of departure: Schleiermacher and the German Romantic Age (see 1.1) as presented in English by André Lefevere (1977). We may recall that in this version the two "roads" open to Schleiermacher's "genuine translator" were described as follows:

> Either the translator leaves the author in peace, as much as possible, and moves the reader towards him; or he leaves the reader in peace, as much as possible, and moves the author towards him. (Lefevere 1977: 74)

Lawrence Venuti (1991, but especially 1995) takes up Schleiermacher's dichotomy as a central issue and draws the following conclusions:

> Admitting (with qualifications like "as much as possible") that translation can never be completely adequate to the foreign text, Schleiermacher allowed the translator to choose between a **domesticating** method, an **ethnocentric reduction** of the foreign text to target-language cultural values, bringing the author back home, and a **foreignizing** method, an **ethnodeviant presure** on those values to register the linguistic and cultural difference of the foreign text, sending the reader abroad. (1995: 20, emphasis added)

The German dichotomy of *Verfremdung* (moving the reader towards the author) and *Entfremdung* (moving the author towards the reader), discussed by Vermeer as "verfremdendes" (alienating) and "angleichendes" (assimilating) translation (Vermeer 1994a), have been rendered here as a "foreignizing" and a "domesticating" method, and as such they have now become standard terminology in English Translation Studies. However, while Schleiermacher certainly made it clear that he preferred moving the reader towards the author, there is nothing in his lecture to indicate that the one method involved evaluations such as "ethnodeviant pressure" versus "ethnocentric reduction" – recognizable as the language of an English-speaking intellectual of the outgoing 20th century. Venuti even intensifies his tone:

> I want to suggest that insofar as foreignizing translation seeks to restrain the eth-nocentric violence of translation, it is highly desirable today, a strategic cultural intervention in the current state of world affairs, pitched against the hegemonic English-language nations and the unequal cultural exchanges in which they engage their global others. Foreignizing translation in English can be a form of

resistance against ethnocentrism and racism, cultural narcissism and imperialism, in the interests of democratic geopolitical relations. (1995: 20)

The notion of "foreignizing translation" is thus made to fit into the framework and
context of late 20th century translation ethics, as seen from a specifically Anglo-
American perspective. Apart from Lefevere, a further "mediator" between the
thinking of Schleiermacher and Venuti was the French theorist Antoine Berman,
in particular his book on German Romanticism *L'Épreuve de l'Étranger: Culture et
traduction dans l'Allemagne romantique* (The trial of the foreign: Culture and
translation in Romantic Germany) (Berman 1984, see too Berman 2000). The
result, as Marilyn Gaddis Rose aptly put it, was that "norms of the American criticism vanguard turned to Continental philosophy, especially German hermeneutics as filtered through French poststructuralism" (1996: 62). From this
perspective Venuti writes his "history of translation", whereby "foreignizing"
translations (e.g. Newman's Homer) are judged as being fundamentally good, and
"domesticating" ones (i.e. "fluent" translations making the translator "invisible", as
in Matthew Arnold's Homer) are seen to be fundamentally bad. As the emotive
terms "ethnocentric violence", "racism", "narcissism" and "imperialism" indicate,
Venuti's language is often provocative and polarizing: in his view (in contrast to
Vermeer), "domestication" exerts violence on the source culture.

In the basic message he wants to get across Venuti is certainly justified. His
actual topic is the unfavourable position of (literary) translators in the Anglo-
American world (including copyright legislation and inadequate pay), and he
points out that by creating fluent and idiomatic English versions ("domesticated"
translations, in fact), they remain "invisible" and repress the foreign element in the
source text.[62] Venuti pleads for the translator's visibility through foreignation, as
by using archaic terms or idiosyncratic word-order that preserve the "foreignness"
of the source text (whether this really produces the desired effect is another issue).
This too must however be understood in the context of the hegemony of English
in the modern globalized world (4.2.3), and Venuti has a strong case where his
demands refer specifically to the Anglo-American market. But his wording is fundamental and generalizing, as against his "history of translation", which, as Pym
aptly points out, is selective and highly coloured:

> The best thing about Venuti's guided tour of English-language translators and the-
> orists is that most of them are tagged with notes on their political connections,
> religious beliefs and occasional dalliances. All the bad ones are associated with lib-
> eral humanism, imperialism, sexism and/or individualism. The few good ones

---

62.   This may explain Venuti's attitude to Helen Lowe-Porter discussed in 3.3.

generally oppose such nasties, in the same way as they oppose fluent translations. (1996: 172)

Nonetheless, since Venuti's book appeared in 1995 the controversy of domestication vs. foreignization has taken a central position in the English-speaking Translation Studies debate. The two notions have spread like memes in Chesterman's sense, as attributed to Venuti, and have largely lost contact with Schleiermacher and the world of German Romanticism – a very different one from the world today. As we saw above (1.1), Schleiermacher himself stressed the importance of understanding an author "through the prism of his nationality and the age in which he lives" (Rübberdt and Salevsky 1997: 302). This applies, not only to his two "methods of translation", but also to other terms such as "half-breeds" (*Blendlinge*) or "nation", which were used from the viewpoint of the early 19th century and cannot be judged according to the criteria of our modern world. It is significant too that Venuti's ideas are most cogently disputed where English is not the target language and the target culture is not Anglo-American, as has been shown by Paloposki and Oittinen (2000) for translations into Finnish (see too Tymoczko 1999). And this is precisely the point: despite his own theory, Venuti has as it were subjected Schleiermacher's notions to an ethnocentric reduction (or cannibalization?) and – as a translator all too visible – "domesticated" them to suit the Anglo-American planetary consciousness of the outgoing 20th century. As such this is cannot be called a new paradigm, but rather evolves new notions from old concepts, and these – despite a fundamental, if not universal claim – refer to the specific situation of the "hegemonic English-language nations" of today. In challenging the hegemonic role of English, the position of translators and the conditions of their work, Venuti is absolutely justified – but the solution to all these problems does not lie merely in "foreignizing" translations. For the cross-cultural communication of today, Schleiermacher's maxim, which was used for the scholars of the time with reference to translating from Classical Antiquity, is simply inadequate.

If we consider the examples of literary prose discussed above, the brief passage from Rushdie's *Midnight's Children* (3.2.1) and the excerpt from Amy Tan's *The Joy Luck Club* (3.3.1) in German translation, also the opening lines of *Der Zauberberg* (3.3) in English translation, we see that "fluency" and an ensuing "invisibility" of the translator was not the real problem. In Rushdie's own hybrid text the English had already been "foreignized" at various levels, the "norm" of the English language already creatively extended in Coseriu's sense to exploit the language potential; similarly Amy Tan creates English structures to reflect the use of Chinese speech as against the same speaker's faulty English. Both the German translations are formally correct, but wooden and one-dimensional rather than fluent. Because of this the dialogue in particular does not match the individual characters of the two speakers concerned, and it is the ensuing incoherence that makes the text "visible" as a translation and presents the basic problem. As was already established with the first few lines of Lowe-Porter's *The Magic Mountain*, they focus on content at the expense of the inner structuring of the text. Strategies for giving expression to these structures could well have been developed, but, as may have emerged from the passages discussed here, they would certainly go beyond merely "foreignizing" the language of the translation.

CHAPTER 5

At the turn of the millenium

State of the discipline

Looking back over the 1990s we can say that it was a time of consolidation in the new discipline of Translation Studies. Fomerly neglected fields were given close attention, the most important possibly being the history of translation and inter- preting – Delisle and Woodsworth 1995, Part II of Baker 1998 and various vol- umes by Vermeer (e.g. 1996, 1996a, 1996b, 2000 and 2000a) – but also translation for stage and screen (3.1.3), or the translation of children's literature (e.g. Oittinen 1993, Marx 1997). Various aspects of Translation Studies were discovered as new fields of research, such as creativity (Kussmaul 2000) or culture-specific facets like humour (Mateo 1995), wordplay (Delabastita 1993) or allusion (Leppihalme 1994). Blank spots were discovered on the disciplinary map, giving rise to a num- ber of pioneering studies as on opera translation (Kaindl 1995) and in particular the various fields of dialogue interpreting (4.1.1). The training of translators and interpreters and the development of new curricula more adequate for the needs of the time became a major field of interest (Dollerup and Loddegaard 1992 and 1994, Hönig 1995, Kussmaul 1995, Dollerup and Appel 1996, Wilss 1996, Freihoff 2001). It was a decade when handbooks, bibliographies and encyclopaedias were compiled (Chan and Pollard 1995, Forstner 1995, Baker 1998, Snell-Hornby et al. 1998). Associations like the European Society for Translation Studies (EST) were founded, new series were devoted to Translation Studies (such as the Benjamins Translation Library or *Studien zur Translation*), new scholarly journals came into existence (*The Translator* in Britain, *Perspectives* in Denmark, *Across* in Hungary), and beside them news magazines like *Language International*[63] and *Language Today* were produced for all those engaged in the "language professions". This gave rise to intensifed interest in special languages, technology and terminology, lead- ing to publications like the *International Who's Who in Translation and Terminol- ogy* (Prado et al. 1995).

---

63. This was created in 1989 to succeed *Language Monthly* (launched by Geoffrey Kingscott in 1983), and was continued until December 2002 (cf. 5.1).

The developments in Translation Studies through the second half of the last century follow clearly the various trends of the times, and parallels can be seen in other disciplines closely linked to it. One good example is Cognitive Science, which first arose in reaction to behaviourism, hence also after the Second World War. There followed an approach called the "computational-representational under-standing of the mind" which shows parallels with Chomsky's Transformational Generative Grammar and the checklist theory (cf. 3.3.1), and this was to become as dominant in cognitive studies as Chomsky's theory was in linguistics. In reaction to this there emerged a third approach known as "parallel distributed processing" or connectionism, which emphasized the associations evoked in the mind by familiar situations, clearly correlating with Rosch's (1973) prototype theory in psychology and with Fillmore's scenes-and-frames semantics (1.3, 3.3.1). The fourth approach, known as "situated or embedded cognition", arose in Cognitive Science in the 1980s, and is seen as a reorientation similar to that in Translation Studies during the same decade. An interaction between the two disciplines then developed dur-ing the 1990s (cf. Wilss 1988, Risku 1998 and 2000). The tendency towards the end of the century, and not only in Translation Studies, was clearly away from strict compartmentalization and towards interdisciplinary cooperation, away from rigid ideology and towards real-life experience (see too the discussion of Cultural Stud-ies in 5.3). The turn of the century, and the role of Translation Studies in it, was (as Bassnett and Lefevere had already predicted in 1990) awaited with high optimism and great expectations. This chapter will attempt to see how far, in the first five years of that century, they have been fulfilled.

5.1   The U-turns – back to square one?

Like many emerging disciplines, translation studies suffers from at least two child-hood diseases: one is that of always reinventing the wheel, and the other, concom-itant with the first, is that of not reading what other people have written, either in the name of (sometimes proud) insularity, or else because one does not even sus-pect that what they might have written might constitute any important contribu-tion to the field. Add to this that many books on translation still claim, with predictable regularity, to be the first to address whatever it is they address. They are aided and abetted in this by the third childhood disease besetting translation studies, namely that of ignoring its own history. This deplorable fact explains why books that would have fit the intellectual climate thirty years ago continue to be published today.

Translation studies would greatly benefit from a more unified discourse, one which all researchers in the field might view as relevant, if not immediately cen-tral, to their own endeavour. It is my contention that such a discourse can, in the final analysis, only be culture-based (which also implies the absence of exclusives aimed at any specific types of translation), that it should fulfill expectations with which texts aspiring to the scientific are usually approached, and that it should contribute to the advancement of knowledge in the field, rather than restating what is already known. (Lefevere 1993: 229–230)

Thus André Lefevere opened a review article in 1993, looking at three (then) new books, two of which became fairly well known, but none of which need concern us at this point. What is more relevant here is that precisely the same words could well have been written ten years later, looking at various publications which appeared after 2000.

In his Preface to Michaela Wolf's anthology of Brazilian essays of 1997, Hans Vermeer expressed similar views to those just quoted:

Wie überall wird (…) heute mehr denn je publiziert, doch wenig wirklich Neues vorgebracht. Manchmal hat man sogar den Eindruck, es sei gerade ein Moment in der modernen Übersetzungshistorie, in dem das Pendel wieder zur Tradition zurückschwingt. Vielleicht fehlt es vielen Praktikern und Theoretikern einfach an der Zeit, sich intensiv mit all den Publikationen, die auf den Markt kommen, auseinanderzusetzen. Kurioserweise sind ja gerade die heute verfügbaren Kommunikationsmöglichkeiten *auch* zu einem Hindernis für eingehende Beschäftigung mit Neuerungen geworden. Man muss 100 Veröffentlichungen lesen, um festzustellen, welches ein Prozent weiterführt. (Vermeer 1997a: 10)

(As everywhere more is published nowadays than ever, but very little is produced that is really new. Sometimes one even gets the impression that this is a time in the modern history of translation when the pendulum is swinging back to the tradition. Perhaps many practitioners and theoreticians simply don't have the time to occupy themselves intensively with all the publications on the market. Curiously enough, it is precisely those means of communication available today that have *also* become a hindrance for intensive preoccupation with innovations. You have to read 100 publications to discover which one per cent takes you further.)

This impression, and particularly the observation that the pendulum is swinging back to the past, was for me confirmed at the close of the Third EST Congress in 2001, when there was an informal general session to give participants the opportunity to comment on the contents and results of the conference. The younger generation in particular were invited to present their opinions. Most striking for anyone familiar with the course of the debate over the last thirty years was the tendency, noticeable both in the topics of the conference programme and in the comments of that closing session, "Back to Linguistics" (Cf. Snell-Hornby 2002).

Is the translatorial wheel to be reinvented yet again? Despite the promise of "new tools and new methods" (Chesterman 2002), it might seem so indeed. This suspicion is reinforced by studies resurrecting the age-old debate on the concept of equivalence (Koller 1995, Halverson 1997), or reintroducing prototype semantics

(Halverson 1999), which as we have seen above (3.3.1) has been extensively discussed in Translation Studies since the early 1980s. Even the use of computer corpora (4.1.2) can be seen as yet another borrowing from linguistics, and with the theme of "translation universals" (Toury 2001, Mauranen and Kujamäki 2004) another favourite concept of Transformational Generative Grammar, so eloquently dismantled by George Steiner in the 1970s (1.2), has been resuscitated into a new academic existence. All in all, it seems that the much feted emancipation of Translation Studies from the discipline of linguistics is embarking on a phase of retrogression. With such fruitful ground as has been marked out in Chapters 2, 3 and 4 above, and with such exciting prospects ahead, what can be the motivation for a "return to linguistics"?

One answer may lie in the academic tradition or school of thought of the individual scholars concerned. "Translation" is still frequently accommodated as a section within traditionally structured language and literature departments – very frequently Departments of English, cf. 4.2.3 – and is hence automatically seen in relation to one or both of these two branches. The functional models on the other hand (2.2, 2.3, 2.4) sought to overcome the traditional thought structures and do not go back to the language/literature divide. While accepting the risk that a broad generalization of this kind involves, I can in fact detect a clear division emerging between the (increasingly dominant) English-speaking debate on the one hand, and other language communities, such as the academic debate carried on in German publications, on the other. What is most striking is that those advocating or implying a "return to linguistics" in the English-speaking debate mostly ignore (or misunderstand) the functional models along with their potential for an independent discipline of Translation Studies.

Sometimes this is explicit and deliberate. Halverson, for example, in her discussion of the concept of equivalence, makes the following statement:

> A similar focus on features of the target system, more specifically the goal/aim/
> intention of the translation, its scopos, underlies another dominant theoretical
> contribution to translation studies, i.e. scopos theory. This theory (…) will not be
> discussed here. What is important to note is that this theory too entails a displace-
> ment of the equivalence concept to a subordinate position as a constraining ele-
> ment in certain kinds of translation only. (1997: 217)

Some reason for not discussing the skopos theory is given in a footnote commenting on the "main lines of demarcation between what are most commonly considered the two main areas in the field,[64] i..e. the 'linguistically oriented school' and its

---

64. I.e. of Translation Studies.

counterpart, the historical-descriptive group" (Halverson 1997: 208). This foot-note runs as follows:

> There are, of course, several other significant approaches to the study of transla-tion, for example the functionalist German tradition (…), the process-oriented approach (…) and deconstructionist approaches (…), to mention only a few. The reduction to two main approaches is a result of a desire to focus on two lines of thought which *exemplify* the underlying philosophical differences. Other approaches will be mentioned, where relevant, as they pertain to the overall argu-ment. The choice of these two particular approaches is also motivated by the fact that scholars working within the general framework of these two approaches have been the most vocal in the debate on the equivalence concept. (1997: 228)

Apart from the fact that there was an immensely heated and protracted debate on the concept of equivalence especially among its opponents during the course of the 1980s (cf. Snell-Hornby 1988), it cannot be convincingly defended by simply ruling out arguments which treat it critically or areas which fail to exemplify it (one is reminded of the treatment of metaphor in transformational grammar). On the contrary, to justify reintroducing a concept which had been so vehemently debated over twenty years and finally discarded by considerable sections of the sci-entific community, it would be essential to state the arguments against the concept and at least endeavour to devalidate them.

A similar criticism must be made against Halverson's discussion of the proto-type concept (Halverson 2000). As we have already seen (3.3.1) this has for many years been a fruitful and familiar notion, first in psychology and linguistics and then in Translation Studies. In Halverson's article (which presents the results of a small empirical study as based on prototype semantics), many decisive contribu-tions to the debate, even the seminal work of Fillmore, and those following him in Translation Studies, are completely ignored. This is a classic confirmation of André Lefevere's two "childhood diseases" in the discipline as diagnosed in 1993: reinventing the wheel and not reading what other people have written. Certainly, we must agree with Vermeer that meanwhile so much has been published that it cannot all be read – what should however be self-evident is a discussion of what is relevant to the field concerned, especially of those contributions which were sem-inal, innovative, provocative or which in some way influenced the course of the academic debate.

The limits of the language/literature approach are illustrated by another study, originally submitted to the University of London as a Ph.D. thesis in 1999, on a topic with immense potential for European Translation Studies: Translation into German during the Nazi regime (Sturge 1999). As research in the field of German studies, this is valuable material meticulously researched, but the topic is also liter-ary translation, and – like many such studies written in English and/or of English provenance – is located firmly within the school of Descriptive Translation Studies. Although the functional approach in general and the skopos theory in particular is directly relevant for translation produced under censorship (or censored subsequently)[65] and would have been highly productive for the topic under discussion, here too it is dismissed in a footnote:

> The "skopos theorists" around Katharina Reiss and Hans Vermeer (see Nord 1997: 27 ff.) talk about fidelity[66] without losing sight of the specificity of the translation in time, culture and commissioning context. Their consideration of translation as a product of the effects the translator wants to achieve in the target language shares ground with the target-oriented approach outlined below; however, they are ultimately interested in the extent of translations' fulfilment of supposedly "correctly identified" goals (Delabatista 1991: 143 f.), an issue of less interest to me here. (Sturge: 1999: 13)

For anyone familiar with the writings of Reiss, Vermeer and Nord, these comments are puzzling, as the scholars concerned seem misunderstood. Reiss and Vermeer (who are not mentioned elsewhere in the study, nor do they appear in the bibliography) are interpreted through Nord in English translation,[67] although the author is not only writing on a German topic but also has a degree in German and would have hence been able to read them in the original. Particularly strange are the "supposedly 'correctly identified' goals" attributed to an article "A False Opposition in Translation Studies: Theoretical versus/and Historical Approaches" by Dirk Delabastita (1991). I cannot find the phrase "'correctly identified' goals" on the pages cited, although there is a brief quote from Snell-Hornby (1988: 47) – hence once again in English – explaining Holz-Mänttäri's theory as communication across cultural barriers. While Delabastita's conclusions are in themselves mystifying for the present author quoted, it is not my aim here to sort out the various misunderstandings and non-communication. Stranger still however is Sturge's conclusion, as based on Delabastita's observations, that the "skopos theorists" present "an issue of less interest to me here". Had she familiarized herself directly with the writings of Reiss, Vermeer and Holz-Mänttäri, she might have come to completely different

---

65. See the discussion of the *Translationsskopos* and the *Translatskopos* under 2.2.

66. This refers to the German term *Fidelität*, which Vermeer introduced in the sense of "intertextual coherence" as against *Äquivalenz*. It is however not identical with the term *fidelity* as used in the English tradition of translation theory (cf. 2.2).

67. This may well explain the misunderstandings. The title of Nord's English version is in itself enough to arouse suspicion: *Translating as a Purposeful Activity* implies that translating is otherwise an activity that is purposeless. But what the skopos theory is concerned with is "Translating as Goal-Driven (or at least Goal-Directed) Action."

conclusions about their relevance for her study, which is a fascinating contribution to Comparative Literature, but remains one-sided from the viewpoint of Translation Studies. This becomes particularly clear in the practical discussion of the case studies, where a large corpus of English texts is compared with their German translations: while the author criticizes the linguistically oriented model of Kitty van Leuven-Zwart (1989/1990) – which centres round microstructural shifts – as not fully suitable for her corpus, it is in part applied, and the discussion hardly goes beyond the level of the surface structures of language. The result is that a large number of linguistic items are compared, but little insight is gained into the texts (i.e. as novels or detective stories) as a whole. This would have been fruitful ground indeed for Margret Ammann's model (3.3.1), but, as quoted above, the "skopos theorists" were not taken into consideration.

A number of similar examples, also by promising scholars of the younger generation, could be cited to illustrate a tendency now observable for some years: the globalization process of the 1990s, along with the ever-increasing dominance of English as the language for publication and scholarly exchange, is influencing the actual content of Translation Studies (cf. 4.2.3). English is often the unquestioned means of communication, and the debate then centres round theories and publications appearing in English. As these theories are mostly connected with departments of (comparative) literature or linguistics, or are based on linguistic approaches (e.g. Hatim and Mason 1990), they continue to focus on essentially literary or linguistic issues: the concept of equivalence or the use of corpora are a case in point. Even where other theoretical approaches have been published in English (e.g. Vermeer 1989, Nord 1997), they tend not to be read for their intended message or for their relevance to the material concerned, but only insofar as they do not conflict with the standpoint already taken. (The footnote trying to explain why they "are not of interest here" often has the function of an academic figleaf.) This usually reflects the perspective, even the planetary consciousness, of the English-speaking world, whether from the viewpoint of an essentially monolingual society or by using English as a lingua franca. It seems that Translation Studies, after the "cultural turn" of the 1980s, the "historical curve" and the "cognitive twist" of the 1990s (see Chesterman 2002), seems at the beginning of the new century to be facing a globalized, hence anglophile levelling off.

Another reason for the trend "Back to Linguistics" may lie in yet another evergreen in the theoretical debate: the divergent views of what the object of study, hence a translation, actually is. The concept of "translation proper" has changed through the centuries, as we could already see with Schleiermacher (1.1). In the 1960s the process of translation was seen essentially as a linguistic operation, and the product was defined as a text equivalent to the source text (1.2, see too Catford 1965) – a vague definition which covered translation exercises at school and university, machine translation and other forms of reproduction of a strictly verbal text seen as consisting of a sequence of sentences, these themselves seen as a string of items. This is reflected in Koller's 1972 conception of translation (quoted under 1.3), but even in his later articles in the 1990s, in which he reaffirms the concept of equivalence and seeks to delimit the object of Translation Studies, no basic change can be detected:

> From a linguistic and text-theoretical perspective, translation can be understood as the *result of a text-processing activity, by means of which a source-language text is transposed into a target-language text. Between the resultant text in L2 (the target-language text) and the source text in L1 (the source-language text) there exists a relationship, which can be designated as a translational or equivalence relation.* (Koller 1995: 196, emphasis Koller)

Equivalence is subsequently termed a relative concept, determined by a range of factors and conditions, ranging from "the world" to the translator's creative inclinations and understanding of the work to the client's guidelines and the declared purpose of the translation (Koller 1995: 197). Despite this gesture to the functional approach, a translation remains dependent on the concept of equivalence, and this in returns still remains vague (contrast Vermeer's definition of translation under 2.2).

Still a bone of contention is the borderline between translation and adaptation, as in drama translation (3.1.3), already dismissed by Bassnett in the 1980s as a "red herring" (1985: 93). Such debates might be resolved if we finally accept Toury's definition that a translation is what is accepted as such. Alternatively, we can take Katharina Reiss's broad view of translation as consisting of the five basic types quoted in 2.2: interlinear, grammar translation, scholarly or documentary translation (Venuti's "foreignization" and Newmark's "semantic translation"), communicative (or instrumental) translation, modifying (or adapting) translation. This last type includes subtitling, dubbing, stage translation, software localization, advertising texts, foreign language versions of press agency texts or the translation of specialized or technical literature for a general public – it is for the most part, as we saw under 3.1, beyond language, and it is certainly beyond equivalence.

The issue of *Logos and Language* on the topic "Translation Studies: Current Theoretical Issues" (2002) , which included the article (Snell-Hornby 2002) from which much of this section was taken, also contained two contributions with a special focus on the relationship between aspects of linguistic research and Translation Studies. Jeremy Munday discussed the issue of corpus lingustics as an "interface for interdisciplinary co-operation". As shown above (4.1.2), this question also arose in the 1980s, whereby some problems (such as the envisaged commercial losses involved in bilingual dictionaries for translators) have meanwhile become partly irrelevant due to the unlimited information available on the Internet and to other technological aids for translators. It is also beyond dispute that language corpora provide a wealth of information for lexicographical projects, in particular monolingual dictionaries. Their direct value for Translation Studies however still remains to be shown, and as yet there are problems that need to be solved. For example, Munday sees one use of computer corpora in

> ….identifying typicalities of the language of a corpus of translated texts. These characteristics of the style of translated language can then be compared to non-translated language. The differences noted may reveal elements of the process of translating and the translation 'norms' at work. Possible characteristic features of translations, known as 'translation universals', suggested by Baker (1993: 244–245), are greater explicitation and use of conventional grammatical structures and an increased frequency of words such as *say*. (Munday 2002: 14)

The major question arising here is what exactly is a "translated text", or in other words, what, in this day and age of hybridity and globalization, is "non-translated language"? In certain set situations the position may be clear: where someone is given an English text produced by a monolingual English native speaker with the specific instructions to "translate this into French" the result may be seen as a "translated text" (and the source text was "non-translated language"). But what about *Midnight's Children* as a postcolonial hybrid text (3.2.1), or the UN text on Morocco, based on French material but intended to function as a source text (4.2.3)? And what about the flood of English-language texts on the Internet, intended to be English but abounding in interferences? What is relevant, the conscious intention to translate with a specific translation brief, or the mere fact of linguistic interference (and in that case how is the language norm to be defined, cf. 1.3)? For the purposes of objective scientific data, Toury's definition of translation as quoted above will not suffice.

After the discussion of norms at the Aston colloquium (3.1.1), Toury wrote these comments:

> One strategic conclusion already drawn is that I will have to remind myself more often, not only that the language I am writing in is not really mine (which I have always been sorely aware of), but that I am addressing audiences whose majority likewise has English as a foreign language. It is not necessarily the same brand of English either, nor does it always represent the same kind of foreignness. (1999: 129)

The question arises whether Toury's English writings – and the many texts produced by the various audiences he mentions – are themselves "non-translated language?"

Another problem connected with comparing multilingual language corpora (apart from the elimination of the basic context, the background situation and the entire cultural component) is the concept of "word" itself, especially when dealing with word frequency or length of text material, because, as Munday himself rightly points out with reference to English and Spanish (2002: 15), what is a "word" varies according to inherent differences in the language systems involved. Moreover, an English word like *say*, as cited above, need by no means be identically lexicalized in other languages or similarly used or reiterated in text-types of other cultures. All this must be considered when presenting sweeping terms like "translation universals".

In discussing George Steiner's *After Babel* (cf. 1.3), Munday describes it as "a book that is stuck in time. Steiner's extensive references to Chomsky's generative-transformational grammar as a support for a universalist view of language, and thus an all-embracing theory of translation, now seem dated." (2001: 167). In reading some recent linguistically based discussions of Translation Studies, I would say that, on the contrary, some attitudes in the discussion unleashed in the 1960s by proponents of generative grammar now seem to have been given a new lease of life. The names and some of the terms may have changed, but in both cases linguistic data are isolated from the cultural background (then termed "extra-linguistic reality"), the concepts of "rules" and "norms" (then "well-formedness" as against "deviance") remain central, and again the debate is characterized by a search for universals, as based on work in English – and it may transpire again, as with generative grammar, that when the phenonema at stake are contrasted with other languages, they can actually prove to be English language-specific (cf. Snell-Hornby 1983).

Munday refers to corpus linguistics as a "methodology" (2002: 12) and not a discipline. In their contribution to the same volume "Machine Translation, Translation Studies and Linguistic Theories", Alan Melby and Deryle Lonsdale describe the space where three areas clearly overlap and discuss "machine translation as a technology that is here to stay as an element of the tapestry of translation." (2002: 39) They begin by referring to the ALPAC report (cf. 1.3), but their contribution is by no means a move back to "Square One". On the contrary, it becomes clear how the role of machine translation has changed since the pipe-dreams of the 1950s, and how it was able to develop into a technology indispensable for today's language industries: firstly, because the lofty ambitions for "Fully Automatic High-Quality Translation" were cut down and replaced by more realistic goals, and secondly because a differentiated range of tools were developed to cater for the differing needs of the translator. As mentioned above (4.2.1), these tools were the subject of innumerable articles during the 1990s and were made available to practitioners through publications such as *Language International*. During those years it also became clear that the issues addressed and the material described in the magazine went well beyond the limits of Translation Studies – an impression confirmed both in the convincing interdisciplinary contribution by Melby and Lonsdale in *Logos and Language* and by the reasons given by the Editors for closing *Language International* in December 2002.[68]

Another – less salutary – impression of mine that thickened over the years while reading such contributions was that this academic world of technology was steadily turning into a male-dominated universe (taking us back to Square One again? – cf. 3.2.2). Precisely this impression was explicitly confirmed in the Final Issue of *Language International* by one its contributors, Anthony Pym:

> For an academic like me, *Language International* and its brethren have been fresh contacts with the world of technology and money. It has taught me the manifold virtues of localization, far superior to the muddy models of translation I come from. This was also a world I might have been able to upset just a little, in the name of something like academic humanism. So let me leave with one parting shot.
>
> I like this place because its relations tend to be masculine. Bert Esselink and Bob Clark are men, as are their editorial predecessors. This has several advantages. For instance, when I get cigarettes from them at conferences, I don't feel obliged to pay them back (as I do with women). The masculinity is certainly a camaraderie of boys-with-toys, playing with technology, as well as gossiping about each other. It also has something to do with envisaging a future, one we will reach if we all look ahead and play in teams. Indeed, many of these pages have reminded me of the pep talks given by football coaches, as opposed to the genealogical critique in fashion in universities (you are what you have come from and not where you are going). This is a masculine world where training is not just the attainment of learning objectives; it is also motivation. I see all that as remarkably masculine, a counterweight to the feminized academy. (2002: 43)

5.2 New paradigms or shifting viewpoints?

At this point we might attempt a – tentative – assessment of what, in the sense of Kuhn (1970) and Vermeer (1994), can be seen as paradigmatic changes or milestones in the development of Translation Studies over the past thirty years, and furthermore what, in the words of Lefevere (1993), has really contributed to the advancement of knowledge in the field. These conclusions are presented, not with the intention of a final verdict, but as food for thought and material for future debate.

---

68. "…it has become increasingly difficult to cover all the changes in language and translation and all the different translation disciplines without losing too much focus. Besides, we now have the Internet: all the information we could possible wish for is there, readily available, 24 hours a day and always up-to-date." (Esselink 2002: 4)

To avoid the danger of being overly subjective or manipulative, I would like to base my conclusions on a matrix that goes beyond what has been described in detail here. As a starting point let us compare the basic content of three different "Introductions to Translation Studies": Werner Koller's *Einführung in die Überset-zungswissenschaft* (1979, 292 p.), Jeremy Munday's *Introducing Translation Studies. Theories and Methods* (2001, 222 p.) and Erich Prunč *Einführung in die Transla-tionswissenschaft. Vol. 1. Orientierungsrahmen* (2001, 388 p.).

Koller 1979 was one of the first books of its kind and thus must be seen as a pioneering effort. In the introduction the author explicitly states that his field is the study of (written) translation as opposed to interpreting (1979: 11–12), and even here he expresses the fear that he might be criticized for trying to introduce something "was es noch nicht in einer Form gibt, die eine einführende Darstellung erlauben würde" (1979: 10) (which doesn't yet exist in a form that would permit an introductory account). The book is divided into eight main chapters. Chapter 1 presents "Basic Aspects" (such as the history of translation, statistics on transla-tion, language policy), Chapter 2 deals with translator training. Chapter 3, with the heading "The Problem of Translation" includes theoretical approaches, as of Levý for literary translation and Jumpelt (1961) for scientific translation, also linguistic theory and translation as communication. Chapter 4 is concerned with the con-cept of translation and aspects of the study of translation (text linguistics, didactics and translation critique), and Chapter 5 discusses definitions and models of the translation process. Chapter 6 deals with the topic of translatability and translation procedures, and Chapter 7 is concerned with the problem of equivalence. The final chapter 8 is devoted to translation critique, discusses models already pre-sented, particularly that of Reiss, and presents an alternative model.

Munday 2001 also excludes "oral translation",[69] but now it is clear that the field of Translation Studies he covers is very well established. There are eleven chapters, each dealing with a specific topic or approach and the scholars associated with them. The introductory Chapter 1 ("main issues") includes Jakobson's triadic sys-tem of translation and discusses the structure of the discipline as sketched by James Holmes. Chapter 2 gives an overview of historical translation theories (including Cicero, Luther, Dolet, Tytler and Schleiermacher). Chapter 3 then deals with the topic of equivalence (e.g. Nida, Newmark, Koller), and Chapter 4 dis-cusses the "translation shift approach" (e.g. Vinay and Darbelnet, Catford, Levý, Van Leuven-Zwart). Chapter 5 is devoted to functional theories of translation (Reiss, Holz-Mänttäri, Vermeer, Nord), and Chapter 6 is concerned with discourse

---

69. See 2001: 4. Meanwhile the same publishers have presented a companion volume *Introduc-ing Interpreting Studies* (Pöchhacker 2004).

and register analysis approaches (Halliday, House, Baker, Hatim and Mason). Chapter 7 looks at "systems theories" (e.g. Toury, Chesterman, Lambert, Van Gorp), and Chapter 8 discusses "Varieties of cultural studies" (e.g. Bassnett, Lefevere, Niranjana, Vieira). Chapter 9 is devoted to the question of the translator's visibility (Berman, Venuti), Chapter 10 to "philosophical theories" (e.g. Steiner, Benjamin, Derrida), while the final Chapter 11 discusses Translation Studies as an interdiscipline (Snell-Hornby, Harvey), with a prognosis for future perspectives.

Prunč 2001 basically includes the study of interpreting in his concept of *Translationswissenschaft*, but only from a general theoretical viewpoint. The book has nine main chapters, and is organized according to problems and issues rather than facts, schools or persons. Chapter 1 is devoted entirely to the issue of the name of the discipline and the act of translation (with Kade's terminology) and the multifarious problems connected with it. Chapter 2 goes into the "dominance of linguistics and the equivalence debate" (Jakobson, Vinay and Darbelnet, Koller, and the text-typology of Reiss). Chapter 3 centres round translation as a cultural transfer, above all as seen by Nida. Chapter 4, with the title "Das finalistische Prinzip der Translation" (the finalistic principle of translation), works from language system to text, including problems of textual conventions and the relation between language and the world around. Chapter 5, "Translatorisches Handeln" (Translatorial Action), spans a range from Sapir and Whorf to the skopos theory, Holz-Mänttäri and Nord. Chapter 6 deals with "comparative and descriptive Translation Studies", these ranging from Russian Formalism, Levý's concept of norm, James Holmes and the "Manipulationists", Toury, Bassnett and Lefevere's cultural turn, along with feminist translation and postcolonialism. Chapter 7 has the topic "Dekonstruktion" and concentrates mainly on the work of Derrida and Benjamin.. The short Chapter 8 presents the work of the Göttingen research project on literary translation (cf. 2.1), and the concluding Chapter 9, entitled "Integration", is an assessment of various terms and approaches in their relation to each other.

From this brief overview of the three books (which does not consider their differing methods of presentation or language focus), various points emerge. The main impression is the breadth of material meanwhile available to Munday and Prunč, hence the blossoming of the discipline since the late 1970s when Koller wrote his *Einführung*, which concentrates mainly on matters of linguistics and language, training and critique. Some topics remain constant: one issue common to all three books is that of equivalence, though with Prunč this is discussed critically and in historical terms as part of the linguistically oriented phase. Munday has a bias towards linguistic or abstract approaches (translation shifts, register analysis, systems, philosophical theories), as represented by the English-speaking community, while Prunč maintains a balance between the functional action theories and the descriptive approach, and his material covers a wide range, including contributions from Slavonic countries. In general, one is aware of the divide, quoted above (2.5) from Toury 1995, between "descriptivists" (DTS) on the one hand and "functionalists" (action theories) on the other (dealt with separately by both Prunč and Munday), also on the differing status of linguistic and cultural aspects in their relevance to translation. Both Prunč and Munday however come to a constructive conclusion, by emphasizing the importance of integration or future collaboration.

This broad trend has been confirmed here. However, this present study is not intended to function as a general or theoretical introduction to the discipline, and a further important criterion has been how a theoretical concept or model could be applied and used – as demonstrated in concrete examples or shown in empirical studies. With this added dimension, we could reach the following conclusions:

There now seems to be a consensus that James Holmes is the first outstanding pioneer of modern Translation Studies as an independent discipline, both in creating suitable terminology and in designing its structure (the main weakness being his neglect of interpreting, also perhaps his literary bias). He only achieved posthumous international recognition however, after his work had been made available to an international public (Holmes 1988), and it is significant that he is hardly mentioned in Koller 1979. Of similar importance, but much less widely acknowledged outside German-speaking countries, is the work of Otto Kade (1968), who also created suitable basic terminology and offered a conception of the discipline that embraced both (conference) interpreting and non-literary texts and included the important dimension of communication theory, thus going beyond the linguistic straitjacket of the time.

New schools of thought then developed during the 1980s, independently of each other, but with much in common, each going back to initial work and bold new concepts created during the late 1970s. This was the time of the paradigmatic changes or, in the words of Vermeer (1994), the (seemingly) straightforward leaps to new points of view. The group of scholars known throughout the English-speaking scientific community today as the "Manipulation School" presented a new paradigm for literary translation as based on the theory of the polysystem (Hermans 1985), creating the school of Descriptive Translation Studies (and with it Toury's – still influential – concept of the translation norm). During the same years two innovative functional approaches were developed in Germany, the skopos theory, which from the outset was presented as a general theory of translation and interpreting (Reiss and Vermeer 1984), and the theory of translatorial action (Holz-Mänttäri 1984). All three approaches focussed on the function of the translation in the target culture, as against equivalence with the source text, but differed in basic concepts (such as the understanding of "function" and "norm") and tenets, the "descriptivists" rejecting any form of evaluation, the "functionalists" favouring it. Initially, the theory of translatorial action was designed for (mainly written) translation in an industrial context, and both functional theories first met with scepticism as to their relevance or suitability for literary translation. New concepts (in particular Nord's concept of "loyalty", also that of "scenes-and-frames") and models (Ammann's model of translation critique) that were developed later opened up new perspectives for the application of the skopos theory to literary texts, as did the cooperation with scholars in literary translation favouring a deconstructionist approach. Furthermore, the dominant cultural (as against linguistic) orientation was taken up by scholars of the "Descriptive" school to mark a "cultural turn" in literary translation (Bassnett and Lefevere 1990), which then became known as a turning point in literary Translation Studies. Thus "descriptive" and "functional" schools of Translation Studies need by no means be dismissed as oppositions per se, they can also, despite differing concepts and varying orientiations, be seen to complement each other.

It was with the further developments and the empirical studies of the 1990s that the new paradigms of the 1980s met their real testing ground. Perhaps the most sensational development in the discipline during the decade was the emergence of Interpreting Studies as a parallel interdiscipline (cooperating with such fields as neurophysiology, psychology and sociology) with its own new fields of study (e.g. media or community interpreting) and its own scientific methods, in particular empirical ones. A new scientific community arose, whereby – to take Lefevere's categorization a stage further – former "disciples" of Translation Studies such as Miriam Shlesinger or Franz Pöchhacker became pioneers of Interpreting Studies. In that field the vision of James Holmes sustained a blank, and approaches focussing on literary translation, whether Descriptive Translation Studies or Deconstruction, could offer little help. However, there was one theoretical approach from Translation Studies that proved highly successful for studies in interpreting, as for conference interpreting (Pöchhacker 1994), and court interpreting (Kadrić 2001): Holz-Mänttäri's model of translatorial action. This was also true for studies in fields of (written) translation which go "beyond language" (e.g. Kaindl 1995 on opera translation) or require subject expertise in a particular (often industrial) setting – see Salmhoferova 2002 for legal translation and Framson (2005) for international marketing. All in all, one can conclude that Holz-Mänttäri's model has proved to be one of the most versatile and productive approaches in varied fields of the discipline of Translation Studies (including interpreting) and deserves far more recognition in the international community than it has had up to now. What has prevented this was discussed above (2.3): Holz-Mänttäri's theoretical work was published in German and in a style that was problematic even for native speakers. The success of research in Think-Aloud Protocols, which also originated in Germany and actually apply to a far more limited field of study than the one treated by Holz-Mänttäri, is largely due to the fact that much of it was published in English and debated in the English-speaking community.

There were of course highly significant innovations in other areas of Translation Studies during the 1990s. A major factor was what Bassnett and Lefevere made famous as the "cultural turn", which inspired a rich amount of work in fields like postcolonial and feminist translation, placing the focus on the vital but hitherto neglected factor of power in translation. Similarly, Toury's concept of "norm" was joined by the other fruitful concept of "meme", this in turn opening up the vital question of ethics (which has by no means been exhausted). The element of nonverbal communication has in my opinion more potential than hitherto assumed (or investigated) in Translation Studies, particularly in forms of translation going "beyond language" as for stage or screen. Conversely, traditional areas like hermeneutics have been given new vitality and immediacy by concepts like *scenes* and *frames* and by new approaches to the concept of text, and to the roles of author and reader. All of these have undoubtedly contributed to the advancement of knowledge in the field of Translation Studies as required by André Lefevere: where they lie on the spectrum between "new paradigm" and "shifting viewpoint" or what type of progress they represent in Vermeer's zigzags and spirals is a judgement that probably varies with the interests and convictions of the individual reader or translation scholar.

5.3 "Make dialogue, not war": Moving towards a "translation turn"

During the closing session of the German Studies Congress in Brazil in 2003, it was agreed that the discipline had moved away from its dogmatic, monolithic standing when German was the great language of scholarship, to a more relative but fruitful position among the plurality of languages and cultures in the globalized world of today with its need for international and intercultural dialogue. As I pointed in the Introduction to this study, these and other insights acclaimed at the Congress as being innovative, had for me been familiar for years from the perspectives we have adopted in Translation Studies. And so this may now be the point to return to Kaindl's discussion of interdisciplinarity (3.1) and the three successive stages of development in the quality of cooperation: "imperialistic", "importing", and "reciprocal". Most of the interdisciplinary studies from the 1990s discussed in this study represent the second stage, and in the first years of the new century it is worth considering what Translation Studies could give or "export" to other disciplines for the final stage of "reciprocal interdisciplinarity".

In the volume *Constructing Cultures* with essays by herself and André Lefevere, Susan Bassnett already included a contribution with the title "The Translation Turn in Cultural Studies" (Bassnett 1998), where she offers some relevant suggestions. The discipline she refers to as Cultural Studies began by being specifically British, and goes back to work from the 1950s and 1960s by Raymond Willams, E.P. Thompson and Richard Hoggart, who founded the Centre for Contemporary Cultural Studies at the University of Birmingham in 1964. As Bassnett points out, this subject went through a process comparable to that of Translation Studies – and indeed to that of linguistics and Cognitive Studies as outlined above (5.) – and she traces the development of the two disciplines in relationship to each other through the last few decades. She maintains that the "translation turn in cultural studies is now well underway" (1998: 136). As a major example she states the type of questions asked about the respective object of study, such as the text.

In the traditional study of literature, for instance, texts were seen as having "some kind of intrinsic universal value of their own that helped them survive down the ages" (1998: 133), whereby Homer and Shakespeare were presented as monolithic universal writers and formed part of a static canon to be venerated by scholars and disciples. As we saw under 2.1, it was the polysystem theory (and the translation scholars who propagated it) that started asking new questions, now standard in Translation Studies, but well outside the interests of traditional literary studies. With Shakespeare, for example:

> ...we would need to consider the complex method of production of the plays in the first place (whether written prior to rehearsals with actors, during rehearsals and transcribed by someone, or written piecemeal as roles for individual actors to modify themselves, similar to the scenarii of the commedia dell'arte), the sources employed in that process of production, the even more complex history of the editing of the plays, the fortunes prior to the eighteenth century, the great Shakespeare boom of early Romanticism, and the gradual process of canonisation that has taken place ever since. We would also need to look at the very different Shakespeares that appear in different cultures: the radical, political author of Central and Eastern Europe, for example, or the high priest of the imperial British ideal who was exported to India and the colonies. And in considering how these differing Shakespeares have been created, we are led back to the role played by translation. (Bassnett 1998: 134–135)

Similar questions were asked with regard to drama translation under 3.1.3, and they show what is now a truism in Translation Studies, but by no means self-evident in traditional literary studies, that any discourse, be it of Shakespeare, Homer, Stoppard or Tagore, does not simply exist "as such", but is always relative to its immediate situation in time and place. As Bassnett concludes, and as was especially clear from the example by the poet Tagore (3.2.1), a comparison of translations of the same text "exposes the fallacy of universal greatness" (1998: 135).

Extending the debate to non-literary translation and interpreting, we could emphasize that Translation Studies opens up new perspectives from which other disciplines – or more especially the world around – might well benefit. It is concerned, not with languages, objects, or cultures as such, but with communication across cultures, which does not merely consist of the sum of all factors involved. And what is not yet adequately recognized is how translation (studies) could help us communicate better – a deficit that sometimes has disastrous results. The caption in the heading of this section "Make dialogue, not war" was used for the title of a lecture I gave in November 2003 at a Conference in Warwick on the theme "The Translation Turn in Cultural Studies" and was inspired – not directly by the hippie motto "Make love not war" – but by a placard held aloft in the streets of London in February 2003 during a demonstration against the imminent war in Iraq. It read "Make tea, not war", and it showed a caricature of the British Prime Minister with a teacup on his head acting as a helmet. It could be said of translation that its main aim is constructive, to "make dialogue", rather than making war, which in its destructiveness is the exact opposite. In attempting to understand and make sense of the source text, the translator tunes in to the other side, as it were, and in creating the target text, s/he formulates a message for the target audience which should be coherent with the target culture. Just how horribly wrong such communication can go if the act of translation as communication fails, could be illustrated by many examples from Iraq since the military conquest. One such incident took place after the war was officially won and occupying soldiers were searching private houses for weapons and undesirable individuals. A high-ranking local personage described to journalists how his villa was ransacked, doors knocked down and furniture demolished, until, after finding nothing of interest, the soldiers put away their weapons, said "Shukran djashilan" (which is what they had been told meant "Thank you very much" in Arabic), and drove away.[70] It was what was understood as the cynicism, the insult behind the phrase meaning "Thank you" that rankled most. But the soldiers had probably never intended to perform a speech-act of thanking. The English phrase "Thank you very much", when used after such military actions, merely has the communicative value of "Well, that's it" – gratitude is not implied. As this example shows, much could have been done to reduce bad feeling in the region during that time if the military personell has been trained as intensively in interlingual and intercultural communication as they had been in using their high-tech weapons. The main lesson for the situation just described, in accordance with the principles of functional translation

---

70. See „Mächtiger Feind", in *Der Spiegel* 27 /2003, p.128.

theories, would have been: don't merely transcode words, but express the necessary information in a way that is appropriate for and understood by the addressee.

Similar stories abound in history, sometimes with devastating consequences. The richest example I know of failed intercultural communication is Lord Macartney's ambitious expedition to China as envoy of George III in 1792 (described in detail in Snell-Hornby 1996c). The aim was to negotiate outlets for British trade (a classic situation for Interpreting Studies), and as Britain then saw herself as the most powerful nation of the globe, Macartney was supremely confident of success (cf. 3.2.1). But the expedition was a complete failure. The Celestial Empire, with its population of 330 million, then one third of the human race, saw itself as the only civilization under heaven, the mission was viewed as yet another tribute offered from an inconsequential envoy, and Macartney's every request was turned down flat. At the crux of the whole entanglement of diplomatic miscommunication was Macartney's refusal to kowtow to the Chinese Emperor Qianlong, in the literal sense of course, which would have involved a ritual of prostrations where the forehead meets the ground nine times; instead he was only willing to bow down on one knee, as he would before his own sovereign (cf. nonverbal communication in translation, 3.1.2). The British revealed themselves in Chinese eyes as a particularly uncouth and obstinate type of barbarian and were coldly shown out of the country.

The story of Lord Macartney's expedition to China is told in fascinating detail in a book by Alain Peyrefitte, published in 1989, with the title *L'Empire Immobile ou Le Choc des Mondes* – Jon Rothschild's English translation has the title *The Collision of Two Civilizations* – thus predating the concept of "clash of cultures" attributed to Samuel Huntington. The entire book is a concrete demonstration of clashing cultures, in other words how communication can go wrong and what consequences can arise when it does. The matter of the kowtow, besides being an issue of power, is a classic example of transcultural miscommunication, though by gesture and not by word. Each side insisted on its own semiotic signs – here the ritual kowtow, there the bended knee – which were given absolute significance. No attempt was made on either side to understand, to interpret or to offer an adequate message for the communication partner. Verbal communication proved equally disastrous. During the audience with the Emperor matters were complicated by ritual, which prohibited direct dialogue between the envoy and the Imperial person: the Emperor's questions to the envoy were first received by the President of the Tribunal of Rites, who transmitted them to the interpreter (a Chinese priest who knew no English, but was reasonably proficient in Latin), who then translated – and for the envoy's reply the procedure was reversed. There was only one person in the entire mission of 700 Englishmen who learnt any Chinese, and that was the 12-year-old son of Macartney's deputy, young Thomas Staunton (the later Sinologist). He actually had the function of Macartney's page (cf. 4.1.1), but the few words he spoke to the Emperor in Chinese proved to be the only real accomplishment in cross-cultural verbal communication during the entire mission.

Similarly defective were the attempts of the British guests to describe and explain the numerous magnificent gifts they had brought for the Emperor. These included Parker lenses, a telescope and an exact replica of the British flagship "Royal Sovereign", and in essence they represented a first attempt to "sell" Western technology to China (cf. 4.2.2). The interpreter during the official inspection of these gifts was again a Latin-speaking priest, an expert clockmaker but without any naval expertise, and it must indeed have been an arduous task to translate deficient nautical Latin into Chinese, especially for an addressee who knew nothing about ships (cf. 2.3). Imperial interest soon flagged and gave way to disdain for such Western trinkets, many of which were found unused and untouched when the palace was sacked over half a century later.

What answers could Translation Studies – from today's viewpoint – have given to all this? Above all the need for professionally trained, bilingual and bicultural interpreters with expertise in the subject areas concerned (cf. 2.2), who could "tune into" the various addressees and their cultural expectations. Secondly, the willingness on both sides – British and Chinese – to recognize the relativity of their own products and world-view (or planetary consciousness, cf. 3.2), and to respect the cultural differences of their partners – a truism in modern marketing and international public relations. These insights would have led to a different quality of discourse and mode of conduct on both sides, and with far-reaching consequences: had Lord Macartney behaved differently, had he presented his offer differently, and had the Chinese Emperor received it differently, history might have taken a different course. As it was, the failure of the British mission set in motion an ominous chain reaction, as Alain Peyrefitte convincingly concludes in his book, leading to the collapse of China with British domination of South East Asia in the 19th century, and then to the renewed and as yet unparalleled "clash of worlds" in the 20th: making war and not dialogue.

Fortunately, there is also a counter-example to prove that the reverse can be true. Exactly 200 years after Macartney set sail for the Far East, Chris Patten, as the last Governor of Hong Kong, embarked on the ambitious task of trying to "sell" democracy to the Chinese. He was amply supported by political advisers, and had at his disposal a team of professionally trained interpreters, well-paid government employees known as "Chinese Language Officers", bilingual in English and Chinese. In this day and age, democracy, at least for any self-respecting citizen of a Western nation, is such a self-evident value in life that the Governor was confident his arguments would win. But these particular negotiations were fraught with difficulty. At the crux of a whole labyrinth of diplomatic wrangling was Patten's refusal to kowtow to the Chinese government, in the metaphorical sense of course, which would have involved an abandonment of his basic principles. Clashing worlds once again? As experienced professionals the interpreters were quite aware both of the problems and the cultural differences involved, and despite some very harsh utterances their declared aim was to "keep up communication".[71] Those experts I later questioned agree that these negotiations achieved the maximum that could reasonably be expected: dialogue, not war, and a successful example of translation as intercultural communication.

Meanwhile Benjamin Barber's dichotomy of "Jihad vs. McWorld" has assumed grim new relevance on the political stage of the new century. The basic problem involved in this particular "clash of worlds" was also briefly addressed in Susan Bassnett's essay:

> The moment for the meeting of cultural studies and translation studies came at exactly the right time for both. For the great debate of the 1990s is the relationship between globalisation, on the one hand, between the increasing interconnectedness of the world-system in commercial, political and communication terms and the rise of nationalisms on the other. Globalisation is a process, certainly: but there is also massive resistance to globalisation. (1998: 132–133)

It would seem that there is also a massive need world-wide for professional translation as cultural mediation. Translation uses language as an instrument for communication, focussing on the addressee and the target text. If Translation Studies is really "destined to continue developing well into the 21st century", as predicted by Bassnett and Lefevere in 1990, its concrete influence and impact must be more clearly felt, both in other academic disciplines and in the world around – and it is up to translation scholars to make the message clear. And then its really great asset must be consolidated: a uniquely fruitful position as an interdiscipline among the plurality of languages and cultures in the world of today with a greater need than ever for international and intercultural dialogue.

---

71. This was a personal communication during an interview in Hong Kong on 21.12.1992.

CHAPTER 6

Translation studies – future perspectives

Eine wahrhaft allgemeine Duldung wird am sichersten erreicht, wenn man das Besondere der einzelnen Menschen und Völkerschaften auf sich beruhen lässt, bey der Überzeugung jedoch festhält, dass das wahrhaft Verdienstliche sich dadurch auszeichnet, dass es der ganzen Menschen angehört. Zu einer solchen Vermittlung und wechselseitigen Anerkennung tragen die Deutschen seit langer Zeit schon bey.

Wer die deutsche Sprache versteht und studirt befindet sich auf dem Markte wo alle Nationen ihre Waren anbieten, er spielt den Dolmetscher indem er sich selbst bereichert.

Und so ist jeder Übersetzer anzusehen, dass er sich als Vermittler dieses allgemein geistigen Handels bemüht, und den Wechseltausch zu befördern sich zum Geschäft macht. Denn, was man auch von der Unzulänglichkeit des Übersetzens sagen mag, so ist und bleibt es doch eins der wichtigsten und würdigsten Geschäfte in dem allgemeinen Weltwesen.

Johann Wolfgang von Goethe to Thomas Carlyle, 20th July 1827 (cit. Tgahrt 1982: 9)

(A truly universal tolerance will most surely be achieved by respecting the special characteristics of individual people and nations while at the same time being convinced that what has real merit stands out because it belongs to all mankind. For a long time the Germans have been contributing towards this kind of mediation and mutual recognition.

Anyone who understands and studies the German language is present on the marketplace where all nations offer their wares, he acts as an interpreter while at the same time enriching himself.

And that is how we should view every translator, as someone who endeavours to mediate in this great intellectual commerce, making it his business to promote the interchange. For say what one will about the shortcomings of translation, it is and will remain one of the most important and most worthy concerns in the whole of world affairs.)

The final sentence of these celebrated lines written by the aging Goethe in a letter of July 20th 1827 to Thomas Carlyle were quoted as a conclusion to *Translation Studies. An Integrated Approach* (Snell-Hornby 1988). From a broad historical perspective one can say that that Goethe's convictions, both as regards the role of the translator in the world and as regards the contribution made by scholars and translators from Germany (a prolific country for translation of all kinds and, as we have seen, for Translation Studies), may still hold true.

What has of course radically changed is the world around. In the globalized world of today, the concept of 'nation' cannot be equated with that one-time ideal of German Romanticism in the early 19th century. However, the vision of a "clearing-house" for intellectual interchange can in principle be seen to have materialized, in particular over the last twenty years, firstly in the range and the sheer quantity of material now translated and interpreted, and secondly in the breadth the new discipline of Translation Studies has meanwhile gained.

This study has attempted to trace the "turns" taken by the discipline during that time, following the "cultural turn" of the 1980s. Meanwhile the concept of the "turn" seems to have become quite popular with translation scholars. Matthew Wing-Kwong Leung (forthcoming) has identified an "ideological turn" in Translation Studies, which however links up directly with our discussion under "Imperial eyes" in 3.2. A popular topic at the time of writing is the sociology of translation (see Chesterman and Gambier, both forthcoming), particularly with reference to the cultural sociology of Pierre Bourdieu (cf. Gouanvic 1997 and Kaindl 2004). But once again the notion of translation sociology was already included in the programme of James Homes (1.4), and, as was pointed out by Michaela Wolf in 1999, it is implicit in the theoretical model of Justa Holz-Mänttäri (2.3, see too 4.1). In her recent study (2005) Wolf detects a "sociological turn" at present under way in Translation Studies. As the topic has been around for so long, it is debatable whether it is now creating a new paradigm in the discipline: at all events translation sociology is a welcome alternative to the purely linguistic approach, and it is an issue of immense importance with a wealth of material for future studies. It also connects up with the problem of ethics addressed under 3.1.1, not only as regards the responsibility of the translator, but also his/her status and role in society. Responsibility for the final product of translation can only be assumed by the translator if s/he is granted it in the first place and is not treated as a "powerless" transcoder providing raw material for further processing by the "real" specialist or artist (cf. 3.1.3). Despite all the work published by translation scholars over the last few decades, and despite the efforts on the part of translators' associations to codify standards, norms and working conditions (cf. the Translator's Charter published by FIT in 1984, discussed in Chesterman 1997: 187–189), as against the meanwhile rather more respected profession of conference interpreters (cf. 4.1.1), the position and image of the translator on the market and in society have hardly improved. Empirical studies such as those by Sobotka (2000), Risku (2004) and Framson (2005) describing the routine tasks performed by translators of today along with the needs and demands of their clients, show that the low public image on the one hand and the results actually achieved (or needed) on the other still lie far apart. A good deal of information (for clients, patrons, publishers and sponsors) and intensive public relations work will be necessary if the translator is to be given appropriate recognition on the global marketplace during the coming years.

The common language of that international marketplace is however not German, as Goethe viewed it nearly two centuries ago, but, at least at the present time, English, and as we have seen (4.2.3), this is usually a globalized form of the language with the reduced function of a convenient lingua franca. But if we want to venture a prognosis for future development, we need to differentiate. In an artificial context as exemplified in international organizations like those of the European Union, the role of language(s) and culture(s) are shifted. The process of integration and political unity involves adaptation, harmonization and standardization, and the resulting institutions are by no means identical with the sum total of the languages and cultures of the member states. Kaisa Koskinen (2004) discusses the concept of culture in the context of her own work as a translator in the European Commission, and with reference to the "culture bumps" or "clashes" she encountered there during the 1990s (Koskinen 2000). Back then she claimed that:

> ...the Commission, or the EU institutions in general, constitute a culture of their own, an institutional and supranational culture that has its own history, shared knowledge, norms and values – and its own idiom (in eleven dialects). In EU translation there is sometimes a need to merely change the linguistic code without reaching outside this multilingual institutional culture (intracultural translation); other documents are addressed to readers outside this EU culture that is more or less foreign to them (intercultural translation). (2004: 145)

Koskinen has meanwhile come to the conclusion that what is described above is not actually a culture, and that the EU institutions are better described as a "discourse system" (2004: 151). I would fully support this term to apply specifically to the framework of international organizations of today (as with the United Nations, see 4.2.3), whereby the word *system* denotes a combination of interrelated and interacting elements forming a collective entity (cf. 2.1). As such it is an abstract term beyond any emotional sense of identity or belonging. Within the specific EU discourse system structures have developed, such as the use of the three working languages (discussed in 4.2.3) for internal use as linguistic codes or as relay languages for interpreting. In this way the principle of democratic multilingualism for all member states can be maintained – and yet implemented with reasonable efficiency.[72] Within discourse systems of this kind languages can well function neutrally as codes and will continue to do so.

Problems of another nature arise however where feelings of identity are addressed and where English is used as the common language for groups representing a number of different cultural traditions – and here there is the danger of a similar resistance to Anglophile dominance as described by Gioconda Belli (4.2) for Latin America. As members of a scientific community working with different languages and cultures, translation scholars need a bilingual and bicultural proficiency similar to that expected of practising translators and interpreters (2.2). This would extend to passive knowledge of languages other than their mother tongue and their active working language, at least for reading purposes. "Passive multilingualism", as already defined by Finkenstaedt and Schröder (1992) may well be the key, not only to transcultural communication among the countries of Europe, but also to a more diversified and more accurate scholarly debate in the discipline of Translation Studies worldwide. This applies particularly to international conferences and publications. If the present trend continues (cf. 4.2.3), and English becomes the sole compulsory language for conference papers and contributions to scholarly journals, there is a danger that the discipline of Translation Studies, having once emancipated itself from linguistics and comparative literature, may finally turn into a province of globalized English departments.

A further problem of Translation Studies, as in other branches of scholarly discourse too, is its metalanguage. As we have seen here (3.1.1) much confusion has been created because basic concepts are differently used, misunderstood or (2.3) not understood at all. Obviously, a school of thought can develop its own terminology, and there is no objection to that as long as the terms are clearly defined (as was the case, for example, with Otto Kade, cf. 1.2). What is important is here again an awareness of the problem and the cultivation of precise, unambiguous definitions that can be related to discourse conventions already in circulation. This is even (and especially) the case when new concepts break away from the old tradition.

Some advances and achievements visible in the "interdiscipline" since *Translation Studies – An Integrated Approach* was first published in 1988, and then since it appeared in a Revised Edition in 1995, have been described and documented here. What has also widely improved, whether due to curricular reform, the Bologna Declaration of 1999, the advancements of technology or the establishment of new programmes, is the range and quality of translator training and degrees in Translation Studies. As emphasized above, what has remained unchanged is the status of

---

72.   Whether it is felt to be satisfactory by citizens of such member states as Estonia, Hungary or Slovakia is of course another problem (cf. Dollerup 1996).

translators in society and the standing of the discipline of Translation Studies among the general public – and it is in my opinion the foremost task of translation scholars over the next few years to try and remedy this situation. It is not the quantity of publications and conferences that is decisive, but their innovative quality and their degree of relevance for our society. In a time dominated by media and publicity, it seems strange that the vital significance of translation and its inherent complexities still remain a message that has not got across – either to the public as a whole or to those responsible for funding and promoting it.

As far as communication within the discipline of Translation Studies is concerned, one can only reiterate André Lefevere's appeal (1993) quoted under 5.1. Of special significance is his observation that work in Translation Studies tends to ignore its own history. This does not only apply to the historical traditions in individual countries, but also to the development within the modern discipline over the last fifty years. A "History of Translation Studies" might be recommended as a compulsory course for future translation scholars. Lefevere also recommends a "more unified discourse" within the discipline. Bearing in mind the "plurality of voices" and the variety of approaches which are a positive characteristic of our subject, one might modify this and recommend at least a "compatible" discourse, even between diverging approaches (and using the precisely defined terminology recommended above). I fully agree with Lefevere that such a discourse must, in the final analysis, be culture-based, reflecting, as Edna Weale so aptly put it, the "different perceptions of the world" (3.1.2). Given such a discourse, and given our plurality of languages, approaches and cultures, there is every reason for optimism that Translation Studies will continue to develop into a success story of the 21st century.

There remains however a further condition for such a success story – and a vital condition for getting the Translation Studies message across to the world outside our scientific community: that this message should be produced, whatever language is used, in a comprehensible, jargon-free style. Too much good work in Translation Studies over the last forty years has been widely ignored or has caused unnecessary misunderstandings because of the opaque and abstract style in which it was written – making it virtually impossible (to revert to Goethe's phrase) for readers to "judge with enjoyment". If Goethe's age, as a heyday of translation in Europe when translators themselves were revered as illustrious men of letters, was characterized by a "Lust am Übersetzen" ("pleasure in translating"), it might be a positive sign for the future if present scholars writing on translation could enable their readers to "enjoy with judgement", generating a genuine and well-deserved pleasure in the discipline of Translation Studies.

References

Aaltonen, Sirkku. 1997. "Translating plays or baking apple pies: A functional approach to the study of drama translation." In *Translation as Intercultural Communication,* M. Snell-Hornby et al. (eds.), 89–97.

ALPAC. 1966. *Machines and Translation.* Washington, DC. NAS/NRC.

Álvarez, Román and Vidal, M. Carmen-África (eds.). 1996. *Translation, Power, Subversion.* (Topics in Translation 8). Clevedon: Multilingual Matters.

Ammann, Margret. 1990. "Anmerkungen zu einer Theorie der Übersetzungskritik und ihrer praktischen Anwendung." *TextConText* 5: 209–250.

Arntz, Reiner. 1986. "Terminologievergleich und internationale Terminologieangleichung." In *Übersetzungswissenschaft – Eine Neuorientierung,* M. Snell-Hornby (ed.), 283–310.

——. 1996. "Der Forschungsbereich 'Sprache und Recht' an der Europäischen Akademie Bozen." *Lebende Sprachen* 1: 5–8.

——. 1999. „Rechtsvergleichung und Kontrastive Terminologiearbeit: Möglichkeiten und Grenzen interdisziplinären Arbeitens." In *Übersetzen von Rechtstexten,* P. Sandrini (ed.), 185–201.

Arrojo, Rosemary. 1986. *Oficina de tradução. A teoria na prática.* São Paolo: Editora Ática.

——. 1992. "As questões teóricas da tradução e a desconstrução do logocentrismo: algumas reflexões." In *O Signo Desconstruído. Implicações para a tradução, a leitura e o ensino,* R. Arrojo (ed.) 71–79, Campinas: Pontes.

——. 1997. "Pierre Menard und eine neue Definition des 'Originals'." In *Übersetzungswissenschaft in Brasilien,* M. Wolf (ed.), 25–34.

——. 1997a. "The 'death' of the author and the limits of the translator's visibility." In *Translation as Intercultural Communication,* M. Snell-Hornby et al. (eds.), 21–32.

Austin, John L. 1962. *How to Do Things with Words.* Oxford: Clarendon.

Baker, Mona. 1993. "Corpus Lingustics and Translation Studies – Implications and Applications." In *Text and Technology. In Honour of John Sinclair,* M. Baker, G. Francis and E. Tognini-Bonelli (eds.), 233–250. Amsterdam/Philadelphia: John Benjamins.

——. 1995. "Corpora in Translation Studies: An Overview and Some Suggestions for Future Research." *Target* 7 (2): 223–243.

——. (ed.) 1998. *Routledge Encyclopedia of Translation Studies.* London/New York: Routledge.

Barber, Benjamin. 1992. "Jihad vs. McWorld." *The Atlantic Monthly* 3: 53–63.

Bar-Hillel, Y. 1960. "The Present State of Automatic Translation of Languages." *Advances in Computers,* Vol. 1, New York: Academic Press.

Barsky, Robert F. 1996. "The Interpreter as Intercultural Agent in Convention Refugee Hearings." *The Translator. Studies in Intercultural Communication.* 2 (1): 45–63.

Barthes, Roland. 1977. *Image, Music, Text.* transl. Stephen Heath. New York: Hill and Wang.

Bassnett(-McGuire), Susan. 1978. "Translating Spatial Poetry: An examination of theatre texts in performance." In *Literature and Translation,* J. S. Holmes et al. (eds.), 161–176.

——. 1980, 2002³. *Translation Studies.* London/New York: Routledge.

——. 1985. "Ways through the Labyrinth. Strategies and Methods for Translating Theatre Texts." In *The Manipulation of Literature,* T. Hermans (ed.), 87–102.

——. 1998. "The Translation Turn in Cultural Studies." In *Constructing Cultures*. S. Bassnett and A. Lefevere (eds.), 123–140.

——. 2000. "Authenticity, travel and translation." In *Translationswissenschaft*, M. Kadrić et al. (eds.), 105–114.

Bassnett, Susan and Lefevere, André (eds.). 1990. *Translation, History and Culture*. London: Pinter.

Bassnett, Susan and Lefevere, André. 1998. *Constructing Cultures. Essays on Literary Translation*. (Topics in Translation 11). Clevedon: Multilingual Matters.

Bassnett, Susan and Trivedi, Harish. 1999. "Introduction. Of colonies, cannibals and vernaculars." In *Post-colonial Translation*, S. Bassnett and H. Trivedi (eds.), 1–18.

Bassnett, Susan and Trivedi, Harish (eds.). 1999a. *Post-colonial Translation. Theory and Practice*. London/New York: Routledge.

Beaugrande, Robert de and Dressler, Wolfgang. 1981. *Einführung in die Textlinguistik*. Tübingen: Niemeyer.

Belli, Gioconda. 1994. "Amerika im Gedächtnis". In *Amerika im Gedächtnis*, O. König et al. (eds.), 11–21.

Benard, Cheryl and Schlaffer, Edit. 1978. *Die ganz gewöhnliche Gewalt in der Ehe. Texte zu einer Soziologie von Macht und Liebe*. Hamburg: Rowohlt.

Berman, Antoine.1984. *L'Épreuve de l'étranger. Culture et traduction dans l'Allemagne romantique*. Paris: Gallimard.

——. 1984/1992. *The Experience of the Foreign. Culture and Translation in Romantic Germany*, transl. S. Heyvaert, New York: SUNY.

——. 2000. "Translation and the trials of the foreign." In *The Translation Studies Reader*, L. Venuti (ed.), 284–297.

Bernardini, Andrea. 2001. *Die Brauchbarkeit zweisprachiger Gesetzesausgaben für den Gerichtsdolmetscher. Dargestellt am Beispiel des italienischen Codice Civile in der deutschen Übersetzung der autonomen Provinz Südtirol*. Vienna: unpubl. doctoral thesis.

Beuren, Daniela. 2005. *Das Konstrukt Frau in der Translation: Elisabeth Schnack übersetzt Carson McCullers*. Graz: Leykam.

Bhabha, Homi K. 1994. *The Location of Culture*. London/New York: Routledge.

Birkenhauer, Klaus and Birkenhauer, Renate. 1989. "Shaping Tools for the Literary Translator's Trade." In *Translation and Lexicography*, M. Snell-Hornby and E. Pöhl (eds.), 89–98.

Bowen, Margareta. 1998. "Community Interpreting." In *Handbuch Translation*, M. Snell-Hornby et al. (eds.), 319–321.

Buck, Timothy. 1995. "Neither the letter nor the spirit. Why most English translations of Thomas Mann are so inadequate." *The Times Literary Supplement* 13.10.1995: 17.

Bühler, Hildegund. 1986. "Linguistic (semantic) and extra-linguistic (pragmatic) criteria for the evaluation of conference interpretation and interpreters." *Multilingua* 5 (4): 231–235.

Carbonell, Ovidio. 1996. "The Exotic Space of Cultural Translation." In *Translation, Power, Subversion*, R.Álvarez and Vidal, M.C-A. (eds.), 79–98.

——. 1997. *Traducir al Otro. Traducción, exotismo, poscolonalismo*. Cuenca: Cuenca Univ. Press

Catford, John C. 1965. *A Linguistic Theory of Translation*. London: Oxford Univ. Press.

Chamberlain, Lori. 1992. "Gender and the Metaphorics of Translation." In *Rethinking Translation*, L. Venuti (ed.), 57–74.

Chan, Sin-wai and Pollard, David (eds.). 1995. *An Encyclopaedia of Translation. Chinese-English. English-Chinese*. Hong Kong: Chinese Univ. Press.

Chen, Tzu-Ann. 2004. *Sprache als identitätsstiftendes Mittel in Amy Tans* The Joy Luck Club. *Eine Übersetzungskritik nach dem Modell von Margret Ammann.* Vienna: unpubl. master's thesis.

Chesterman, Andrew. 1993. "From 'Is' to 'Ought': Laws, Norms and Strategies in Translation Studies." *Target* 5(1): 1–20.

———. 1997. *Memes of Translation. The Spread of Ideas in Translation Theory.* (Benjamins Translation Library 22), Amsterdam/Philadelphia: John Benjamins.

———. 2002. "On the Interdisciplinarity of Translation Studies." *Logos and Language* 3 (1): 1–9.

———. Forthcoming. "Questions in the Sociology of Translation", in *Translation Studies,* J. F. Duarte et al. (eds.)

Chesterman, Andrew, Gallardo San Salvador, Natividad, Gambier, Yves (eds.). 2000. *Translation in Context. Selected Contributions from the EST Congress, Granada 1998* (Benjamins Translation Library 39). Amsterdam/Philadelphia: John Benjamins.

Chomsky, Noam. 1957. *Syntactic Structures.* The Hague: Mouton.

———. 1965. *Aspects of the Theory of Syntax.* Cambridge: MIT Press.

Clyne, Michael. 1991. "Zu kulturellen Unterschieden in der Produktion und Wahrnehmung englischer und deutscher wissenschaftlicher Texte." *Info DaF* 18 (4): 376–383.

"Code for the use of new technologies in conference interpretation." 1997. *AIIC Bulletin* XXVI (2): 23–25.

Coseriu, Eugenio. 1970. "System, Norm und Rede." In *Sprache, Strukturen und Funktionen.* E. Coseriu, 193–212. Tübingen: Narr.

———. 1971. "Thesen zum Thema 'Sprache und Dichtung'." In *Beiträge zur Textlinguistik,* W.-D. Stempel (ed.), 183–188. München: Fink.

Cronin, Michael. 1998. "Game theory and translation." In *Routledge Encyclopedia of Translation Studies,* M. Baker (ed.), 91–93.

———. 2000. *Across the Lines: Travel, Language, Translation.* Cork: Cork Univ. Press.

———. 2002. "The Empire talks back: Orality, Heteronomy and the Cultural Turn in Interpreting Studies." In *The Interpreting Studies Reader,* F. Pöchhacker and M. Shlesinger (eds.), 387–397.

Cruz Romão, Tito Livio. 2000. "Die Problematik der Übersetzung von Begriffen aus afrobrasilianischen Religionen." In *Translationswissenschaft,* M. Kadrić et al. (eds.), 227–239.

Crystal, David. 1997. *English as a Global Language.* Cambridge: Cambridge Univ. Press.

Dawkins, Richard. 1976. *The Selfish Gene.* Oxford: Oxford Univ. Press.

———. 1982. *The Extended Phenotype: The Gene as the Unit of Selection.* Oxford/San Francisco: Freeman.

Delabastita, Dirk. 1991. "A False Opposition in Translation Studies: Theoretical versus/and Historical Approaches." *Target* 3(2): 137–152.

———. 1993. *There's a Double Tongue. An Investigation into the Translation of Shakespeare's Wordplay.* Amsterdam: Rodopi.

Delisle, Jean. 1998. "Canadian tradition." In *Routledge Encyclopedia of Translation Studies,* M. Baker (ed.), 356–365.

Delisle, Jean and Woodsworth, Judith (eds.). 1995. *Translators through History* (Benjamins Translation Library 13). Amsterdam/Philadelphia: John Benjamins.

Derrida, Jacques. 1978. *Positions,* transl. Alan Bass, Chicago: Chicago Univ. Press.

Didaoui, Mohammed. 1996. *Communication interferences in a multilingual environment. The role of translators.* Vienna: unpubl. doctoral thesis.

Diller, Hans-Jürgen and Kornelius, Joachim. 1978. *Linguistische Probleme der Übersetzung.* Tübingen: Niemeyer.

Dingwaney, Anuradha and Maier, Carol (eds.). 1995. *Between Languages and Cultures. Translation and Cross-Cultural Texts.* Pittsburgh: Pittsburgh Univ. Press.

Dizdar, Dilek. 1997. "Die Norm brechen. Möglichkeiten eines neuen Vokabulars in der Translationswissenschaft." *TextConText* 11 (1): 129–147.

Dollerup, Cay. 1996. "Language Work at the European Union." In *Translation Horizons,* M. Gaddis Rose (ed.), 297–314.

———. 2000. "English: Axes for a target language." In *Translation into Non-Mother Tongues,* M. Grosman et al. (eds.), 61–70.

Dollerup, Cay, and Loddegaard, Anne (eds.). 1992. *Teaching Translation and Interpreting. Training, Talent and Experience. Papers from the First* Language International *Conference Elsinore, Denmark, 31 May – 2 June* 1991. Amsterdam/Philadelphia: John Benjamins.

———. (eds.). 1994. *Teaching Translation and Interpreting 2. Insights, Aims, Visions. Papers from the Second* Language International *Conference Elsinore, Denmark 4-6 June 1993.* (Benjamins Translation Library 5). Amsterdam/Philadelphia: John Benjamins.

Dollerup, Cay and Appel, Vibeke (eds.). 1996. *Teaching Translation and Interpreting 3. New Horizons. Papers from the Third* Language International *Conference Elsinore,Denmark 9-11 June 1995.*(Benjamins Translation Library 16). Amsterdam/Philadelphia: John Benjamins.

Driesen, Christiane. 1998. "Gerichtsdolmetschen." In *Handbuch Translation,* M. Snell-Hornby et al. (eds.), 312–316.

Drosdowski, Günther et al (eds.). 1996[3]. *Duden Deutsches Universalwörterbuch.* Mannheim: Duden.

Dryden, John. 1962. *Of dramatic poesy,* ed. George Watson. London: Dent.

Duarte, João Ferreira, Assis Rosa, Alexandra and Seruya, Teresa (eds.). Forthcoming. *Translation Studies. A Crossroads of Disciplines.* Amsterdam/Philadelphia: John Benjamins.

Eco, Umberto. 1985[3]. *Lector in fabula. La cooperazione interpretativa nei tesi narrativi.* Milan: Bompiani.

El-Akramy, Ursula. 2001. "Caroline Schlegel-Schelling: Salonnière und Shakespeare-Übersetzin." In *Übersetzung aus aller Frauen Länder,* S. Messner and M. Wolf (eds.), 71–76.

Esselink, Bert. 2002. Editorial, *Language International* 14 (6): 4.

Fillmore, Charles J. 1977. "Scenes-and-frames semantics." In *Linguistic Structures Processing,* A. Zampolli (ed.), 55–81. Amsterdam: N. Holland.

Finkenstaedt, Thomas and Schröder, Konrad. 1992. *Sprachen im Europa von morgen.* Berlin/München: Langenscheidt.

Fischer-Lichte, Erika. 1983. *Das System der theatralischen Zeichen.* Tübingen: Narr.

Flotow, Luise von. 1997. *Gender and Translation. Translation in an 'Era of Feminism'.* Ottawa: Ottawa Univ. Press.

———. 1998. "Feministische Aspekte." In *Handbuch Translation,* M. Snell-Hornby et al. (eds.), 130–132.

———. 2001. "Genderkonzepte im Wandel. Übersetzungspolitische Überlegungen." In *Übersetzung aus aller Frauen Länder,* S. Messner and M. Wolf (eds.), 49–59.

Forstner, Martin (ed.). 1995. *C.I.U.T.I. Conférence Internationale Permanente d'Instituts Universitaires de Traducteurs et Interprètes.Translation and Interpreting Studies at C.I.U.T.I. Institutes. Formation des Traducteurs et des Interprètes dans les Instituts de la C.I.U.T.I. Die Studiengänge Übersetzen und Dolmetschen an den C.I.U.T.I-Instituten.* European Community.

Framson, Elke Anna. 2005. *Translation in der internationalen Marketingkommunikation. Funktionen und Aufgaben für Translatoren im globalisierten Handel.* Vienna: unpubl. doctoral thesis.

Freihoff, Roland. 2001. *Kernfragen der Übersetzerausbildung. Curriculumentwicklung – Praxis und Theorie der Translation.* Vaasa: Vaasa Univ. Press.

Frenz, Horst (ed.). 1969. *Nobel Lectures on Literature.* London: Nobel Foundation.

Gadamer, Hans-Georg. 1960. *Wahrheit und Methode. Grundzüge einer philosophischen Hermeneutik.* Tübingen: Mohr.

Gaddis Rose, Marilyn. 1996. "Like the Paths Around Combray, Humanistic Translation Theories Diverge and Converge." In *Translation Horizons*, M. Gaddis Rose (ed.), 59–67.

———. (ed.) 1996a. *Translation Horizons. Beyond the Boundaries of* Translation Spectrum. *Translation Perspectives IX 1996. A Collection of Essays Situating and Proposing New Directions and Major Issues in Translation Studies.* Binghamton: SUNY.

Gamal, Muhammed, "Court interpreting." In *Routledge Encyclopedia of Translation Studies*, M. Baker (ed.), 53–56.

Gambier, Yves. Forthcoming. "Pour une socio-traduction", in *Translation Studies*, J. F.Duarte et al.

Gambier, Yves and Snell-Hornby, Mary (eds.). 1995. *Problemi e Tendenze nella Didattica dell'Interpretazione e della Traduzione / Problems and Trends in the Teaching of Interpreting and Translation.* Misano Adriatico: Koiné.

Gambier, Yves and Gottlieb, Henrik (eds.). 2001. *(Multi) Media Translation. Concepts, Practices, and Research.* (Benjamins Translation Library 34). Amsterdam/Philadelphia: John Benjamins.

Gawlas, Christine. 2004. *Nachrichten – heißer Draht zwischen Lebenswelten. Kulturtransfer im internationalen Pressewesen.* Frankfurt: Lang.

Gentzler, Edwin. 1998. Foreword to *Constructing Cultures*, S. Bassnett and A. Lefevere (eds.), ix–xxii.

Gerhardt, Stefan. 1998. "Software-Lokalisierung." In *Handbuch Translation*, M. Snell-Hornby et al. (eds.), 213–217.

Gibbels, Elisabeth. 2004. *Mary Wollstonecraft zwischen Feminismus und Opportunismus. Die diskursiven Strategien in deutschen Übersetzungen von "A Vindication of the Rights of Woman".* Tübingen: Narr.

Gile, Daniel. 1994. "Opening up in Interpretation Studies." In *Translation Studies. An Interdiscipline,* M. Snell-Hornby et al. (eds.), 149–158.

———. 1998. "Conference and simultaneous interpreting." In *Routledge Encyclopedia of Translation Studies*, M. Baker (ed.), 40–45.

Godard, Barbara. 1990. "Theorizing Feminist Discourse/Translation." In *Translation, History and Culture*, S. Bassnett and A. Lefevere (eds.), 87–96.

Göhring, Heinz. 1977. "Interkulturelle Kommunikation: Die Überwindung der Trennung von Fremdsprachen- und Landeskundeunterricht durch einen integrierten Fremdverhaltensunterricht." In *Kongressberichte der 8. Jahrestagung der Gesellschaft für Angewandte Linguistik GAL e.V.*, Vol. IV, 9–13. Mainz.

Goodenough, Ward H. 1964. "Cultural Anthropology and Linguistics." In *Language in Culture and Society. A Reader in Linguistics and Anthropology*, D. Hymes (ed.), 36–40. New York: Harper & Row.

Göpferich, Susanne. 1998. "Paralleltexte." In *Handbuch Translation*, M. Snell-Hornby et al. (eds.), 184–186.

————. 2002. *Textproduktion im Zeitalter der Globalisierung. Entwicklung einer Didaktik des Wissenstransfers*. (Studien zur Translation 15). Tübingen: Stauffenburg.

Gottlieb, Henrik. 1994. "Subtitling: Diagonal Translation." *Perspectives, Studies in Translatology* 2 (1): 101–121.

Gouanvic, Jean-Marie. 1997. "Pour une sociologie de la traduction: le cas de la littérature américaine traduite en France après la Seconde Guerre mondiale (1945–1960)." In *Translation as Intercultural Communication*, M. Snell-Hornby et al. (eds.), 33–44.

Grbić, Nadja. 1998. "Gebärdensprachdolmetschen." In *Handbuch Translation*, M. Snell-Hornby et al. (eds.), 321–324.

Grbić, Nadja and Wolf, Michaela (eds.). 1997. *Text – Kultur – Kommunikation. Translation als Forschungsaufgabe. Festschrift aus Anlass des 50jährigen Bestehens des Instituts für Übersetzer- und Dolmetscherausbildung an der Universität Graz*. (Studien zur Translation 4). Tübingen: Stauffenburg.

Grbić, Nadja and Wolf, Michaela. 1998. "Strategien des geschlechtsneutralen Ausdrucks." In *Handbuch Translation*, M. Snell-Hornby et al. (eds.), 294–296.

Grosman, Meta, Kadrić, Mira, Kovaičič, Irena and Snell-Hornby, Mary (eds.). 2000. *Translation into Non-Mother Tongues. In Professional Practice and Training*. (Studien zur Translation 8). Tübingen: Stauffenburg.

Gutt, Ernst August. 1991. *Translation and Relevance. Cognition and Context*. Oxford: Blackwell.

Haag, Ansgar. 1984. "Übersetzen für das Theater: Am Beispiel William Shakespeare." *Babel* 30: 218–224.

Halliday, Michael A.K. 1976. *System and Function in Language. Selected Papers*. Ed. G. R. Kress, Cambridge: Cambridge Univ. Press.

Halliday, Michael A.K. and Hasan, Ruqaia. 1976. *Cohesion in English*. London: Longman.

Halverson, Sandra. 1997. "The Concept of Equivalence in Translation Studies: Much Ado about Something." *Target* 9 (2): 207–233.

————. 1999. "Conceptual Work and the 'Translation' Concept." *Target* 11 (1): 1–31.

————. 2000. "Prototype effects in the 'translation' category." In *Translation in Context*, A. Chesterman et al. (eds.) 3–16.

Hanks, Patrick Long, Thomas Hill and Urdang, Lawrence (eds.). 1979. *Collins Dictionary of the English Language* (CED). London/Glasgow: Collins.

Hansen, Gyde and Hönig, Hans G.. 2000. "Kabine oder Bibliothek? Überlegungen zur Entwicklung eines interinstitutionell anwendbaren Versuchsdesigns zur Erforschung der mentalen Prozesse beim Übersetzen." In *Translationswissenschaft*, M. Kadrić et al. (eds.), 319–338.

Hasada, Rie. 1997. "Some aspects of Japanese cultural ethos embedded in nonverbal communicative behavior." In *Nonverbal Communication and Translation*, F. Poyatos (ed.), 83–103.

Hatim, Basil. 1998. "Pragmatics and translation." In *Routledge Encyclopedia of Translation Studies*, M. Baker (ed.), 179–183.

Hatim, Basil and Ian Mason. 1990. *Discourse and the Translator*. London: Longman.

Hermans, Theo (ed.) 1985. *The Manipulation of Literature. Studies in Literary Translation*. London: Croom Helm.

————. 1991. "Translational Norms and Correct Translations." In *Translation Studies: The State of the Art*, K. van Leuven-Zwart and T. Naaijkens (eds.), 155–169.

————. 1996. "Norms and the Determination of Translation. A Theoretical Framework." In *Translation, Power, Subversion*, R. Álvarez and M.. C-Á. Vidal (eds.), 25–51.

————. 1998 "Descriptive Translation Studies." In *Handbuch Translation*, M. Snell-Hornby (eds.), 96–100.

Heynold, Christian. 1998. "Satelliten-Konferenzdolmetschen." In *Handbuch Translation,* M. Snell-Hornby et al. (eds.), 324–326.

Hohn, Stefanie. 1998. "Philologisch-historische Tradition." In *Handbuch Translation,* M. Snell-Hornby et al. (eds.), 91–95.

Holmes, James S. 1987. "The name and nature of translation studies." *Indian Journal of Applied Linguistics* 13 (2): 9–24.

——. 1988. *Translated! Papers on Literary Translation and Translation Studies.* Amsterdam: Rodopi.

Holmes, James S., Lambert, José and Van den Broeck, Raymond (eds.). 1978. *Literature and Translation: New Perspectives in Literary Studies.* Leuven: ACCO.

Holz-Mänttäri, Justa. 1984. *Translatorisches Handeln. Theorie und Methode.* Helsinki: Suomalainen Tiedeakatemia.

——. 1984a. "Sichtbarmachung und Beurteilung translatorischer Leistungen bei der Ausbildung von Berufstranslatoren." In *Die Theorie des Übersetzens und ihr Aufschlusswert für die Übersetzungs- und Dolmetschdidaktik,* W. Wilss and G. Thome (eds.), 176–185.

——. 1986. "Translatorisches Handeln – theoretisch fundierte Berufsprofile." In *Übersetzungswissenschaft – Eine Neuorientierung,* M. Snell-Hornby (ed.), 348–374.

——. 1989. „Interferenz als naturbedingtes Rezeptionsdefizit – ein Beitrag aus translatologischer Sicht." In *Interferenz in der Translation,* H. Schmidt (ed.), 129–134.

Holz-Mänttäri, Justa and Nord, Christiane (eds.). 1993. *Traducere Navem. Festschrift für Katharina Reiss zum 70. Geburtstag.* (Studia Translatologica A.3), Tampere: Tampere Univ. Press.

Hönig, Hans G. 1991. "Holmes' 'Mapping Theory' and the Landscape of Mental Translation Processes." In *Translation Studies: The State of the Art,* K. van Leuven-Zwart and T. Naaijkens (eds.), 91–101.

——. 1995. *Konstruktives Übersetzen.* (Studien zur Translation 1). Tübingen: Stauffenburg.

——. 2004. "Einige späte Einsichten und ein Ausblick." In *Übersetzungswissenschaft Dolmetschwissenschaft,* W. Pöckl (ed.), 133–140.

Hönig, Hans G. and Kussmaul, Paul. 1982. *Strategie der Übersetzung. Ein Lehr- und Arbeitsbuch.* Tübingen: Narr.

Hörmanseder, Fabienne. 2002. *Text und Publikum. Kriterien für eine bühnenwirksame Übersetzung im Hinblick auf eine Kooperation zwischen Translatologen und Bühnenexperten.* Vienna: unpubl. doctoral thesis.

House, Juliane. 1977. *A Model for Translation Quality Assessment.* Tübingen: Narr.

Iser, Wolfgang. 1976. *Der Akt des Lesens. Theorie ästhetischer Wirkung.* München: Fink.

Isham, William P. 1998. "Signed language interpreting." In *Routledge Encyclopedia of Translation Studies,* M. Baker (ed.), 231–235.

Ivarsson, Jan. 1992. *Subtitling for the Media.* Stockholm: Transedit.

Jääskeläinen, Riitta. 1989. "Translation Assignment in Professional vs. Non-professional Translation: A Think-Aloud Protocol Study." In *The Translation Process,* C. Séguinot (ed.), 87–98.

Jäger, Gert. 1975. *Translation und Translationslinguistik,* Halle: Bibliographisches Institut.

Jakobson, Roman, 1959. "On Linguistic Aspects of Translation." In *On Translation,* R. Brower (ed.), 232–239. Cambridge, Mass.

Jettmarová, Zuzana, Piotrowska, Maria and Zauberga, Ieva. 1997. "New advertising markets as target areas for translation." In *Translation as Intercultural Communication,* M. Snell-Hornby et al. (eds.), 185–194.

Jumpelt, R.W. 1961. *Die Übersetzung naturwissenschaftlicher und technischer Literatur: Sprachliche Maßstäbe und Methoden zur Bestimmung ihrer Wesenszüge und Probleme.* (Langenscheidt-Bibliothek für Wissenschaft und Praxis 1). Berlin: Langenscheidt.

Kade, Otto. 1965. "Perspektiven der Dolmetscherausbildung an der Karl-Marx-Universität." *Fremdsprachen* 9 (2): 1–5, 24–25.

———. 1968. *Zufall und Gesetzmäßigkeit in der Übersetzung.* Supplement to *Fremdsprachen 1.* Leipzig: Enzyklopädie.

———. 1970. "Zur linguistischen Erforschung des Simultandolmetschens (Ein Beitrag zum Verhältnis von Sprach- und Übersetzungswissenschaft)." In *Actes du Xe Congrès International des Linguistes,* 1069–1078. Bucharest.

———. 1973. "Zum Verhältnis von "idealem Translator" als wissenschaftlicher Hilfskonstruktion und optimalem Sprachmittler als Ausbildungsziel." *Neue Beiträge zu Grundfragen der Übersetzungswissenschaft.* Supplement to *Fremdsprachen* 5 (6): 179–190.

Kadrić, Mira. 2001. *Dolmetschen bei Gericht. Erwartungen, Anforderungen, Kompetenzen.* Vienna: Vienna Univ. Press.

Kadrić, Mira, Kaindl, Klaus and Pöchhacker, Franz (eds.). 2000. *Translationswissenschaft. Festschrift für Mary Snell-Hornby zum 60. Geburtstag.* Tübingen: Stauffenburg.

Kaindl, Klaus. 1995. *Die Oper als Textgestalt. Perspektiven einer interdisziplinären Übersetzungswissenschaft.* (Studien zur Translation 2), Tübingen: Stauffenburg.

———. 1997. "Von Hauptdarstellern und Statisten: Zur Rolle des Textes im translationswissenschaftlichen Handlungsspiel." In *Text – Kultur – Kommunikation,* N. Grbić and M. Wolf (eds.), 53–65.

———. 2004. *Übersetzungswissenschaft im interdisziplinären Dialog. Am Beispiel der Comicübersetzung.* (Studien zur Translation 16), Tübingen: Stauffenburg.

Kaiser-Cooke, Michèle. 2003. *Translation, Evolution und Cyberspace. Eine Synthese von Theorie, Praxis und Lehre.* Frankfurt: Lang.

Kenny, Dorothy. 1998. "Corpora in translation studies." In *Routledge Encyclopedia of Translation Studies,* M. Baker (ed.), 50–53.

———. 1998a. "Equivalence." In *Routledge Encyclopedia of Translation Studies,* M. Baker (ed.), 77–80.

Kittel, Harald and Poltermann, Andreas. 1998. "German tradition." In *Routledge Encyclopedia of Translation Studies,* M. Baker (ed.), 418–428.

Kluge, Friedrich. 1975. *Etymologisches Wörterbuch der deutschen Sprache.* Berlin: de Gruyter.

Koller, Werner. 1972. *Grundprobleme der Übersetzungstheorie. Unter besonderer Berücksichtigung schwedisch-deutscher Übersetzungsfälle.* Bern: Francke.

———. 1979. *Einführung in die Übersetzungswissenschaft.* Heidelberg: Quelle & Meyer.

———. 1995. "The Concept of Equivalence and the Object of Translation Studies." *Target* 7 (2): 191–222.

König, Otto, Renner, Franz and Wolf, Michaela (eds.). 1994. *Amerika im Gedächtnis. "500 Jahre Widerstand in Lateinamerika". Eine Selbstbeschreibung.* Vienna: Böhlau.

Koskinen, Kaisa. 2000. "Institutional illusions: Translating in the EU Commission". *The Translator* 6 (1): 49–65.

———. 2004. "Shared culture? Reflections on recent trends in Translation Studies". *Target* 16 (1): 143–156.

Krings, Hans-P. 1986. *Was in den Köpfen von Übersetzern vorgeht. Eine empirische Untersuchung zur Struktur des Übersetzungsprozesses an fortgeschrittenen Französischlernern.* (TBL 291). Tübingen: Narr.

——. 1988. "Blick in die 'black box' – Eine Fallstudie zum Übersetzungsprozess bei Berufs-übersetzern." In *Textlinguistik und Fachsprache. Akten des Internationalen übersetzungs-wissenschaftlichen AILA-Symposions, Hildesheim 13.-16. April 1987*, R. Arntz (ed.), 303–412. Hildesheim: Olms.

Krishnan, Mini. 1995. Preface to *Pandavapuram*, Sethu, v.

Kufnerová, Zlata and Osers, Ewald. 1998. "Czech tradition." In *Routledge Encyclopedia of Translation Studies*, M. Baker (ed.), 376–383.

Kuhiwczak, Piotr. 1990. "Translation as Appropriation: The Case of Milan Kundera's *The Joke*." In *Translation, History and Culture*, S. Bassnett and A. Lefevere (eds.), 118–130.

Kuhn, Thomas S. 1970². *The structure of scientific revolutions*. Chicago: Chicago Univ. Press.

Kurth, Ernst-Norbert. 1995. *Metaphernübersetzung. Dargestellt an grotesken Metaphern im Frühwerk Charles Dickens in der Wiedergabe deutscher Übersetzungen*. Frankfurt: Lang.

Kurz, Ingrid. 1994. "A look into the 'black box' – EEG probability mapping during mental simultaneous interpreting." In *Translation Studies. An Interdiscipline*, M. Snell-Hornby et al. (eds.) 199–207.

——. 1996. *Simultandolmetschen als Gegenstand der interdisziplinären Forschung*. Vienna: Vienna Univ. Press.

——. 1997. "Getting the message across – Simultaneous interpreting for the media." In *Translation as Intercultural Communication*, M. Snell-Hornby et al.(eds.), 195–205.

——. 2000. "Tagungsort Genf/Nairobi/Wien. Zu einigen Aspekten des Teledolmetschens." In *Translationswissenschaft*, M. Kadrić et al. (eds.), 291–302.

Kurz, Ingrid and Klaus Kaindl (eds.) 2005. *Wortklauber, Sinnverdreher, Brückenbauer? ÜbersetzerInnen und DolmetscherInnen als literarische Geschöpfe*. Münster: LIT-Verlag.

Kussmaul, Paul. 1986. "Übersetzen als Entscheidungsprozess. Die Rolle der Fehleranalyse in der Übersetzungsdidaktik." In *Übersetzungswissenschaft – Eine Neuorientierung*, M. Snell-Hornby (ed.), 206–229.

——. 1989. „Interferenzen im Übersetzungsprozess – Diagnose und Therapie." In *Interferenz in der Translation*, H. Schmidt (ed.), 19–28.

——. 1994. "Möglichkeiten einer empirisch begründeten Übersetzungsdidaktik." In *Translation Studies. An Interdiscipline*, M. Snell-Hornby et al. (eds.), 377–386.

——. 1995. *Training the Translator*. (Benjamins Translation Library 10). Amsterdam/Philadelphia: John Benjamins.

——. 1997. "Comprehension processes and translation. A think-aloud protocol study." In *Translation as Intercultural Communication*, M. Snell-Hornby et al. (eds.), 239–248.

——. 1998. "Philologische Texte." In *Handbuch Translation*, M. Snell-Hornby et al. (eds.), 235–236.

——. 2000. *Kreatives Übersetzen*. (Studien zur Translation 10).Tübingen: Stauffenburg.

——. 2004. "Entwicklung miterlebt." In *Übersetzungswissenschaft Dolmetschwissenschaft*, W. Pöckl (ed.), 221–226.

Language International 8 / 6 1996. "Profile of a linguist. Dr. Eugene Nida. Patriarch of Translation Studies", 8–9.

Lefevere, André. 1977. *Translating Literature. The German Tradition from Luther to Rosenzweig* (Approaches to Translation 4). Assen/Amsterdam: Van Gorcum.

——. 1985. "Why Waste our Time on Rewrites? The Trouble with Interpretation and the Role of Rewriting in an Alternative Paradigm." In *The Manipulation of Literature*, T. Hermans (ed.), 215–243.

———. 1992. *Translation, Rewriting and the Manipulation of Literary Fame.* London/New York: Routledge.

———. 1993. "Discourses on Translation: Recent, Less Recent and to Come." *Target* 5 (2):, 229–241.

Lefevere, André and Bassnett, Susan. 1990. "Introduction: Proust's Grandmother and the Thousand and One Nights: The 'Cultural Turn' in Translation Studies." In *Translation, History and Culture,* S. Bassnett and A. Lefevere (eds.), 1–13.

Leisi, Ernst. 1953/1975. *Der Wortinhalt. Seine Struktur im Deutschen und Englischen.* Heidelberg: Quelle & Meyer.

———. 1973. *Praxis der englischen Semantik.* Heidelberg: Winter.

Leppihalme, Ritva. 1994. *Culture Bumps. On the translation of allusions.* Helsinki: Helsinki Univ. Press.

Levý, Jiří. 1967/2000. "Translation as a Decision Process." In *To Honor Roman Jakobson. Essays on the Occasion of his 70th Birthday,* repr. *The Translation Studies Reader,* L. Venuti (ed.). 148–171.

———. 1969. *Die literarische Übersetzung. Theorie einer Kunstgattung,* transl. W. Schamschula, Frankfurt: Athenäum.

Limbeck, Sonja. 2005. *"Familienkonferenz". Eine funktionale Übersetzungskritik der deutschen Fassung von Thomas Gordons "Parent Effectiveness Training",* Vienna: unpubl. master's thesis.

Lisa, Claudia. 1993. *Die Übersetzung des modernen Musicals. Am Beispiel von* Les Misérables. Vienna: unpubl. master's thesis.

Longley, Patricia. 1984. "What is a Community Interpreter?" *The Incorporated Linguist* 23 (3): 178–181.

Lörscher, Wolfgang. 1991. *Translation Performance, Translation Process, and Translation Strategies. A Psycholinguistic Investigation.* Tübingen: Narr.

Lotbinière-Harwood, Susanne de. (1991) *Re-Belle et Infidèle. La Traduction comme pratique de réécriture au féminin/The Body Bilingual. Translation as a Rewriting in the Feminine.* Toronto: The Women's Press / Montréal: Les éditions du remue-ménage.

Luke, David. 1995. "Translating Thomas Mann." *The Times Literary Supplement,* 8.12.1995: 15.

Luyken, Georg-Michael, Herbst, Thomas, Langham-Brown, Jo, Reid, Helen and Spinhof, Hermann (eds.). *Overcoming Language Barriers in Television. Dubbing and Subtitling for the European Audience.* Manchester: European Institute for the Media.

Manhart, Sibylle. 1996. *Zum übersetzungswissenschaftlichen Aspekt der Filmsynchronisation in Theorie und Praxis: Eine interdisziplinäre Betrachtung.* Vienna: unpubl. doctoral thesis.

Marx, Sonia. 1997. *Klassiker der Jugendliteratur in Übersetzungen.* Struwwelpeter, Max und Moritz, Pinocchio *im deutsch-italienischen Dialog.* Padua: Padua Univ. Press.

Mateo, Marta. 1995. *La traducción del humor. Las comedias inglesas en espanol.* Oviedo: Oviedo Univ. Press.

Mauranen, Anna and Kujamäki, Pekka (eds.). 2004. *Translation Universals. Do they exist?.* (Benjamins Translation Library 48). Amsterdam/Philadelphia: John Benjamins.

Mehrez, Samía. 1992. "Translation and the postcolonial experience: The francophone North African text." In *Rethinking Translation,* L. Venuti (ed.), 120–138.

Melby, Alan K, and Lonsdale, Deryle W. 2002. "Machine Translation, Translation Studies, and Linguistic Theories." *Logos and Language* 3 (1): 39–57.

Messner, Sabine and Wolf, Michaela (eds.). 2001. *Übersetzung aus aller Frauen Länder. Beiträge zu Theorie und Praxis weiblicher Realität in der Translation.* Graz: Leykam.

Morris, Ruth. 1995. "The Moral Dilemmas of Court Interpreting." *The Translator. Studies in Intercultural Communication* 1 (1): 25–46.

Moser-Mercer, Barbara. 1986. "Schnittstelle Mensch/Maschine: Interaktion oder Konfrontation?" In *Übersetzungswissenschaft – Eine Neuorientierung*, M.Snell-Hornby (ed.), 311–330.

Munday, Jeremy. 2001. *Introducing Translation Studies. Theories and applications.* London/New York: Routledge.

———. 2002. "Translation Studies and Corpus Linguistics: An interface for interdisciplinary co-operation." *Logos and Language* 3 (1): 11–20.

Müntefering, Matthias. 2002. "Dubbing in Deutschland. Cultural and Industrial Considerations." *Language International* 14(2): 14–16.

Navarro, Fernando. 1997. "Which is the world's most important language?" *Lebende Sprachen* 42: 5–10.

Neubert, Albrecht. 1977. "Übersetzungswissenschaft in soziolinguistischer Sicht." *Übersetzungswissenschaftliche Beiträge 1.* 52–59. Leipzig: Enzyklopädie.

———. 1986. "Dichtung und Wahrheit des zweisprachigen Wörterbuchs." In *Sitzungsberichte der Sächsischen Akademie der Wissenschaften zu Leipzig*, Vol.126, 4, 1–23.

———. 1989. "Interference between Languages and between Texts." In *Interferenz in der Translation*, H. Schmidt (ed.), 56–64.

———. 1992. "Von der kommunikationswissenschaftlichen Begründung der Translation zur computergestützten Realisierung des Übersetzens: theoretische und empirische Voraussetzungen für ein translatorisches Expertensystem." In *Wissenschaftliche Grundlagen der Sprachmittlung*, H. Salevsky (ed.), 25–37. Frankfurt: Lang.

Newmark, Peter. 1981. *Approaches to Translation.* Oxford: Pergamon.

———. 1985. "The Translation of Metaphor." In *The Ubiquity of Metaphor*, W. Paprotté and R. Dirven (eds.), 295–326. Amsterdam/Philadelphia: John Benjamins.

Nida, Eugene A. 1964. *Toward a Science of Translating. With special reference to principles and procedures involved in Bible translating.* Leiden: Brill.

Nida, Eugene A. and Charles Taber. 1969. *The Theory and Practice of Translation.* Leiden: Brill.

Niranjana, Tejaswini. 1992. *Siting Translation. History, Post-structuralism, and the Colonial Context.* Berkeley: Univ. of California Press.

Nord, Christiana. 1988. *Textanalyse und Übersetzen. Theoretische Grundlagen, Methode und didaktische Anwendung einer übersetzungsrelevanten Textanalyse.* Heidelberg: Groos.

———. 1989. "Loyalität statt Treue. Vorschläge zu einer funktionalen Übersetzungstypologie." *Lebende Sprachen* 3, 100–105.

———. 1991. "Scopos, Loyalty, and Translational Conventions." *Target* 3(1): 91–109.

———. 1997. *Translating as a Purposeful Activity.* Manchester: St. Jerome.

Oittinen, Riitta. 1993. *I am Me – I am Other: On the Dialogics of Translating for Children.* Tampere: Tampere Univ. Press.

Paepcke, Fritz. 1986. *Im Übersetzen leben. Übersetzen und Textvergleich.* Ed. K. Berger and H.-M. Speier, Tübingen: Narr.

Paloposki, Outi and Oittinen, Riitta. 2000. "The domesticated foreign." In *Translation in Context.* A. Chesterman et al. (eds.), 373–390.

Petioky, Viktor. 1997. "Zur nichtliterarischen Übersetzungstätigkeit in der Donaumonarchie." In *Ars transferendi. Sprache, Übersetzung, Interkulturalität. Festschrift für Nikolai Salnikow zum 65. Geburtstag*, D. Huber and E. Worbs (eds.), 351–372. Frankfurt: Lang.

Peyrefitte, Alain. 1989. *L'Empire Immobile ou Le Choc des Mondes. Récit historique.* Paris: Fayard.

——. 1992. *The Collision of Two Civilisations. The British Expedition to China in 1792–4,* transl. J. Rothschild, London: Harvill.

Pisek, Gerhard. 1994. *Die große Illusion: Probleme und Möglichkeiten der Filmsynchronisation.* Trier: WTV.

Plecher, Renate. 1998. *Das frauenkulturelle Weltbild als Basis für Übersetzungen aus fremden Kulturen. Am Beispiel jamaicanischer Literatur.* Vienna: unpubl. doctoral thesis.

Pluta, Aga. 1998. *Textsorte "Baubescheid". Textsortenkonventionen im deutschsprachigen Baubescheid und "Baubescheid-Counterparts" in polnischer und englischer Sprache.* Vienna: unpubl. master's thesis.

Pöchhacker, Franz. 1994. *Simultandolmetschen als komplexes Handeln.* Tübingen: Narr.

——. 1997. "'Clinton speaks German': A case study of live broadcast simultaneous interpreting." In *Translation as Intercultural Communication,* M. Snell-Hornby at al. (eds.), 207–216.

——. 1997a. *Kommunikation mit Nichtdeutschsprachigen in Wiener Gesundheits- und Sozialeinrichtungen.* Vienna: MA/Dezernat für Gesundheitsplanung.

——. 1998. "Simultandolmetschen." In *Handbuch Translation,* M. Snell-Hornby et al. (eds.), 301–304.

——. 2000. *Dolmetschen: Konzeptuelle Grundlagen und deskriptive Untersuchungen.* (Studien zur Translation 7). Tübingen: Stauffenburg.

——. 2004. *Introducing Interpreting Studies.* London/New York: Routledge.

——. 2004a. "Fachliche Entwicklung – persönliche Genese." In *Übersetzungswissenschaft Dolmetschwissenschaft,* W. Pöckl (ed.) 259–264.

Pöchhacker, Franz and Kadrić, Mira. 1999. "The Hospital Cleaner as Healthcare Interpreter: A Case Study." In *Dialogue Interpreting,* Special Issue of *The Translator. Studies in Intercultural Communication* 5 (2): 161–178.

Pöchhacker, Franz and Miriam Shlesinger (eds.). 2002. *The Interpreting Studies Reader.* London/New York: Routledge.

Pöckl, Wolfgang (ed.). 2004. *Übersetzungswissenschaft Dolmetschwissenschaft. Wege in eine neue Disziplin.* Wien: Praesens.

Pollard, David. 1995. "Body language in Chinese-English Translation." In *An Encyclopaedia of Translation,* S-W. Chan and D. Pollard (eds.), 70–77.

Poyatos, Fernando. 1993. "Aspects of Nonverbal Communication in Literature." In *Traducere Navem,* J. Holz-Mänttäri and C. Nord (eds.), 137–151.

——. (ed.). 1997. *Nonverbal Communication and Translation. New Perspectives and Challenges in Literature, Interpretation and the Media.* (Benjamins Translation Library 17) Amsterdam/Philadelphia: John Benjamins.

——. 1997a. "Aspects, problems and challenges of nonverbal communication in literary translation." In *Nonverbal Communication and Translation,* F. Poyatos (ed.), 17–47.

——. 1997b. "The reality of multichannel verbal-nonverbal communication in simultaneous and consecutive interpretation." In *Nonverbal Communication and Translation,* F. Poyatos (ed.), 249–282.

Prado, Daniel, Kingscott, Geoffrey, Baddé, Karl and Galinski, Christian (eds.). 1995. *International Who's Who in Translation & Terminology / Traduction et Terminologie Répertoire biographique international.* Paris: Union latine.

Prasad, G.J.V. 1999. "Writing translation: the strange case of the Indian English novel." In *Postcolonial Translation,* S. Bassnett and H. Trivedi (eds.), 41–57.

Pratt, Mary Louise. 1992. *Imperial Eyes. Travel Writing and Transculturation*. London/New York: Routledge.

Prunč, Erich. 2001. *Einführung in die Translationswissenschaft*. Band 1, *Orientierungsrahmen*. Graz: Institut für Translationswissenschaft.

Pusch, Luise F. 1984. *Das Deutsche als Männersprache. Aufsätze und Glossen zur feministischen Linguistik*. Frankfurt: Suhrkamp.

Pym, Anthony. 1996. "Venuti's Visibility." *Target* 8 (1): 165–177.

———. 1997. *Pour une Éthique du Traducteur*. Artois: Artois Univ. Press.

———. (ed.). 2001. *The Return to Ethics*. Special Issue of *The Translator. Studies in Intercultural Communication* 7(2).

———. 2002. "Sayonara *Language International*. A few words of farewell from past and present contributors." *Language International* 14 (6): 43.

Quine, Willard Van Orman. 1960. *Word and Object*. Cambridge: MIT Press.

Quirk, Randolph and Greenbaum, Sydney. 1973. *A University Grammar of English*. London: Longman.

Radnitzky, Gerard. 1968/1970². *Contemporary Schools of Metascience*. Göteborg: Göteborg Univ. Press.

Reiss, Katharina. 1971. *Möglichkeiten und Grenzen der Übersetzungskritik. Kategorien und Kriterien für eine sachgerechte Beurteilung von Übersetzungen* (Hueber Hochschulreihe 12). München: Hueber.

———. 1990. "Brief an den Herausgeber." *Lebende Sprachen* 4: 185.

———. 1995. *Grundfragen der Übersetzungswissenschaft. Wiener Vorlesungen von Katharina Reiss*, ed. M. Snell-Hornby and M. Kadrić. Vienna: Vienna Univ. Press.

———. 2000. *Translation Criticism – The Potentials and Limitations. Categories and Criteria for Translation Quality Assessment*, transl. E. F. Rhodes, Manchester: St. Jerome.

Reiss, Katharina and Hans J. Vermeer. 1984. *Grundlegung einer allgemeinen Translationstheorie*. Tübingen: Niemeyer.

Resch, Renate. 1998. "Oedipus und die Folgen: Die Metaphorik der Translationswissenschaft." *Target* 10(2): 335–351.

———. 2000. "Werbetexte – multisemiotisch, intertextuell und zapper-gerecht: Neue Herausforderungen für ÜbersetzerInnen und Translationswissenschaft." In *Translationswissenschaft*, M. Kadrić et al (eds.), 183–193.

Rintelen, Fritz-Joachim von. 1974. "Wissenschaften, Wirklichkeit und Sinn." In *Internationales Jahrbuch für interdisziplinäre Forschung*, R. Schwarz (ed.), 235–262.

Risku, Hanna. 1998. *Translatorische Kompetenz. Kognitive Grundlagen des Übersetzens als Expertentätigkeit*.. (Studien zur Translation 5). Tübingen: Stauffenburg.

———. 2000. "*Situated Translation* und *Situated Cognition*: ungleiche Schwestern." In *Translationswissenschaft*, M. Kadrić et al.(eds.) 81–91.

———. 2004. *Translationsmanagement. Interkulturelle Fachkommunikation im Informationszeitalter*. (Translationswissenschaft 1). Tübingen: Narr.

Robinson, Douglas. 1991. *The Translator's Turn*. Baltimore: Johns Hopkins Univ. Press.

———. 1998. „Free translation." In *Routledge Encyclopedia of Translation Studies*, M. Baker (ed.), 87–90.

———. 1998a. „Literal translation." In *Routledge Encyclopedia of Translation Studies*, M. Baker (ed.), 125–130.

Rosch, Eleanor. 1973. "Natural categories." *Cognitive Psychology* 4: 328–350.

Rübberdt, Irene and Salevsky, Heidemarie. 1997. "New ideas from historical concepts: Schleiermacher and modern translation theory." In *Translation as Intercultural Communication*, M. Snell-Hornby et al. (eds.), 301–312.

Rushdie, Salman. 1983. *Mitternachtskinder,* transl. K. Graf, München/Zürich: Piper.

———. 1991. *Imaginary Homelands.* New Delhi: Penguin.

Said, Edward. 1978. *Orientalism.* London/New York: Routledge.

Salevsky, Heidemarie (ed.). 1992. *Wissenschaftliche Grundlagen der Sprachmittlung. Berliner Beiträge zur Übersetzungswissenschaft.* Frankfurt: Lang.

———.1994. "Schleiermacher-Kolloquium 1993." *TextConText* 9, 159–162.

Salmhoferova, Nadezda. 2002. *Das Rollenbild der Übersetzenden im Prozess der interkulturellen juristischen Kommunikation.* Vienna: unpubl. doctoral thesis.

Sandrini, Peter (ed.) 1999. *Übersetzen von Rechtstexten. Fachkommunikation im Spannungsfeld zwischen Rechtsordnung und Sprache.* (Forum für Fachsprachen-Forschung 54). Tübingen: Narr.

Šarčević, Susan. 1990. "Strategiebedingtes Übersetzen aus den kleineren Sprachen im Fachbereich Jura." *Babel* 36 (3): 155–166.

———. 1994. "Translation and the law: An interdisciplinary approach." In *Translation Studies. An Interdiscipline*, M. Snell-Hornby et al. (eds.), 301–307.

Schäfer, Jürgen (ed.). 1981. *Commonwealth-Literatur.* Bern: Francke.

Schäffner, Christina. 1998. „Metaphern." In *Handbuch Translation,* M. Snell-Hornby et al. (eds.), 280–285.

———. 1998a. "Action (theory of 'translatorial action')." In *Routledge Encyclopedia of Translation Studies*, M. Baker (ed.), 3–5.

———. 1998b. "Skopos theory." In *Routledge Encyclopedia of Translation Studies*, M. Baker (ed.), 235–238.

———. (ed.). 1999. *Translation and Norms.* Clevedon: Multilingual Matters.

Schäffner, Christina and Adab, Beverly. 1997. "Translation as intercultural communication – Contact as conflict." In *Translation as Intercultural Communication*, M. Snell-Hornby et al. (eds.), 325–337.

Schleiermacher, Friedrich. 1993. *Hermeneutik und Kritik,* ed. M. Frank. Frankfurt: Suhrkamp.

Schmid, Annemarie. 1994. "Gruppenprotokolle – ein Einblick in die black box des Übersetzens." *TextConText* 9: 121–146.

———. 2000. "'Systemische Kulturtheorie' – relevant für die Translation?". In *Translationswissenschaft*, M. Kadrić et al (eds.), 51–65.

Schmidt, Heide (ed.). 1989. *Interferenz in der Translation.* (Übersetzungswissenschaftliche Beiträge 12). Leipzig: Enzyklopädie.

Schmitt, Peter A. 1998. "Technische Arbeitsmittel." In *Handbuch Translation,* M. Snell-Hornby et al (eds.), 186–199.

———. 1999. *Translation und Technik.* (Studien zur Translation 6). Tübingen: Stauffenburg.

———. 2000. (ed.) *Paradigmenwechsel in der Translation. Festschrift für Albrecht Neubert zum 70. Geburtstag.* Tübingen: Stauffenburg.

Schopp, Jürgen. 1994. "Typographie als Translationsproblem." In *Translation Studies. An Interdiscipline*, M. Snell-Hornby et al. (eds.), 349–360.

———. 1998. "Typographie und Layout." In *Handbuch Translation*, M. Snell-Hornby et al. (eds.) 199–204.

———. 2005. *"Gut zum Druck"? Typographie und Layout im Übersetzungsprozess.* Tampere: Tampere Univ. Press.

Schwarz, Richard. 1974. "Interdisziplinarität der Wissenschaften als Problem und Aufgabe heute." In *Internationales Jahrbuch für interdisziplinäre Forschung*, R. Schwarz (ed.), 1–131.

Schwarz, Richard (ed.). 1974. *Internationales Jahrbuch für interdisziplinäre Forschung. Wissenschaft als interdisziplinäres Problem*. Berlin: de Gruyter.

Searle, John R. 1969. *Speech acts. An essay in the philosophy of language*. Cambridge: Cambridge Univ. Press.

Séguinot, Candace (ed.) 1989. *The Translation Process*. Toronto: York University.

———. 1994. "Translation and Advertising: Going Global." *Current Issues in Language and Society* 1(3): 249–265.

Seleskovitch, Danica. 1992. "De la pratique à la théorie /Von der Praxis zur Theorie." In *Wissenschaftliche Grundlagen der Sprachmittlung*, H. Salevsky (ed.), 38–55.

Seleskovitch, Danica and Lederer, Marianne. 1984. *Interpréter pour traduire*. Paris: Didier.

Sengupta, Mahasweta. 1990. "Translation, Colonialism and Poetics: Rabindranath Tagore in Two Worlds." In *Translation, History and Culture*, S. Bassnett and A. Lefevere (eds.), 56–63.

Sethu(madhavan), A. 1995. *Pandavapuram*, transl. P. Javakumar, Madras: Macmillan India.

Simon, Sherry. 1996. *Gender and Translation. Culture and Identity and the Politics of Transmission*. London/New York: Routledge.

———. 1999. "Translating and interlingual creation in the contact zone: border writing in Quebec." In *Postcolonial Translation*, S. Bassnett and H. Trivedi (eds.), 58–74.

Sinclair, John M. (ed.). 1987. *Looking up. An Account of the COBUILD Project in lexical computing*. London: Collins.

Singerman, Robert. 2002. *Jewish Translation History. A bibliography of bibliographies and studies*. (Benjamins Translation Library 44). Amsterdam/Philadelphia: John Benjamins.

Smith Veronica and Klein-Braley, Christine. 1997. "Advertising – A five-stage strategy for translation." In *Translation as Intercultural Communication*, M. Snell-Hornby et al. (eds.), 173–184.

Snell-Hornby, Mary. 1983. *Verb-descriptivity in German and English. A contrastive study in semantic fields*. Heidelberg: Winter.

———. 1984. "Sprechbare Sprache – Spielbarer Text. Zur Problematik der Bühnenübersetzung." In *Modes of Interpretation. Essays Presented to Ernst Leisi on the Occasion of his 65th Birthday*, R.J. Watts and U. Weidmann (eds.), 101–116. Tübingen: Narr.

———. (ed.). 1986/1994². *Übersetzungswissenschaft – Eine Neuorientierung. Zur Integrierung von Theorie und Praxis* (UTB 1415). Tübingen: Francke.

———. 1988/1995². *Translation Studies. An Integrated Approach*. Amsterdam/Philadelphia: John Benjamins.

———. 1988a. "*Angst* und *fear* – Wirklichkeit, Wörterbuch, Übersetzung." In *Angst. Interdisziplinäre Vorlesungsreihe der Privatdozenten der Philosophischen Fakultät I der Universität Zürich im Wintersemester 1987/88*, H.-J. Braun and A. Schwarz (eds), 105–119, Zürich: Verlag der Fachvereine.

———. 1989. „Andere Länder, andere Sitten. Zum Problem der kulturbedingten Interferenz in der Translation." In *Interferenz in der Translation*, H. Schmidt (ed.), 135–143.

———. 1989a. „Zur sprachlichen Norm in der literarischen Übersetzung." *Bulletin CILA* 49, 51–60.

———. 1990. "Linguistic transcoding or Cultural Transfer? A Critique of Translation Theory in Germany." In *Translation, History and Culture*, S.Bassnett and A. Lefevere (eds.), 79–86.

———. 1991. „Translation Studies – Art, Science or Utopia?" In *Translation Studies: The State of the Art*, K. Van Leuven-Zwart and T. Naaijkens (eds.), 13–23.

———. 1992. "The professional translator of tomorrow: language specialist or all-round expert?" In *Teaching Translation and Interpreting*, C.Dollerup and A. Loddegaard (eds.), 9–22.

———. 1992a. "Translation as a cultural shock: Diagnosis and therapy." In *Language and Civilization. A Concerted Profusion of Essays and Studies in Honour of Otto Hietsch*, C. Blank (ed.), 341–355. Frankfurt: Lang.

———. (ed.). 1992b. *Translation in Mitteleuropa. Beiträge aus dem Mitteleuropäischen Symposium am Institut für Übersetzer- und Dolmetscherausbildung der Universität Wien, 11.-13. November 1991.* (Folia Translatologica 1). Prague: Charles Univ. Press.

———. 1993. "Der Text als Partitur: Möglichkeiten und Grenzen der multimedialen Übersetzung." In *Traducere Navem*, J. Holz-Mänttäri and C. Nord (eds.), 335–350.

———. 1995. "On Models and Structures and Target Text Cultures: Methods of Assessing Literary Translations." In *La Traducció Literaria*, J.M. Borillo (ed.), 43–58. Castelló: Univ.Jaume I.

———. 1996. "'All the world's a stage': Multimedial translation – constraint or potential?" In *Traduzione multimediale per il cinema, la televisione e la scena*, C Heiss and R.M. Bottelieri Bosinelli (eds.), 29–45. Forlí: CLUEB.

———. 1996a. „Übersetzungswissenschaft: Eine neue Disziplin für eine alte Kunst?" In *Translation und Text. Ausgewählte Vorträge*, 9–24. Vienna: Vienna Univ. Press.

———. 1996b. "The translator's dictionary – An academic dream?" In *Translation und Text. Ausgewählte Vorträge*, 90–96. Vienna: Vienna Univ. Press.

———. 1996c. "Interdiscipline or 'clash or worlds'? – Translation Studies in the 1990s." In *Translation und Text. Ausgewählte Vorträge*, 140–152. Vienna: Vienna Univ. Press.

———. 1997. "'Is this a dagger which I see before me?': The non-verbal language of drama." In *Nonverbal Communication and Translation*, F. Poyatos (ed.), 187–201.

———. 1997a. "Written to be Spoken: The Audio-Medial Text in Translation." In *Text Typology and Translation*, A. Trosborg (ed.), 277–290.

———. 1997b. "The Integrated Linguist: On Combining Methods of Translation Critique." In *Modelle der Translation. Festschrift für Albrecht Neubert*, G. Wotjak and H. Schmidt (eds.), 73–88. Frankfurt: Vervuert.

———. 1997c. "Released from the grip of Empire: lingua franca as target culture?" In *La palabra vertida. Investigaciones en torno a la traducción*, M.A.Vega and R.. Martíno (eds.), 45–56. Madrid: Complutense.

———. 1998. "Kontrastive Linguistik." In *Handbuch Translation*, M. Snell-Hornby et al. (eds.), 66–70.

———. 1998a. "Audiomediale Texte." In *Handbuch Translation*, M. Snell-Hornby et al. (eds.), 273–274.

———. 1999. "The 'Ultimate Confort': Word, Text and the Translation of Tourist Brochures." In *Word, Text, Translation. Liber Amicorum for Peter Newmark*, G. Anderman and M. Rogers (eds.), 95–103. Clevedon: Multilingual Matters.

———. 2000. "'McLanguage': The identity of English as an issue in translation today." In *Translation into Non-Mother Tongues*, M. Grosman et al. (eds.), 35–44.

———. 2000a. "Communicating in the Global Village: On Language, Translation and Cultural Identity." In *Translation in the Global Village*, C. Schäffner (ed.), Clevedon: Multilingual Matters.

———. 2001. "The space 'in between'. What is a hybrid text?" *Across Languages and Cultures* 2 (2): 207–216.

————. 2002. "Back to Square One? – On the troubled relation between Translation Studies and Linguistics." *Logos and Language* 3 (1): 21–30.

————. 2002a. "Übersetzen als interdisiplinäres Handeln. Über neue Formen des kulturellen Transfers." In *Übersetzung als Medium des Kulturverstehens und sozialer Integration*, J. Renn, J. Straub and S. Shimada (eds.), 144–160. Frankfürt: Campus.

————. 2003. "Re-creating the hybrid text: postcolonial Indian writings and the European scene." *Linguistica Antverpiensia* 2: 178–189.

————. 2003a. "Loyalität in der literarischen Übersetzung: Zwischen 'Abbildung' und Kreativität." In *Traducta Navis. Festschrift zum 60. Geburtstag von Christiane Nord*, B. Nord and P.A. Schmitt (eds.), 231–240. Tübingen: Stauffenburg.

————. 2003b. "Translationskultur und Politik. Wege und Irrwege der Kommunikation." *Studia Germanica Posnaniensia* 19: 79–93.

————. 2005. " 'Small smile': Berühmte Übersetzerin als Liebesobjekt", in: *Wortklauber, Sinnverdreher, Brückenbauer?*, I. Kurz and K.Kaindl (eds.), 173–180.

————. 2005a. "Of catfish and blue bananas: scenes-and-frames-semantics as a contrastive 'knowledge system' for translation." In *Knowledge Systems and Translation*, H.v. Dam, J. Engberg, H. Gerzymisch-Arbogast (eds.), 193–206. Berlin/New York: de Gruyter.

Snell-Hornby, Mary and Pöhl, Esther (eds.). 1989. *Translation and Lexicography. Papers from the EURALEX Colloquium, Innsbruck, 2–5 July 1987* (Special Monograph of *Paintbrush*, Journal of Poetry, Translation and Letters), Kirksville MO; repr. Amsterdam/Philadelphia: John Benjamins.

————, Franz Pöchhacker and Klaus Kaindl (eds.). 1994. *Translation Studies. An Interdiscipline* (Benjamins Translation Library 2). Amsterdam/Philadelphia: John Benjamins.

————, and Kadrić, Mira (eds.). 1995. *Grundfragen der Übersetzungswissenschaft. Wiener Vorlesungen von Katharina Reiss*. Vienna: Vienna Univ. Press.

————, Jettmarová, Zuzana and Kaindl, Klaus (eds.). 1997. *Translation as Intercultural Communication. Selected Papers from the EST Congress – Prague 1995* (Benjamins Translation Library 20) . Amsterdam/Philadelphia: John Benjamins.

————, Hönig, Hans G., Kussmaul, Paul and Schmitt, Peter A. (eds.). 1998. *Handbuch Translation*. Tübingen: Stauffenburg.

Sobotka, Eveline. 2000. "Translationsaufträge aus Kundensicht." In *Translationswissenschaft*, M. Kadrić et al. (eds.) 353–362.

Spillner, Bernd. 1980. "Semiotische Aspekte der Übersetzung von Comics-Texten." In *Semiotik und Übersetzen*, W. Wilss (ed.), 73–86. Tübingen: Narr.

Stecconi, Ubaldo. 2000. "A semiotic analysis of the translation-original relationship." In *Translationswissenschaft*, M. Kadrić et al. (eds.), 93–101.

Steiner, George. 1975. *After Babel. Aspects of Language and Translation*. London: Oxford Univ. Press.

Stellbrink, Hans-Jürgen. 1985. "Die Tätigkeit des Dolmetschers und Übersetzers in der Industrie: Meistens nicht wie im Lehrbuch," Guest Lecture Heidelberg 1.2.1985, unpubl.ms.

Stoll, Karl-Heinz. 2000. "Zukunftsperspektiven der Translation." In *Paradigmenwechsel in der Translation*. P. A. Schmitt (ed.), 235–264.

Stolze, Radegundis. 1982. *Grundlagen der Textübersetzung*. Heidelberg: Groos.

————. 1999. "Expertenwissen des juristischen Fachübersetzers." In *Übersetzen von Rechtstexten*, ed. P. Sandrini, 45–62.

————. 2003. *Hermeneutik und Translation*. Tübingen: Narr.

Stoppard, Tom. 1986. Preface to *Dalliance* and *Undiscovered Country*, adapted from Arthur Schnitzler. London: Faber.

Störig, Hans J. (ed.) 1963. *Das Problem des Übersetzens*, Stuttgart: Henry Goverts Verlag.

Strolz, Birgit. 1992. *Theorie und Praxis des Simultandolmetschens. Argumente für einen kontextuellen top-down Ansatz der Verarbeitung und Produktion von Sprache.* Vienna, unpubl. doctoral thesis.

———. 2000. "Translation versus Transkodieren beim Simultandolmetschen: Ergebnisse einer empirischen Untersuchung." In *Translationswissenschaft*, M. Kadrić et al (eds.), 271–290.

Sturge, Kathryn E. 1999. 'The Alien Within': *Translation into German during the Nazi Regime.* London: unpubl. Ph.D. thesis.

Svejcer, A.D. 1989. "Literal Translation as a Product of Interference." In *Interferenz in der Translation*, H. Schmidt (ed.), 39–44.

Tan, Amy. 1996. "Mother Tongue." In *Asian American Literature: A Brief Introduction and Anthology*, S.Wong (ed.). New York: Harper Collins.

Tesnière, Lucien. 1969. *Eléments de syntaxe structurale.* Paris: Klincksieck.

Tgahrt, Reinhard (ed.). 1982. *Weltliteratur. Die Lust am Übersetzen im Jahrhundert Goethes.* München: Kösel.

Thieme, Karl, Hermann, Alfred and Glässer, Edgar. 1956. *Beiträge zur Geschichte des Dolmetschens.* München: Isar.

Tilly, Charles. 1997. "How Empires End." In *After Empire. Multiethnic Societies and Nation-Building. The Soviet Union and the Russian, Ottoman and Habsburg Empires*, K. Barkey and M. von Hagen (eds.), 1–11. Oxford: Westview.

Tirkkonen-Condit, Sonja. 1989. "Professional vs. Non-Professional Translation: A Think-Aloud Protocol Study." In *The Translation Process*, C. Séguinot (ed.), 73–85.

Toury, Gideon. 1977. *Translational Norms and Literary Translation into Hebrew, 1930–1945.* Tel Aviv: Porter Institute.

———. 1978. "The Nature and Role of Norms in Literary Translation." In *Literature and Translation*, J. S. Holmes et al. (eds.), 83–100.

———. 1980. *In Search of a Theory of Translation.* Tel Aviv: Porter Institute.

———. 1985. "A Rationale for Descriptive Translation Studies." In *The Manipulation of Literature*, T. Hermans (ed.), 16–41.

———. 1995. *Descriptive Translation Studies and Beyond.* (Benjamins Translation Library 4). Amsterdam/Philadelphia: John Benjamins.

———. 1999. "Some of Us are Finally Talking to Each Other. Would it Mark the Beginning of a True Dialogue? Comments on Responses." In *Translation and Norms*, C. Schäffner (ed.), 129–132.

———. 2001. "Probabilistic Explanations in Translation Studies: Universals – Or a Challenge to the Very Concept?" Paper given at the Third EST Congress, Translation Studies: Claims, Changes and Challenges August 30 – September 1, 2001, Copenhagen.

Tristan, Flora. 1983. *Meine Reise nach Peru. Fahrten einer Paria.* Transl. Friedrich Wolfzettel. Frankfurt: Insel.

Trömel-Plötz, Senta. 1984. *Gewalt durch Sprache. Die Vergewaltigung von Frauen in Gesprächen.* Frankfurt: Fischer.

Trosborg, Anna (ed.). 1997. *Text Typology and Translation.* (Benjamins Translation Library 26). Amsterdam/Philadelphia: John Benjamins.

Tymoczko, Maria. 1999. *Translation in a Postcolonial Context.* Manchester: St. Jerome.

Tytler, Alexander Fraser, Lord Woodhouselee. 1978. *Essay on the Principles of Translation*, ed. J.F. Huntsman. Amsterdam/Philadelphia: John Benjamins.

Van den Broeck, Raymond, 1988. Introduction to J. Holmes, *Translated!* 1988, 1–5.

Van Leuven-Zwart, Kitty. 1989, 1990. "Translation and Original. Similarities and Dissimilarities." *Target* 1(2): 151–181 and 2(1): 69–95.

Van Leuven-Zwart, Kitty and Naaijkens, Tom (eds.). 1991. *Translation Studies: The State of the Art. Proceedings of the First James S Holmes Symposium on Translation Studies*. Amsterdam: Rodopi.

Vandaele, Jereon (ed.). 2002. *Translating Humour*. Special Issue of *The Translator. Studies in Intercultural Communication* 8(2).

Vannerem, Mia and Snell-Hornby, Mary. 1986. "Die Szene hinter dem Text. 'Scenes-and-frames semantics' in der Übersetzung." In *Übersetzungswissenschaft – Eine Neuorientierung*, M. Snell-Hornby (ed.) 184–205.

Venuti, Lawrence. 1986. "The Translator's Invisibility." *Criticism* 28: 179–212.

——. 1991. "Genealogies of Translation Theory: Schleiermacher." *TTR* 4 (2): 125–150.

——, (ed.). 1992. *Rethinking Translation. Discourse, Subjectivity, Ideology*. London: Routledge.

——. 1994. "Translation and the Formation of Cultural Identities." *Current Issues in Language and Society* 1(3): 201–217.

——. 1995. *The Translator's Invisibility. A history of translation*. (Translation Studies 5). London/New York: Routledge.

——. 1995a. "Translating Thomas Mann." *The Times Literary Supplement*, 24.11.1995:17.

——. 1998. *The Scandals of Translation. Towards an ethics of difference.*London/New York: Routledge.

——. (ed.) . 2000. *The Translation Studies Reader*. London/New York: Routledge.

Vermeer, Hans J. 1978. "Ein Rahmen für eine allgemeine Translationstheorie." *Lebende Sprachen* 23: 99–102.

——. 1983. *Aufsätze zur Translationstheorie*. Heidelberg: mimeo.

——. 1984. "Textkohärenz in Übersetzungstheorie und –didaktik." In *Die Theorie des Übersetzens und ihr Aufschlusswert für die Übersetzungs- und Dolmetschdidaktik*, W.Wilss and G. Thome (eds.), 46–51.

——. 1986. "Übersetzen als kultureller Transfer." In *Übersetzungswissenschaft – Eine Neuorientierung*, M. Snell-Hornby (ed.), 30–53.

——. 1989. "Scopos and Commission in Translational Action." In *Readings in Translation Theory*. A. Chesterman (ed.), 99–104. Helsinki: Oy Finn Lectura Ab.

——. (ed.). 1989a. *Kulturspezifik des translatorischen Handelns*. Heidelberg: mimeo.

——. 1992. *Skizzen zu einer Geschichte der Translation*. Frankfurt: Verlag für Interkulturelle Kommunikation.

——. 1994. „Translation today. Old and new problems." In *Translation Studies. An Interdiscipline*. M. Snell-Hornby et al. (eds.), 3–16.

——. 1994a. "Hermeneutik und Übersetzung(swissenschaft)." *TextConText* 9 (3): 163–182.

——. 1995. *A skopos theory of translation. (Some arguments for and against.)* Heidelberg: mimeo.

——. 1996. *Das Übersetzen im Mittelalter (13. und 14. Jahrhundert)*. Vol. 1. *Das arabisch-lateinische Mittelalter*. Heidelberg: TextConText.

——. 1996a. *Das Übersetzen im Mittelalter. (13. und 14. Jahrhundert)*. Vol. 2. *Deutsch als Zielsprache*. Heidelberg: TextConText.

———. 1996b. *Das Übersetzen im Mittelalter (13. und 14. Jahrhundert)*. Vol. 3. *Literaturverzeich-nis und Register*. Heidelberg: TextConText.

———. 1997. "Translation and the 'Meme'." *Target* 9 (1): 155–166.

———. 1997a. Preface to *Übersetzungswissenschaft in Brasilien*, M. Wolf (ed.), 9–11.

———. 1998. "Starting to Unask What Translatology Is About." *Target* 10 (1): 41–68.

———. 2000. *Das Übersetzen in Renaissance und Humanismus (15. und 16. Jahrhundert)*. Vol. 1. *Westeuropa*. Heidelberg: TextConText.

———. 2000a. *Das Übersetzen in Renaissance und Humanismus (15. und 16. Jahrhundert)*. Vol. 2. *Der deutschsprachige Raum. Literatur und Indices*. Heidelberg: TextConText.

———. 2003. „Die sieben Grade einer Translationstheorie." *Studia Germanica Posnaniensia* 19: 19–38.

Vermeer, Hans J. and Heidrun Witte. 1990. *Mögen Sie Zistrosen? Scenes und frames und channels im translatorischen Handeln*. Heidelberg: Groos.

Viaggio, Sergio. 1997. "Kinesics and the simultaneous interpreter: The advantages of listening with one's eyes and speaking with one's body." In *Nonverbal Communication and Transla-tion*, F. Poyatos (ed.), 283–292.

Vieira, Else Ribeiro Pires. 1994. "A postmodern translational aesthetics in Brazil." In *Translation Studies. An Interdiscipline*, M. Snell-Hornby et al. (eds), 65–72.

Villareal, Corazon. 1994. *Translating the Sugilanon: Re-framing the Sign*. Quezon City: Univ. of the Philippines Press.

Vinay, Jean-Paul and Jean Darbelnet. 1958. *Stylistique comparée du Français et de l'Anglais. Méthode de traduction*. Paris: Didier.

———. 1995. *Comparative Stylistics of French and English: A Methodology for Translation*, transl. J. Sager. (Benjamins Translation Library 11) Amsterdam/Philadelphia: John Benjamins.

Violante-Cassetta, Patricia. 1996. "Jack in the Year 2000." In *Problemi e Tendenze nella Didattica dell'Interpretazione e della Traduzione*, Y. Gambier and M. Snell-Hornby (eds), 199–213.

Vogt, Elisabeth. 2002. *Robert McNamaras* In Retrospect. The Tragedy and Lessons of Vietnam *in der deutschen Übersetzung* Vietnam. Das Trauma einer Weltmacht. *Eine Übersetzungs-kritik nach dem Modell von Margret Ammann*. Vienna: unpubl. master's thesis.

Walter, Ulrike. 2001. "Die Auswirkungen der Erwerbsmöglichkeit auf Leben und Werk von Übersetzerinnen: Louise Gottsched und Sophie Mereau im Vergleich." In *Übersetzung aus aller Frauen Länder*, S. Messner and M. Wolf (eds), 63–76.

Weale, Edna. 1997. "From Babel to Brussels: Conference interpreting and the art of the impos-sible." In *Nonverbal Communication and Translation*, F. Poyatos (ed.), 295–312.

Weaver, Warren. 1955. „Translation, a memorandum, 15.07.1949." In *Machine Translation of Languages*, W.N. Locke and A.D. Booth (eds), 15–23.New York.

Weinreich, Uriel. 1966. „Explorations in semantic theory." In *Current Trends in Linguistics* 3, T. A. Sebeok (ed.), 395–477.

Wertheimer, Max. 1912/1959. *Productive Thinking*. Chicago: Chicago Univ. Press.

Widdowson, Henry. 1994. "The ownership of English." *The TESOL Quarterly* 28: 377–389.

Wildblood, Alan. 2002. "Subtitle is not a Translation. A day in the life of a subtitler." *Language International* 14/2: 40–43.

Wilss, Wolfram. 1977. *Übersetzungswissenschaft. Probleme und Methoden*. Stuttgart: Klett.

———. 1988. *Kognition und Übersetzen. Zur Theorie und Praxis der menschlichen und maschinellen Übersetzung*. Tübingen: Niemeyer.

————. 1989. „Interferenzerscheinungen beim Übersetzen. Fremdsprache – Grundsprache / Vorschläge zu einer prozeduralen Analyse." In *Interferenz in der Translation,* H. Schmidt (ed.), 7–18.

————. 1996. *Übersetzungsunterricht. Begriffliche Grundlagen und methodische Orientierungen.* Tübingen: Narr.

————. 2000. "Interdisziplinarität: ein neues übersetzungswissenschaftliches Paradigma?" In *Paradigmenwechsel in der Translation,* P.A. Schmitt (ed.), 265–278.

————. 2004. "Verschlungene Wege zum Ziel. Der unorthodoxe Werdegang eines Universitätsprofessors." In *Übersetzungswissenschaft Dolmetschwissenschaft,* W.Pöckl (ed.), 393–398.

Wilss, Wolfram and Gisela Thome (eds.). 1984. *Die Theorie des Übersetzens und ihr Aufschlusswert für die Übersetzungs- und Dolmetschdidaktik. Akten des Internationalen Kolloquiums der Association Internationale de Linguistique Appliquée (AILA), Saarbrücken, 25.-30. Juli 1983.* Tübingen: Narr.

Wing-Kwong Leung, Matthew. Forthcoming. "The Ideological Turn in Translation Studies." In *Translation Studies,* J. F. Duarte et al. (eds.)

Witte, Heidrun. 1987. "Die Kulturkompetenz des Translators – Theoretisch-abstrakter Begriff oder realisierbares Konzept?" *TextConText* 2 (2/3): 109–136.

Wittgenstein, Ludwig. 1953. *Philosophical Investigations.* Oxford: Blackwell.

Wolf, Michaela (ed.), 1997. *Übersetzungswissenschaft in Brasilien. Beiträge zum Status von "Original" und Übersetzung.* (Studien zur Translation 3).Tübingen: Stauffenburg.

————. 1999. "Zum 'sozialen Sinn' in der Translation. Translationssoziologische Implikationen von Pierre Bourdieus Kultursoziologie." *Arcadia. Zeitschrift für Allgemeine und Vergleichende Literaturwissenschaft* 34(2): 262–275.

————. 2000. " ,Du weißt, dass ich Slawe, Deutscher, Italiener bin'. Hybridität in Original und Übersetzung am Beispiel Scipio Slatapers *Il Mio Carso."* In *Translationswissenschaft,* M. Kadrić et al. (eds.), 115–131.

————. 2005. *Die vielsprachige Seele Kakaniens. Translation als soziale und kulturelle Praxis in der Habsburgermonarchie 1848 bis 1918.* Graz: unpubl. postdoctoral thesis..

Wotjak, Gerd. 2000. „War das die Leipziger Übersetzungswissenschaftliche Schule?" In *Paradigmenwechsel in der Translation.* P.A. Schmitt (ed.), 279–304.

Yau, Shun-chiu. 1997. "The identification of gestural images in Chinese literary expressions." In *Nonverbal Communication and Translation,* F. Poyatos (ed.), 68–82.

Zajic, Susanne. 1994. *Atembarkeit, Spielbarkeit, Sprechbarkeit. Zur Problematik der Bühnenübersetzung.* Vienna: unpubl. master's thesis.

Subject index

Author index

In the series *Benjamins Translation Library* the following titles have been published thus far or are scheduled for publication:

37 **TIRKKONEN-CONDIT, Sonja and Riitta JÄÄSKELÄINEN (eds.):** Tapping and Mapping the Processes of Translation and Interpreting. Outlooks on empirical research. 2000. x, 176 pp.

36 **SCHMID, Monika S.:** Translating the Elusive. Marked word order and subjectivity in English-German translation. 1999. xii, 174 pp.

35 **SOMERS, Harold (ed.):** Computers and Translation. A translator's guide. 2003. xvi, 351 pp.

34 **GAMBIER, Yves and Henrik GOTTLIEB (eds.):** (Multi) Media Translation. Concepts, practices, and research. 2001. xx, 300 pp.

33 **GILE, Daniel, Helle V. DAM, Friedel DUBSLAFF, Bodil MARTINSEN and Anne SCHJOLDAGER (eds.):** Getting Started in Interpreting Research. Methodological reflections, personal accounts and advice for beginners. 2001. xiv, 255 pp.

32 **BEEBY, Allison, Doris ENSINGER and Marisa PRESAS (eds.):** Investigating Translation. Selected papers from the 4th International Congress on Translation, Barcelona, 1998. 2000. xiv, 296 pp.

31 **ROBERTS, Roda P., Silvana E. CARR, Diana ABRAHAM and Aideen DUFOUR (eds.):** The Critical Link 2: Interpreters in the Community. Selected papers from the Second International Conference on Interpreting in legal, health and social service settings, Vancouver, BC, Canada, 19–23 May 1998. 2000. vii, 316 pp.

30 **DOLLERUP, Cay:** Tales and Translation. The Grimm Tales from Pan-Germanic narratives to shared international fairytales. 1999. xiv, 384 pp.

29 **WILSS, Wolfram:** Translation and Interpreting in the 20th Century. Focus on German. 1999. xiii, 256 pp.

28 **SETTON, Robin:** Simultaneous Interpretation. A cognitive-pragmatic analysis. 1999. xvi, 397 pp.

27 **BEYLARD-OZEROFF, Ann, Jana KRÁLOVÁ and Barbara MOSER-MERCER (eds.):** Translators' Strategies and Creativity. Selected Papers from the 9th International Conference on Translation and Interpreting, Prague, September 1995. In honor of Jiří Levý and Anton Popovič. 1998. xiv, 230 pp.

26 **TROSBORG, Anna (ed.):** Text Typology and Translation. 1997. xvi, 342 pp.

25 **POLLARD, David E. (ed.):** Translation and Creation. Readings of Western Literature in Early Modern China, 1840–1918. 1998. vi, 336 pp.

24 **ORERO, Pilar and Juan C. SAGER (eds.):** The Translator's Dialogue. Giovanni Pontiero. 1997. xiv, 252 pp.

23 **GAMBIER, Yves, Daniel GILE and Christopher TAYLOR (eds.):** Conference Interpreting: Current Trends in Research. Proceedings of the International Conference on Interpreting: What do we know and how? 1997. iv, 246 pp.

22 **CHESTERMAN, Andrew:** Memes of Translation. The spread of ideas in translation theory. 1997. vii, 219 pp.

21 **BUSH, Peter and Kirsten MALMKJÆR (eds.):** Rimbaud's Rainbow. Literary translation in higher education. 1998. x, 200 pp.

20 **SNELL-HORNBY, Mary, Zuzana JETTMAROVÁ and Klaus KAINDL (eds.):** Translation as Intercultural Communication. Selected papers from the EST Congress, Prague 1995. 1997. x, 354 pp.

19 **CARR, Silvana E., Roda P. ROBERTS, Aideen DUFOUR and Dini STEYN (eds.):** The Critical Link: Interpreters in the Community. Papers from the 1st international conference on interpreting in legal, health and social service settings, Geneva Park, Canada, 1–4 June 1995. 1997. viii, 322 pp.

18 **SOMERS, Harold (ed.):** Terminology, LSP and Translation. Studies in language engineering in honour of Juan C. Sager. 1996. xii, 250 pp.

17 **POYATOS, Fernando (ed.):** Nonverbal Communication and Translation. New perspectives and challenges in literature, interpretation and the media. 1997. xii, 361 pp.

16 **DOLLERUP, Cay and Vibeke APPEL (eds.):** Teaching Translation and Interpreting 3. New Horizons. Papers from the Third Language International Conference, Elsinore, Denmark, 1995. 1996. viii, 338 pp.

15 **WILSS, Wolfram:** Knowledge and Skills in Translator Behavior. 1996. xiii, 259 pp.

14 **MELBY, Alan K. and Terry WARNER:** The Possibility of Language. A discussion of the nature of language, with implications for human and machine translation. 1995. xxvi, 276 pp.

13 **DELISLE, Jean and Judith WOODSWORTH (eds.):** Translators through History. 1995. xvi, 346 pp.

12 **BERGENHOLTZ, Henning and Sven TARP (eds.):** Manual of Specialised Lexicography. The preparation of specialised dictionaries. 1995. 256 pp.

11 **VINAY, Jean-Paul and Jean DARBELNET:** Comparative Stylistics of French and English. A methodology for translation. Translated and edited by Juan C. Sager, M.-J. Hamel. 1995. xx, 359 pp.

10 **KUSSMAUL, Paul:** Training the Translator. 1995. x, 178 pp.

9 **REY, Alain:** Essays on Terminology. Translated by Juan C. Sager. With an introduction by Bruno de Bessé. 1995. xiv, 223 pp.

8 **GILE, Daniel:** Basic Concepts and Models for Interpreter and Translator Training. 1995. xvi, 278 pp.

7 **BEAUGRANDE, Robert de, Abdullah SHUNNAQ and Mohamed Helmy HELIEL (eds.):** Language, Discourse and Translation in the West and Middle East. 1994. xii, 256 pp.

6 **EDWARDS, Alicia B.:** The Practice of Court Interpreting. 1995. xiii, 192 pp.

5 **DOLLERUP, Cay and Annette LINDEGAARD (eds.):** Teaching Translation and Interpreting 2. Insights, aims and visions. Papers from the Second Language International Conference Elsinore, 1993. 1994. viii, 358 pp.

4 **TOURY, Gideon:** Descriptive Translation Studies – and beyond. 1995. viii, 312 pp.

3 **LAMBERT, Sylvie and Barbara MOSER-MERCER (eds.):** Bridging the Gap. Empirical research in simultaneous interpretation. 1994. 362 pp.

2 **SNELL-HORNBY, Mary, Franz PÖCHHACKER and Klaus KAINDL (eds.):** Translation Studies: An Interdiscipline. Selected papers from the Translation Studies Congress, Vienna, 1992. 1994. xii, 438 pp.

1 **SAGER, Juan C.:** Language Engineering and Translation. Consequences of automation. 1994. xx, 345 pp.